Christopher Marlowe

EDWARD II

Christopher Marlowe

EDWARD II

WITH RELATED TEXTS

Edited, with Introduction and Notes,
by Stephen J. Lynch

Hackett Publishing Company, Inc.
Indianapolis/Cambridge

For further information, please address
  Hackett Publishing Company, Inc.
  P.O. Box 44937
  Indianapolis, Indiana 46244-0937

  www.hackettpublishing.com

Cover design by Brian Rak
Interior design by Elizabeth L. Wilson and Laura Clark
Composition by William Hartman

Library of Congress Cataloging-in-Publication Data
Marlowe, Christopher, 1564–1593.
    [Edward the Second]
    Edward II : with related texts / Christopher Marlowe ;
edited, with introduction and notes, by Stephen J. Lynch.
        pages cm
    Includes bibliographical references.
    ISBN 978-1-62466-238-6 (pbk.) — ISBN 978-1-62466-255-3 (cloth)
    1. Edward II, King of England, 1284–1327—Drama.
    I. Lynch, Stephen J., 1955– editor. II. Title.
    PR2665.A2L96 2015
    822'.3—dc23   2014029047

CONTENTS

PREFACE

I have attempted to make this edition of *Edward II* as reader-friendly as possible, but also suitable for in-depth study of the play. Spelling and punctuation have been modernized throughout, including all selections in the appendix of Related Texts. For ease of reading, I have added marginal glosses for all obscure words, along with generous footnotes explaining more complex thematic and textual issues. The selection of related texts offers students the opportunity for more advanced study of the play within the relevant contexts of early modern culture. All of the related texts were published before or during the life of Marlowe, and thus are texts that Marlowe likely read—or at least knew about from conversations with fellow students at Cambridge or colleagues in London.

LIFE OF MARLOWE[1]

According to the coroner's report, Christopher Marlowe met with Ingram Frizer, Nicholas Skerres, and Robert Poley at the house of a widow in Deptford on May 30, 1593. After dinner, Marlowe and Frizer exchanged insults in a heated argument over the bill. Marlowe grabbed Frizer's dagger and wounded him twice in the head, but then Frizer managed to seize the dagger and inflict a fatal wound above Marlowe's right eye. It was a sudden and violent end to a life that began twenty-nine years earlier as the son of a Canterbury shoemaker.

Christopher Marlowe was baptized on February 26, 1564, exactly two months before the baptism of William Shakespeare. He was the eldest son in a family of nine children. No record survives of Marlowe's early education, but at age fourteen he won a scholarship to the prestigious King's School in Canterbury, and two years later he entered Corpus Christi College, Cambridge, where he was awarded an Archbishop Parker scholarship. The Parker scholarship provided financial support for three years of study toward the BA, and an additional three years of support for students who intended to earn an MA and then enter the church. Marlowe completed both degrees (BA in 1584, MA in 1587), but he never entered the clergy. His decision may have been motivated not only by personal inclination but also by limited opportunities for clerical employment. Though holders of the BA earned the legal status of "gentlemen," Marlowe (as the son of a shoemaker) lacked the family connections and social prestige that usually were necessary to secure anything but a low-paying position as a parish priest.

Marlowe's literary career began while he was still a student at Cambridge, when he translated Ovid's *Amores* and probably wrote his first play, *Dido, Queen of Carthage*. After moving to London in 1587, he rose to fame with *Tamburlaine the Great* and the sequel *Tamburlaine the Great, Part Two*—plays that set a new standard for dramatic blank verse (what Ben Jonson famously called "Marlowe's mighty line"). During the next five years, Marlowe wrote four additional plays, though the exact order of composition is uncertain: *The Jew of Malta*, *Doctor Faustus*, *The Massacre at Paris*, and *Edward II*. He also composed the narrative poem *Hero and Leander* and translated the first book of Lucan's *Civil Wars*.

---

1. The following section is an adaptation of "Life of Marlowe" from Christopher Marlowe, *The Jew of Malta*, edited by Stephen J. Lynch (Indianapolis: Hackett Publishing, 2009), viii–xiv.

As an MA student at Cambridge, Marlowe apparently began supplementing his income by working as a spy for the Elizabethan secret service. Evidence for his espionage activities is circumstantial but compelling. Not only was he absent from Cambridge for weeks and sometimes months at a time, but in 1587 a rumor circulated that Marlowe had gone to Rheims in France. Since Rheims was the location of an English Catholic seminary, the rumor provoked suspicion that Marlowe had converted to Catholicism—an action that would have disqualified him for an MA degree. In response, the Queen's Privy Council sent a letter to the Cambridge authorities, assuring them of Marlowe's loyalty:

> Whereas it was reported that Christopher Morley [Marlowe] was determined to have gone beyond the sea to Rheims and there to remain, their Lordships [members of the Queen's Privy Council] thought good to certify that he had no such intent, but that in all actions he had behaved himself orderly and discreetly whereby he had done her Majesty good service, and deserved to be rewarded for his faithful dealing. (qtd. in Riggs 180)

The "good service" performed by Marlowe is never specified. But if Marlowe did in fact travel to Rheims in service of the English government, it seems likely that he was employed as a spy or messenger in the service of agents who had infiltrated the Catholic seminary.

Marlowe's involvement with the Elizabethan secret service seems all the more plausible in light of the fact that he often ran into trouble with the law, and yet he consistently evaded serious punishment—apparently because he enjoyed special protection from authorities at court. In 1589 Marlowe got into a fight with an innkeeper named William Bradley. Marlowe's friend and fellow poet Thomas Watson attempted to break up the fight, but Bradley turned on Watson, and in self-defense Watson fatally stabbed Bradley in the chest. Both Watson and Marlowe were arrested and charged with murder. Watson spent five months in prison before he was pardoned by the queen, but Marlowe was freed after twelve days in Newgate prison.

In 1592 Marlowe traveled to the Dutch town of Flushing with Richard Baines (a professional spy and informer) and a goldsmith named Gifford Gilbert. The three men set up an operation to counterfeit coins, but soon after the first coins were minted Baines turned in his partners to the authorities. The English governor of Flushing, Sir Robert Sidney, reported in his letter to Lord Burghley (chief adviser to Queen Elizabeth) that both Baines and Marlowe claimed that they participated in the coining scheme only "to see the goldsmith's cunning," and, curiously, Marlowe and Baines accused each other of "intent to go to the enemy, or to Rome" (qtd. in Riggs 274–75). All three men were then sent back to England for further interrogation by Lord Burghley. Though counterfeiting was legally defined as an act of treason, and thus punishable by death, Marlowe was apparently released unpunished. (The evidence is sketchy, but it is possible that the coining operation was part of a government espionage plan to lure treasonous English Catholics into a trap.)

In May of the same year, Marlowe was again in court, this time for threats he made against two constables in London. Once again, Marlowe went unpunished, though the judge ordered him under penalty of a bond to "keep the peace." A few months later, in September 1592, Marlowe was back in Canterbury where he was accused of attacking a man with a stick and dagger. The case was settled out of court.

Marlowe's troubles with the law turned far more serious in May 1593. Thomas Kyd, a fellow playwright and author of *The Spanish Tragedy*, was arrested on charges of libel against the state. His room was searched, and heretical papers were discovered. Under torture Kyd protested that the papers were the work of Marlowe, with whom he had shared a room two years earlier. Marlowe was arrested on May 18, but, unlike Kyd, Marlowe was not tortured. He was held for two days and then ordered to report to the Queen's Privy Council on a daily basis. In the meantime, Richard Baines (one of the partners in the counterfeiting scheme) was employed by the Privy Council to gather information on Marlowe. Baines did not disappoint. Within a week, he submitted the following report:

A note containing the opinion of one Christopher Marly [Marlowe] concerning his damnable judgment of religion, and scorn of God's word:

That the Indians, and many authors of antiquity, have assuredly written of above 16 thousand years ago, whereas Adam is proved to have lived within six thousand years.

He affirmeth that Moses was but a juggler, and that one Harriot[2] being Sir W. Raleigh's man can do more than he. . . .

That the beginning of religion was only to keep men in awe. . . .

That Christ was a bastard and his mother dishonest.

That he was the son of a carpenter, and that if the Jews among whom he was born did crucify him, they best knew him and whence he came.

---

2. Thomas Harriot (1560–1621) was an astronomer and mathematician, employed as a tutor by Sir Walter Raleigh.

That Christ deserved better to die than Barabbas, and that the Jews made a good choice, though Barabbas were both a thief and a murderer.

That if there be any God or any good religion, then it is in the Papists, because the service of God is performed with more ceremonies, as elevation of the mass, organs, singing men, shaven crowns, etc. That all Protestants are hypocritical asses. . . .

That St. John the Evangelist was bedfellow to Christ and leaned always in his bosom; that he used him as the sinners of Sodom.

That all they that love not tobacco and boys are fools. . . .

That he had as good a right to coin as the Queen of England, and that he was acquainted with one Poole, a prisoner in Newgate, who hath great skill in mixture of metals, and having learned some things of him, he meant through help of a cunning stamp-maker to coin French crowns, pistolets, and English shillings.

That if Christ would have instituted the sacrament with more ceremonial reverence, it would have been had in more admiration; that it would have been much better being administered in a tobacco pipe.

That the angel Gabriel was bawd to the Holy Ghost, because he brought the salutation to Mary.

That one Richard Cholmley hath confessed that he was persuaded by Marlowe's reasons to become an atheist.

Baines concludes his note with the claim that Marlowe "almost into every company he cometh, he persuades men to atheism" and that "all men in Christianity ought to endeavor that the mouth of so dangerous a member may be stopped."[3] When Queen Elizabeth was shown a copy of the Baines Note, she reportedly ordered her Privy Council to "prosecute it to the full" (see Riggs 329).

Within a few days Marlowe was dead. Suspicion naturally falls on the members of the Privy Council, for whom Marlowe must have seemed an unruly and growing liability. It is also possible, however, that any number of people who closely associated with Marlowe may have feared they would be implicated in charges of atheism, libel, or even treason. In any case, the

---

3. For the complete Baines Note, see Honan, 374–75. The term "atheism" in the sixteenth century often meant not the denial of the existence of God but the denial of essential Christian doctrines, such as the divinity of Christ, the immortality of the soul, or the existence of heaven and hell.

death of Marlowe seems suspicious in a variety of ways: not only in the timing of his death (just days after the Privy Council became alarmed about Marlowe's behavior) but also in the reported details about how Marlowe was killed and the sordid nature of the men involved.

The official inquest by the queen's coroner, William Danby, claims that Marlowe met Ingram Frizer, Nicholas Skerres, and Robert Poley at ten in the morning on May 30, 1593, at the house of a widow in Deptford (perhaps an inn or tavern). All three men were shady characters: Frizer and Skerres were petty criminals employed by Thomas Walsingham, second cousin of Sir Francis Walsingham (who ran the queen's secret service until his death in 1590), and Poley was a professional informer employed by Lord Burghley (who assumed control over the secret service after Walsingham). Marlowe and his companions ate lunch and then took a leisurely walk in the garden. At the hour of six, they returned for dinner, but soon after dining Frizer and Marlowe began to exchange "diverse malicious words" in a heated argument over "*le recknynge*" (payment of the bill). According to the report, Marlowe was lying on a bed, and Frizer was sitting between Poley and Skerres on a bench with his back to Marlowe, when, suddenly, Marlowe grabbed Frizer's dagger and wounded him twice in the head. Frizer could not escape because he was sitting between Skerres and Poley (who apparently did nothing to intervene), but he somehow managed to turn around, grab hold of the dagger, and plunge it into the head of Marlowe, inflicting a two-inch-deep wound above the right eye. Marlowe died instantly. The queen's coroner gathered a jury of men who concluded on oath that Frizer acted in self-defense.

Though the coroner may have investigated the death with due diligence, at least some of what he was told by the men involved may have been fabricated to cover up a planned assassination. In the light of Marlowe's past history, it does not seem surprising that he would have reacted violently to insults, but Marlowe may have been deliberately provoked, and in any case the reported details of the death and the alleged innocence of Frizer seem rather suspicious. Adding to the suspicion is the fact that four weeks later the queen signed Frizer's pardon.[4]

Soon after the death of Marlowe, Thomas Kyd wrote two letters to Thomas Puckering (Lord Keeper of the Privy Seal) in an effort to defend himself against the charge of atheism and in hope of regaining the favor of his patron, Lord Strange. The first letter apparently repeats the claims Kyd made under torture—that the heretical papers found in his room belonged to Marlowe, and that the papers were accidentally shuffled together with

---

4. The complete text of the Coroner's Inquest (originally in Latin) is translated in Honan, appendix 3.

his own papers when they shared a room two years earlier. Kyd then describes Marlowe as "irreligious" and "intemperate and cruel of heart." In his second letter to Puckering, Kyd expands on Marlowe's blasphemes, including details that closely accord with the allegations in the Baines Note:

> Pleaseth it your honorable Lordship touching Marlowe's monstrous opinions as I cannot but with an aggrieved conscience think on him or them so can I but particularize few in respect of them that kept him greater company . . . .
>
> First it was his custom . . . to jest at the divine scriptures, gibe at prayers, and strive in argument to frustrate and confute what hath been spoke or writ by prophets and such holy men.
>
> He would report St. John to be our savior Christ's Alexis.[5] I cover it with reverence and trembling that is that Christ did love him with an extraordinary love. . . .
>
> That things esteemed to be done by divine power might have as well been done by observation of men.[6]

Neither Baines nor Kyd was a reliable witness who could be trusted to give an impartial account of Marlowe, yet nevertheless their accusations against Marlowe cohere on basic points: Marlowe apparently scoffed at religious rituals, denied the authenticity of sacred scripture, and alleged a homoerotic relationship between Christ and St. John. Moreover, five additional contemporaries of Marlowe described him as an atheist or blasphemer, and at least four more Elizabethans made similar accusations by way of pseudonyms (see Riggs 4). All such evidence is no more than hearsay—but the hearsay is consistent.

Marlowe's reputation as a political and religious heretic was likely reinforced by the hero-villains he created for the public stage. Tamburlaine, though born a lowly Scythian shepherd, conquers an empire, heaps abuse on anointed kings, blasphemes against "Mohamet," and even burns the Koran on stage (*2 Tam.* 5.1.171–84); Doctor Faustus defies all religious orthodoxy as he sells his soul to the devil; and, in the *Jew of Malta*, the prologue "Machevil" dismisses religion as a "childish toy" (Prol. 14) and discredits the divine right of kings as an aristocratic myth: "Might first made kings" (Prol. 20). It is not possible to discern the extent to which Marlowe may have projected himself into such stage characters. Nonetheless, such

5. Alexis was a young boy loved by the shepherd Corydon in Virgil's *Second Eclogue*.
6. Kyd's letters to Puckering are included in Honan, appendixes 4 and 5.

characters (whether Marlowe liked it or not) would have inevitably shaped public perceptions of Marlowe.

Yet even if Marlowe blasphemed with abandon and actively preached atheism, as his contemporaries reported, we cannot be sure whether Marlowe spoke his intellectual convictions, or blathered drunken nonsense, or perhaps went about London spouting off such opinions in a scheme to lure heretics and traitors into a trap. Indeed, if Marlowe was a spy in the secret service, he may have been routinely employed to enact the role of enemy of the English church and state. He may have acted the role all too convincingly, perhaps because the role suited his genuine beliefs and attitudes—but of that we can never be sure.

INTRODUCTION TO *EDWARD II*

No records survive indicating how Marlowe's audiences responded to the horrific murder of the king in *Edward II*. Though Elizabethan sensibilities were most likely toughened by familiarity with spectacles of human suffering in the form of public executions of criminals and traitors, Marlowe's audiences may have found the staging of Edward's death particularly scandalous. The victim was not a criminal but an anointed king, and the mode of execution was especially humiliating and sadistic. Indeed, a sense of scandal has lingered well into modern times. After performances during the reigns of Elizabeth and James, there were no further recorded performances until William Poel staged the play in 1903. In deference to Victorian sensibilities, Poel abridged the murder scene and hid the stage action behind a screen. More recently, Derek Jarman, in his 1991 film adaptation of the play, also altered the ending, though for quite different reasons. Jarman presents the murder as a dream sequence, after which the king awakens to see the approach of the would-be murderer, who promptly tosses the iron spit into the water and proceeds to kiss the frightened king—a violation of the play, but an apparent vindication of the king's homoeroticism.[1]

The horrific mode of execution was not the invention of Marlowe. The historical event was described in graphic detail in the major source for the play, Holinshed's *Chronicles*:

> . . . they came suddenly one night into the chamber where he lay in bed fast asleep, and with heavy featherbeds or a table (as some write) being cast upon him, they kept him down and withal put into his fundament an horn, and through the same they thrust up into his body an hot spit, or (as other have) through the pipe of a trumpet, a plumber's instrument of iron made very hot, the which passing up into his entrails, and being rolled to and fro, burnt the same, but so as no appearance of any wound or hurt outwardly might be once perceived.[2]

The first printed text of the play, the 1594 quarto, does not include any stage directions for the murder of the king—perhaps because the printer feared censorship, or perhaps because Marlowe neglected to include them

1. For descriptions of the 1903 William Poel production, see Stewart 82–83 and Geckle 78–80.

2. See selections from Holinshed's *Chronicles* in Related Texts.

in his manuscript. The dialogue in the murder scene, however, strongly indicates that the stage action follows the events as described in Holinshed. Early in the scene, Lightborn requests three things—a featherbed, a table, and a red-hot spit (5.5.30–33)—the very instruments used in Holinshed.[3]

No other tragic hero in Marlowe's plays endures such a humiliating fate. Tamburlaine remains unbroken (and dies while giving final instructions to his sons), Faustus refuses to repent and is ultimately torn apart by devils, and Barabas is consumed in a burning cauldron (while continuing to curse his enemies)—all are to some degree heroic and defiant. Only Edward suffers such degradation. Indeed, it is possible that Holinshed's account of the execution of King Edward may have been the event that especially attracted the attention of Marlowe and provoked his interest in writing the stage play.

Edward and Gaveston

From the start, the play seems designed to disturb and unsettle the audience. Gaveston enters the stage and speaks of his love for the king in homoerotic terms. Edward's letter calling Gaveston back from exile in France contains "amorous lines" (1.1.6), and Gaveston likens himself to the mythical Leander who swam the Hellespont to meet his beloved Hero—an analogy that boldly configures King Edward as the erotic and feminine object of Gaveston's desires. Though the language of male friendship in Elizabethan culture often overlapped with the language of erotic love, Marlowe steps beyond playful ambiguity: Gaveston walks "arm in arm" with Edward and leans "on the shoulder of the king," while Edward "hangs about his neck . . . and whispers in his ears" (1.2.20–23, 51–52), and later Gaveston taunts the irate barons by sitting beside Edward on the throne (1.4.8–9)—literally and symbolically usurping the place of the queen. Like all Elizabethan playwrights, Marlowe wrote under conditions of censorship, and thus Edward and Gaveston are never explicitly described as lovers. But a wide range of images, allusions, and stage actions clearly suggest the erotic nature of their relationship.

3. Stephen Orgel argues that Marlowe did not follow Holinshed, but instead the king on stage is merely pressed to death with the featherbed and table (see Orgel 47–48). Orgel's argument is plausible but difficult to reconcile with the fact that Lightborn requests a "spit," and he insists it be "red hot" (5.5.30). Moreover, after the murder, Matrevis fears that the king's "cry will raise the town" (5.5.114). Such a "cry" (also mentioned in Holinshed) would be unlikely if the king died from suffocation.

Like the medieval stage Vice, Gaveston plays the role of the manipulative tempter, speaking directly to the audience and boasting of his plans to seduce the pliant king with forbidden pleasures. Appropriately compared to Helen of Troy, "the Greekish strumpet" (2.5.15), Gaveston also appears as a masculine *femme fatale*, posing a monstrous triple threat to the English state: He helps destroy the king's sanctified marriage to Isabella; he is a "sly inveigling Frenchman" (1.2.57) who dresses in Italian style and is thus a source of alien contamination in the English court; and he is a social and political upstart, a disrupter of proper hierarchy, "hardly . . . a gentleman by birth" (1.4.29), who longs to "share the kingdom" (1.1.2) with Edward.

Gaveston is repeatedly called the king's "minion"—a term for a male favorite, often (but not always) suggesting homosexual lover. To the dismay of the barons, however, Gaveston is no mere plaything or submissive object of the king's desire. Instead, he dominates the court, and like a Lord of Misrule, he turns the world topsy-turvy. Under the spell of Gaveston, Edward casts the queen aside and disregards the barons, while he offers the lowly Gaveston an assortment of noble titles, along with the power of the Great Seal and free access to the king's treasury (see 1.1.166–67). As the royal court is turned into a world of endless festivity, the serious business of governing the state and defending the land from invaders is blithely ignored.

Friendship and Love

Edward II was the first play on the English stage to depict a homoerotic relationship as a central concern and—as the play develops—in a relatively sympathetic light. Though the king and his minion are rarely free from the taint of epicurean pleasure-seeking, their relationship evolves into the most admirable in the play, and they rise in audience sympathy—if only by default—as the queen and Mortimer descend into ruthless Machiavellian scheming. Unlike his enemies, Edward genuinely prizes personal loyalty and friendship. But in the hostile world of the play, Edward's public responsibilities as king and his personal desire for friendship are hopelessly and tragically at odds—he cannot have both. By pursuing friendship with Gaveston, he nearly ruins the kingdom.

Yet Edward's passionate plea for the value of friendship seems difficult to dismiss:

> *Mortimer.* Why should you love him whom the world hates so?
> *Edward.* Because he loves me more than all the world. (1.4.76–77)

The words "friend" and "friendship" appear fifty-eight times in the play and seem continually to evoke the ideals of friendship described by Plato, Cicero, and Montaigne. In Plato's *Symposium*, Aristophanes tells of primordial double creatures, who are split apart by Jove and thus long for reunion with their other selves. Similarly, Cicero describes friendship as a relationship of complete mutuality, loyalty, and devotion, in which the friend becomes "another self." And Montaigne comments, "I am but half myself," after the death of his beloved friend.[4] Likewise, in the play Edward sees Gaveston as his other self:

> Embrace me, Gaveston, as I do thee.
> Why shouldst thou kneel? Knowest thou not who I am?
> Thy friend, thy self, another Gaveston! (1.1.140–42)

And later, when Gaveston is banished, Edward again evokes the Ciceronian notion of a friend as another self: "I from myself am banished" (1.4.118).

Cicero argues that only virtuous men can be true friends, but Cicero requires not ideal, perfected virtues but only the kinds of virtues possible in the world: "let us interpret the word 'virtue' by the familiar usage of our everyday life and speech, and not in pompous phrase apply to it the precise standards which certain philosophers use" (see Related Texts). Even by ordinary standards, Edward and Gaveston fall short in their virtues, yet Edward's devotion to Gaveston, and his generosity in promoting Gaveston with noble titles, seems in accord with Cicero's dictum that a friend should do all he can to raise the status of his friend (though Cicero calls for prudent limits). Even Edward's disregard of Isabella accords with Montaigne's view of the superiority of friendship over all other commitments—including marriage. When Edward is defeated and taken prisoner in act 4, he equates the loss of his friends with the loss of life itself—"And go I must. Life, farewell, with my friends!" (4.7.98)—a sentiment not far from the views of Cicero and Montaigne. Desiring too much of a good thing, Edward pursues friendship to an extreme, in reckless disregard of his political and marital obligations.

As every audience member realizes, the relationship of Edward and Gaveston is more than a friendship. At the center of the play is the sin that dare not speak its name. Indeed, the word "sodomy" never appears in the play or in Holinshed's account of the reign of Edward. As Emily Bartels argues, the absence of the word in Holinshed ironically tends to amplify the nature of the offense.[5] Though Holinshed's language is

---

4. See selections from Plato, Cicero, and Montaigne in Related Texts.
5. See Bartels 150–51.

highly suggestive—Gaveston lured the king into "heinous vices," "disordered doings," and "filthy and dishonorable exercises"—the vagueness of such terms encourages readers to suspect an array of sordid possibilities. Likewise, Marlowe's play includes remarks about the king's "looseness" (4.1.7, 4.4.11)—unspecified accusations that suggest a wide range of dark and illicit actions.

Sodomy was a vague and fuzzy concept in medieval and early modern Europe, and was often associated with a variety of supposedly related moral and criminal offenses, including heresy, witchcraft, sedition, and treason.[6] St. Thomas Aquinas, drawing from St. Paul and St. Augustine, defined sodomy with relative precision—"copulation with an undue sex, male with male, or female with female"—but Aquinas categorized sodomy with an assortment of sexual behaviors "from which generation cannot follow" (*ST* II–II.154.11). All such nonprocreative sexual acts, according to Aquinas, run contrary to the order of creation (and thus are offensive to the Creator). Moreover, Aquinas classified disordered sexual acts within the broader context of intemperate actions, including all varieties of the seven deadly sins.

During the Reformation, the scholastic categories and subcategories of Aquinas tended to blur into an amorphous stew of human depravity. John Calvin, in his *Commentary upon Genesis*, interprets the biblical narrative of Sodom and Gomorrah not as a story about sodomy in the limited sense but as a story about cities fallen into utter depravity: "they were not infected with one vice alone, but . . . were fallen to all boldness of sinning" (see Related Texts). The fact that the men of Sodom demanded sexual access to the men (actually angels) in Lot's house is barely mentioned in Calvin's analysis. Instead, his focus is on the larger concept of disordered sins. According to Calvin, the people of Sodom had fallen into "divers lusts" and a "great heap of wickedness." The proper social order had collapsed as the old men failed to exert their authority over the young, and the young lost all sense of virtue and modesty. The particulars of Sodom's "great heap of wickedness" are left vague by Calvin, with the implication that all imaginable sins of degenerate humanity were shamefully practiced in the doomed city.

Marlowe himself was accused of sodomy, and the accusations against him took the usual form of linking sodomy with an assortment of related offenses, including atheism, blasphemy, and even counterfeiting.[7] By

---

6. For early modern views of homoeroticism, see the studies of Bray, Smith, Stymeist, and Crewe.

7. See the report on Marlowe by Richard Baines and the comments by Thomas Kyd in the preceding section on the "Life of Marlowe."

implication, Marlowe led a disordered life, and one disorder led to the next: An unnatural desire for "tobacco and boys" led to an unnatural and perverse affection for counterfeiting coins. "Sin will pluck on sin" (*R3* 4.2.64), as we are told by Shakespeare's humpback king. In the play, Marlowe dramatizes a wide range of disordered, "sodomitic" actions: adulterous violations of the sanctity of marriage, disorderly acts of political ambition, and treasonous plans to depose and ultimately kill an anointed king. From a Calvinistic perspective, much of the action in the play seems a "great heap of wickedness"—a reflection of Sodom in all its infamy.

Ironically, Marlowe presents the most sodomitic relationship in the play as least offensive. Though the nobles are called "unnatural" in their rebellion against the king (3.2.86, 4.6.9), and Edward is called "unnatural" in his harsh vengeance on the nobles (3.3.33, 4.1.8), the term "unnatural" is never used to describe the relationship of Edward and Gaveston—not even by their enemies. Also, neither Edward nor Gaveston is represented according to the model of the "feminized" sodomite. Elizabethan moralists disparaged homoerotic love not only as a violation of the natural order but also because the passive partner was unnaturally "feminized." As Bruce Smith argues, the term "Ganymede" was often used in a derogatory sense to describe the younger, socially inferior, passive partner, while the active "masculine" role was less stigmatized (see Smith 195–96). The relationship that Marlowe presents on stage does not fit the often denigrated model. Instead, Marlowe followed the intriguing precedent found in his primary historical source. In Holinshed, Gaveston and Edward are described as boyhood friends of similar age, and neither man is passive or feminized, especially not Gaveston: "For being a goodly gentleman and a stout, as would not once yield an inch to any of them [the barons], which worthily procured him great envy amongst the chiefest peers of all the realm." In Holinshed and the play, Gaveston is the social inferior of the king, but the king grants noble titles to Gaveston and thus elevates his social standing.

In the play, Edward and Gaveston are "feminized" in particular images, but only briefly and inconsistently. Gaveston describes himself as Leander in relation to Edward as the feminine Hero. But their roles are reversed when Edward describes himself as Hercules and Gaveston as the boy Hylas (1.1.143), and later when the queen describes the king as Jove and Gaveston as young Ganymede (1.4.180). In the play at large, Edward and Gaveston are not represented in the traditional sodomitic roles of masculine man and feminized man but in the mode of mutuality and friendship—reflecting the ideals of Cicero and Montaigne.

Though Gaveston enters the play as a Vice figure and a Lord of Misrule, his love for the king evolves as the play develops. His tearful farewell to the king as he departs for Ireland indicates genuine affection: "For every look, my lord, drops down a tear; / Seeing I must go, do not renew my sorrow" (1.4.136–37). And when he is captured by the barons and confronts the imminence of his own death, Gaveston's only desire is to see Edward one last time—a desire without any political or economic motive: "Sweet sovereign, yet I come / To see thee ere I die!" (2.5.93–94). Moreover, the dishonorable trickery of Warwick (in violating his word by not allowing Gaveston a final meeting with Edward) makes Gaveston's constancy and devotion to the king seem all the more virtuous. Marlowe develops a similar pattern in depicting the relationship of Edward and Spencer, although the king's friendship with his new favorite is not so obsessive—and not clearly sexual. Edward embraces Spencer (3.2.177) and repeatedly calls him "sweet Spencer" (3.1.144, 4.7.72, 4.7.95), but no one refers to Spencer as the king's "minion." Regardless of the exact nature of their relationship, Spencer begins in act 2 as a cynical social climber, but in act 4 he goes to his death completely devoted to the king:

> O, is he gone? Is noble Edward gone,
> Parted from hence, never to see us more?
> Rend, sphere of heaven, and fire, forsake thy orb!
> Earth, melt to air! Gone is my sovereign,
> Gone, gone, alas, never to make return. (4.7.99–103)

While the queen and Mortimer become more malicious and Machiavellian as the play develops, the intimate friends of Edward become more loyal and virtuous.

Yet however sympathetic Edward may appear in his capacity for devoted friendship (and for eliciting friendship from others), Marlowe does not allow the audience to ignore his political failures. In terms of the microcosm-macrocosm analogy so familiar to Elizabethans, Edward is a weak king who cannot govern himself—and thus cannot govern his kingdom. With his "giddy brain . . . frantic" for love of Gaveston (1.4.314–15), Edward is overcome by his unruly passions as he is overmastered by his unruly barons. Though a king, he has no interest in governing but desires only to "frolic" with his minion (1.2.67, 1.4.73, 2.3.17). The irate barons may be proud and ambitious, but they express legitimate concerns for the tottering state. In his misrule and financial negligence, Edward exposes English lands to foreign invasion. The pesky Scots cross the northern borders, while French troops invade English territories on the continent, and the "wild O'Neil, with swarms of Irish kerns" raid English settlements in Ireland (see 2.2.161–66). In effect, the sodomite king exposes the body politic to sodomitic penetration by foreign invaders. For Marlowe's audiences in the early 1590s—anxious over the ongoing treat of a Spanish invasion—Edward's self-absorbed indifference to the defense of the nation would not seem a trivial offense.

In contrast to Queen Elizabeth's carefully cultivated image as the Virgin Queen who sacrificed personal happiness in order to serve the people of England—even to the extent of donning a suit of armor in 1588 to defend the homeland—Edward would seem an abysmal failure as king. Yet Marlowe continues to sustain a modulated and balanced portrayal of Edward, so that at times Edward appears analogous to Elizabeth. When the archbishop of Canterbury threatens the king with excommunication, Edward's response—"Why should a king be subject to a priest?" (1.4.96)— would clearly evoke the defiance of both Elizabeth and Henry VIII to the threat of excommunication and foreign meddling by the bishop of Rome. Under the threat of Elizabethan censorship, such analogies had to be subtle and understated, but at least momentarily Marlowe presents his sodomite king as the very incarnation of Tudor nationalism.

Unruly Nobles

The Ovidian myth of Actaeon and Diana, evoked by Gaveston in the opening scene, provides an apt analogy for the tragic fate of King Edward. Actaeon violated the natural order by spying on the goddess Diana bathing in a pool, and in consequence Actaeon is justly killed by his own hunting dogs. Likewise, Edward seeks forbidden erotic knowledge, and in turn he is hunted down by his rebellious barons and eventually killed. The Actaeon myth, however, casts a long shadow over the play and also anticipates the tragic fate of the nobles. As Edward transgresses the natural procreative order, the nobles transgress the natural political order. In their insistence that Gaveston not be recalled from banishment, the barons act with unruly boldness. Early in the first scene, the barons not only threaten Gaveston but directly threaten the king: "either change your mind, / Or look to see the throne, where you should sit, / To float in blood" (1.1.129–31). The barons violate the natural order of royal authority, and, like Actaeon, they are destroyed—hunted down by Edward and his loyal supporters in act 3 (and though Mortimer is spared, he is undone by the son of Edward in the final scene).

Throughout the play, Marlowe straddles the political fault line between the natural rights of the king and the natural rights of the nobles. Kent— the most reliable choric voice in the play—speaks at various points for both positions. He defends Edward against the threatening barons in act 1, but later he denounces the "Unnatural king," who slaughters his own noblemen (4.1.8), and by the end of the play, Kent returns to his original position, denouncing Mortimer and Isabella for their "unnatural revolt" against the "lawful king" (4.6.4–9). Lurking beneath the text is the doctrine—highly contested in early modern Europe—of the divine right of kings (the doctrine that monarchs rule by divine will, and should never be judged or opposed by any human authority). Homilies in favor of divine right were preached from the pulpit on a regular basis in all the churches in England and thus would have been intimately familiar to Marlowe's audiences.[8] Opposing views—familiar at least to more literate playgoers—were expressed in various treatises, most of them Protestant, that argued against the sacred and sacramental status of royal authority, and in defense of the right of the people (by way of Parliament) to depose an immoral and irresponsible king.[9] In the play, Marlowe keeps both views in active tension—perhaps with the effect of discrediting and demystifying the claims of both the king and the nobles to any "natural" political order (and thus implicitly endorsing more contingent political views, such as those in Machiavelli's *Prince* and *Discourses*).

Appropriately, the ambitious and unnatural nobles seem relatively indifferent to the unnatural sexual proclivities of the king. Their resentful comments about Gaveston may even suggest a petulant jealousy on the part of the barons. What they most desire is to be in the position of their hated rival—although for political, not sexual, favors. Mortimer Senior attempts to calm young Mortimer by assuring him that many great men have had their minions:

> The mightiest kings have had their minions:
> Great Alexander loved Hephaestion,
> The conquering Hercules for Hylas wept,
> And for Patroclus stern Achilles drooped.
> And not kings only, but the wisest men:
> The Roman Tully loved Octavius,
> Grave Socrates, wild Alcibiades.
> Then let his grace, whose youth is flexible,
> And promiseth as much as we can wish,
> Freely enjoy that vain lightheaded earl,
> For riper years will wean him from such toys. (1.4.391–401)

---

8. See *An Homily against Disobedience and Willful Rebellion* in Related Texts.

9. See John Ponet's *A Short Treatise of Politic Power* and the anonymous *Vindiciae contra Tyrannos: A Defense of Liberty against Tyrants* in Related Texts.

Implicit in the speech of Mortimer Senior is the medieval and early modern assumption that homoeroticism is not the inclination of a particular group but a symptom of the depraved and fallen condition of all humanity, and thus a behavior that anyone could fall into, and grow out of. In response, Mortimer Junior expresses the real issue for the nobles—not sex, but power:

> Uncle, his wanton humor grieves not me,
> But this I scorn, that one so basely born
> Should by his sovereign's favor grow so pert,
> And riot it with the treasure of the realm. (1.4.402–5)

In the zero-sum game of medieval politics, the offices and favors bestowed on Gaveston are offices and favors that will not be granted to the barons. In the political calculations of young Mortimer, the only "natural" force in the play, or at least the only force that he recognizes, is Machiavellian self-interest and the will to power.

Isabella and Mortimer

The sodomitic love of Edward and Gaveston in acts 1–2 is mirrored in the adulterous love of Isabella and Mortimer in acts 4–5. Indeed, Gaveston and Mortimer are closely paralleled figures. As Gaveston pursues self-advancement through love of the king, Mortimer pursues political power by way of the queen.

In adapting Holinshed's *Chronicles* for the stage, Marlowe's most prominent changes were to the roles of Mortimer and Isabella. In Holinshed, the queen is barely mentioned until the last quarter of the narrative. She takes no part in the banishment or recall of Gaveston, and she emerges as a major figure only after she is sent to France on a diplomatic mission to help resolve disputes over territories in France held as fiefs by the English king. At the French court, she is "drawn and allured" into "evil counsel" by unnamed courtiers, and eventually she hatches a plan for rebellion against Edward. Likewise, Mortimer does not appear as a major figure in Holinshed until late in the narrative when he escapes from the Tower of London and flees to France where he joins the queen's rebellion.

In reworking his source material, Marlowe greatly expands the roles of Isabella and Mortimer, developing them as major figures from the start. In effect, Marlowe reads into the historical narrative possible motivations in Isabella and Mortimer that Holinshed never mentions. Holinshed eventually reveals (in the early pages of his history of Edward III) that Mortimer and the queen were lovers, and that she became pregnant by Mortimer. In the play, Marlowe backdates the adulterous affair and suggests in the opening scenes the possibility of an illicit—though teasingly enigmatic—relationship. In Isabella's first encounter with Mortimer on stage, she affectionately calls him "gentle Mortimer" and "sweet Mortimer" (1.2.47, 81), but at the same time she seems entirely devoted to Edward, and indeed she appears as a model of saintly patience and virtue. She is even willing to endure a "melancholy life" and allow her husband to "frolic with his minion" (1.2.66–67), and she begs Mortimer not to oppose or take arms against the king. Edward calls her a "French strumpet," and Gaveston names "Mortimer" as her lover (1.4.145–47), but these accusations seem baseless and malicious. Pembroke's description of Isabella as a "saint" (1.4.190) seems far more reliable. In act 2, however, the queen makes the early accusations against her seem credible when she confides to Mortimer: "So well hast thou deserved, sweet Mortimer, / As Isabel could live with thee forever" (2.4.59–60). And by act 4 their adulterous affair is confirmed by Kent: "for Mortimer / And Isabel do kiss while they conspire" (4.6.12–13). When exactly did the change occur? Did the queen present a face of love to the king out of genuine loyalty and devotion? Or was she, even in act 1, secretly weighing her options and testing the waters with Mortimer?[10]

Any interpretation of Isabella depends on a moment in the play in which we cannot hear a word she says. After the barons reject her request for Gaveston's return from banishment, Isabella turns to Mortimer:

> Sweet Mortimer, sit down by me a while,
> And I will tell thee reasons of such weight
> As thou wilt soon subscribe to his repeal. (1.4.225–27)

The queen and Mortimer then speak privately, so there is no telling what exactly the queen says, although it is clear that she convinces Mortimer to support the return of Gaveston. Moments later, when the barons stubbornly reject Mortimer's appeal, Isabella urges the barons to listen to Mortimer—as though she knows exactly what he is about to say:

> *Queen.* Yet, good my lord, hear what he can allege.
> *Warwick.* All that he speaks is nothing; we are resolved.

---

10. As Sara Deats argues, Isabella seems to perform the roles that are most advantageous to her in response to political exigencies. At first she plays the role of "patient Griselda," but later she changes to a "scheming Jezebel." See Deats 166–67.

> *Mortimer.* Do you not wish that Gaveston were dead?
> *Pembroke.* I would he were.
> *Mortimer.* Why then, my lord, give me but leave to speak.
>   (1.4.250–54)

Did the queen in private conversation with Mortimer plead for the recall of Gaveston in self-sacrificial and loving devotion to the king? And did Mortimer then improvise the added possibility that Gaveston could be killed? Or did Isabella hatch the entire plan? When Lancaster asks the obvious question—"but how chance this was not done before?"—Mortimer responds, "Because, my lords, it was not thought upon" (1.4.272–73). Did it take a woman, a sly Machiavellian she-fox, to first propose the idea?

Was Isabella at the start of the play a long-suffering saint? Or was she all along a manipulative and supersubtle Frenchwoman, and did she plead for the return of Gaveston so that he would be killed and she could reclaim her position beside the king? And when Gaveston is executed, and the king turns his affections immediately to Spencer, does the queen then pursue her options with Mortimer?

The unknowable and secretive motives of Isabella are mirrored in the dark and secretive motivations of Mortimer. What exactly does Mortimer want early in the play? To rid the kingdom of sycophants? To depose the king? To kill the king? To make himself king? It becomes clear by act 5 that he wants it all. But did he harbor those motives in act 1, or do his motives change and evolve? The play offers various hints but not certainty. Early in the play, Mortimer is the first baron to mention the possibility of deposing Edward: "The king shall lose his crown, for we have power, / And courage too, to be revenged at full" (1.2.59–60). Later, when the barons attack Tynemouth Castle, Lancaster announces their limited strategic goals—"None be so hardy as to touch the king, / But neither spare you Gaveston nor his friends" (2.3.27–28)—but after they breech the walls, Mortimer immediately says to the queen, "tell us where's the king?" (2.4.30). Does Mortimer's eagerness to find the king indicate dark, barely restrained thoughts of regicide?

The hidden motives of Isabella and Mortimer are implicitly linked to the hidden and unseen sodomitic actions of Edward and Gaveston. In both cases, that which is secretive and private evokes a range of nefarious and illicit suspicions. Moreover, the adulterous, treasonous, and regicidal offenses of Mortimer and Isabella—as violations of the divinely sanctioned natural order—would have evoked further associations with the unnatural actions of Edward and his minion.

Royal Sodomite or Saintly Martyr?

In acts 4–5, the rebellious Mortimer and Isabella rise in power and decline in moral standing, while the king loses power but gains in dignity and virtue (a pattern imitated by Shakespeare in *Richard II*). At the end of act 4, King Edward, hounded by his enemies and taking refuge with monks in the abbey, expresses longings he had never before shown:

> Come, Spencer, come, Baldock, come sit down by me;
> Make trial now of that philosophy
> That in our famous nurseries of arts
> Thou sucked'st from Plato and from Aristotle.
> [*To the Abbot*] Father, this life contemplative is heaven;
> O that I might this life in quiet lead! (4.7.16–21)

A desire for escape from the cares of the world is suggested earlier in the play when Edward offers to give his kingdom to the barons if only they would allow him "some nook or corner . . . To frolic with my dearest Gaveston" (1.4.72–73). With the monks, however, Edward longs not for the pleasures of the mundane world but for the "life contemplative" of learning and prayer. In terms of platonic allegory, Edward begins to ascend the ladder of love, seeking beauty and goodness in higher forms. He begins to evolve from a "wild Alcibiades" to a "Grave Socrates" (1.4.397).

In Holinshed's *Chronicles*, the defeated and imprisoned king fully repents for his misdeeds: "And lastly he besought the lords now in his misery to forgive him such offenses as he had committed against them." In Marlowe's play, however, Edward's repentance is partial and erratic at best. He continues to speak of his "guiltless life" (5.1.73), and his moments of self-understanding are fleeting and inconsistent:

> Commend me to my son, and bid him rule
> Better than I. Yet how have I transgressed,
> Unless it be with too much clemency? (5.1.121–23)

He wavers in his repentance as he wavers in his willingness to surrender the crown. Anticipating Shakespeare's Gloucester, who is cured of despair only to fall into "ill thoughts again" (*KL* 5.2.9), Edward's movements toward redemption are uneven and recidivistic. He longs for eternal life—"Now, sweet God of Heaven, / Make me despise this transitory pomp, / And sit for aye enthronizèd in heaven" (5.1.107–9)—but his desire for spiritual transcendence is weighed down with confusion and sulking self-pity.

A tragic hero who suffers into wisdom is not the usual fare from Marlowe. Yet in *Edward II* Marlowe charts a course distinctly different from his earlier works. While Tamburlaine, Barabas, and Faustus possess enormous strength and power from the start, Edward begins as an underachiever—a misfit king, weak and incompetent, incapable of ruling or defending his kingdom. The trajectory of *Edward II* aligns more closely with the tragedies of Aeschylus and Sophocles (and anticipates the mature tragedies of Shakespeare). As Edward loses power, he gains in wisdom—although, like Gloucester and Lear, his gains are partial, erratic, and confused (modeled perhaps more on lived experience than on literary precursors).

Considering the ruinous civil disorder during Edward's reign, Holinshed is surprisingly favorable in his final assessment of the king, even suggesting a saintly power after his death:

> The fame went that by this Edward the second, after his death, many miracles were wrought. So that the like opinion of him was conceived as before had been of earl Thomas of Lancaster, namely amongst the common people. . . .
>
> And albeit in his youth he [Edward] fell into certain light crimes, and after by the company and counsel of evil men was induced unto more heinous vices, yet was it thought that he purged the same by repentance, and patiently suffered many reproofs, and finally death itself (as before ye have heard) after a most cruel manner.

Marlowe makes no mention of miracles after the death of Edward, but he clearly develops Holinshed's suggestions of a repentant king. And while Holinshed suggests saintly virtues in both Lancaster and Edward, Marlowe develops such indications only for Edward. While Lancaster and the barons go to their deaths with only perfunctory comments about the afterlife, Edward endures a prolonged process of purgatorial suffering. Marlowe reserves the possibility of spiritual transformation exclusively for his sodomite king—perhaps with a vicious sense of irony, although the final scenes may suggest otherwise.

Though devoted only to himself and Gaveston early in the play, in prison Edward shows the first signs of concern for his royal lineage and the future of England—appropriate concerns for a virtuous king. After a considerable display of histrionic reluctance, he surrenders his crown with the understanding that his son would assume the throne (and as many in the audience would know, Edward III will prove a heroic warrior-king who will defeat the French at Crecy and Calais). Marlowe also develops an emerging and impressive stoic virtue in the king. Though poisoned, starved, and sleep-deprived by his jailers, Edward endures all (see 5.5.1–11)—in contrast to his luxurious and epicurean pursuits earlier in the play.

As many scholars have noted, providential themes are muted in *Edward II*. Unlike the history plays of Shakespeare, Marlowe's play offers no prophetic voices that speak for divine justice and an impending final reckoning, nor are there any supernatural signs and wonders indicating a larger cosmic plan at work. The world of Marlowe's history play is far too gritty and dark, a world of political maneuvering and visceral ambitions, with little room for spiritual transcendence. And yet Edward, in the final scenes, may prove the exception. Moments before his execution, Edward's mind is focused not on Gaveston or Spencer but on his God:

> Yet stay a while; forbear thy bloody hand,
> And let me see the stroke before it comes,
> That even then when I shall lose my life,
> My mind may be more steadfast on my God. (5.5.75–78)

The potential for martyrdom in Edward is emphasized in a series of Christ analogies. When captured by Leicester and his men, Edward offers his own heart in a gesture of Christlike self-sacrifice to save his companions: "Here, man, rip up this panting breast of mine, / And take my heart in rescue of my friends" (4.7.66–67). The ironic comment of his executioner—"These hands were never stained with innocent blood" (5.5.81)—clearly echoes the words of Pilate before Christ (see Matt. 27:24). And the penultimate words of Edward in the play—"Assist me, sweet God, and receive my soul!" (5.5.109)—evoke the final words of Christ on the cross—"And Jesus cried with a loud voice, and said, Father, into thine hands I commend my spirit" (Luke 23:46).[11] Moreover, while Holinshed mentions nothing about the duration of the king's imprisonment, in the play Edward twice refers to his imprisonment for "ten days" (5.5.60, 5.5.94)—an allusion perhaps to the imprisoned faithful in the book of Revelation who endure suffering but are promised eternal salvation: "Behold, it shall come to pass, that the devil shall cast some of you into prison, that ye may be tried, and ye shall have tribulation ten days; be thou faithful unto the death, and I will give thee the

---

11. Patrick Ryan argues that Edward also endures some of the humiliations of Christ not mentioned in the passion narratives of the New Testament but widely believed, in medieval and early modern Europe, to be foreshadowed in the Old Testament. Like Edward, Jesus, after his arrest, was supposedly shaved (as was the sheep led to the slaughter in Isaiah 53:7), and, like Edward, Jesus was believed to have been placed in a filthy dungeon (as the prophet Jeremiah was lowered into a filthy cistern in Jeremiah 38:6). See Ryan 465–90.

crown of life" (Rev. 2:10). Such an apocalyptic allusion would have been far less obscure during the religious upheavals of the sixteenth century.

Allegorically, as Edward becomes a Christ figure, Mortimer becomes a devil figure, in league with the murderer Lightborn, a character without precedent in the historical sources, and with a name that evokes "Lucifer."[12] By hiring Lightborn to kill the king, Mortimer becomes the prime instigator in the rape-execution of Edward. Disdainful of Gaveston's intimacy with the king early in the play, Mortimer now (with the aid of Lightborn) ironically enacts the sodomitic role of Gaveston—with red-hot vengeance.

Neither in Holinshed nor in the stage play do the murderers ever speak of the method of execution as punishment for the king's sexual offenses. Their concern is only with performing the murder by a method that will leave no evidence of the crime—no outward marks of violence on the body of the king. In the play, however, the homoerotic affections of the king are more developed, and thus the stage action would likely appear to Marlowe's audiences as symbolic—a torturous reenactment of the sin of sodomy, an image of Dantesque *contrapasso*.[13] Yet the overall response of audience members to the horrific stage action is difficult to assess and has been much debated by scholars. Would the murder have been seen primarily as an act of poetic justice and a moral indictment of the sodomite king? Or does the abhorrent mode of execution redound on the inhuman cruelty of Mortimer? Or does the action perhaps discredit the traditional moral order that would affirm the justice of the deed?

Though the play gestures toward martyrdom for the king, very few people could see or read this play and feel any sense of confidence in the king's redemption. His suffering is far too degrading, and indeed Marlowe seems to make every effort to intensify the suffering of Edward by combining the most repugnant details from the chronicles of Holinshed and Stow—and then pushing the degradation of the king even further. In the shaving episode in Stow's *Annals of England* (an event without counterpart in Holinshed), the tormenters of the king shave him with water from a "ditch," while in Marlowe's play his jailers use "puddle water" from a sewage channel in a vicious parody of baptism (5.3.27–30).[14] And in

---

12. Harry Levin notes that "Lightborn" appears as the name of one of the devils in the Chester mystery plays (see Levin 101).

13. Dante, however, is far more kind and gentle with the sodomites of his underworld. In *Inferno*, canto 15, the sodomites wander about in a sterile and fiery desert (not an especially horrific fate). In Protestant England, the work of Dante was generally unavailable and unread, but notions of poetic justice and *contrapasso* were commonplace in sermons, literature, and traditional iconography.

14. See selections from Stow's *Annals of England* in Related Texts.

Holinshed's *Chronicles*, the king is imprisoned in a "chamber *over* a foul filthy dungeon, full of dead carrion," while in the play the king is not over but "*in* a vault up to the knees in water" (5.5.2, italics added). The horrific murder of the king, however, seems virtually the same in Holinshed and in the play—even Marlowe could not improve on that. The degrading humiliations of Edward in act 5 would likely leave the audience to wonder: Does the king endure the purgatorial suffering of a sinner moving toward salvation, or does he endure the putative suffering of the hopelessly damned? In platonic terms, does Edward ascend from the lower levels of carnal love to higher ideals of love, or does he end allegorically (and literally) in a "cave of care" (5.1.32), lingering in darkness and confusion?

Does Marlowe make Edward a Christ figure only to scandalously degrade him? Or does Marlowe degrade him in order to show Edward's emerging tenacity for stoic endurance and spiritual transcendence? Edward's last words are not even words but instead an animal "cry," loud enough to "raise the town" (5.5.114)—perhaps echoed a decade later in Lear's agonizing howls over the body of his murdered daughter (*KL* 5.3.262). The higher values of compassion and transcendent understanding might be sustained even in the hostile territory of *King Lear*, but can they be sustained by a king standing knee-deep in sewage?

Marlowe is often seen as a radical, an outsider, a voice of denial and contempt, and certainly Marlowe provided abundant evidence to support such a view. In his brief career as a playwright, he entertained audiences with an impressive assortment of hero-villains: a Scythian shepherd who defeats and humiliates anointed kings and defiantly burns the Koran on stage, a Maltese Jew who exposes the hypocrisy and villainy of the Christians who exploit him, and an overeducated Wittenberg doctor who defies divine law and makes an alliance with the forces of hell. In *Edward II*, Marlowe may tease the audience with touches of Christian allegory and biblical allusions, only to conclude with flowing channels of sewage and a perverse anal crucifixion—a full-scale assault on the values that most of his audience would have held as sacred. But it is also possible that Marlowe, like many conflicted and tortured souls, never stopped believing in the very things he defied.

BIBLIOGRAPHY

Editions of *Edward II*

Marlowe, Christopher. *The Troublesome Reign and Lamentable Death of Edward the Second*. London, 1594. STC 17437.

Marlowe, Christopher. *Edward the Second*. Facsimile of 1594 Quarto. Edited by W. W. Greg. Malone Society Reprints. Oxford: Oxford University Press, 1925.

Marlowe, Christopher. *Edward the Second*. Edited by Charles R. Forker. Manchester: Manchester University Press, 1994.

Marlowe, Christopher. *Edward the Second*. Edited by Mathew R. Martin. Ontario: Broadview, 2010.

Marlowe, Christopher. *Edward the Second*. Edited by Martin Wiggins and Robert Lindsey. 2nd ed. London: A & C Black, 1997.

Marlowe, Christopher. *Doctor Faustus and Other Plays*. Edited by David Bevington and Eric Rasmussen. Oxford: Oxford University Press, 1995.

Primary Sources

Aquinas, St. Thomas. *Summa Theologiae*. Translated by the Fathers of the English Dominican Province. Westminster: Christian Classics, 1981.

Bale, John. *First Two Parts of the Acts of English Votaries*. London, 1551. STC 1273.5.

Bible. Geneva translation. London, 1587. STC 2146.

Calvin, John. *Commentary upon the First Book of Moses Called Genesis*. 1554. Translated by Thomas Tymme. London, 1578. STC 4393.

Cicero, Marcus Tullius. *De Senectute, De Amicitia, De Divinatione [On Old Age, On Friendship, On Divination]*. Translated by William A. Falconer. Loeb Classical Library. Cambridge, MA: Harvard University Press, 1923.

Dante. *Inferno*. Translated by Anthony Esolen. New York: Modern Library, 2005.

Estienne, Henri. *A World of Wonders, or An introduction to a treatise touching the conformity of ancient and modern wonders, or A preparative treatise to* the Apology for Herodotus. 1566. Translated by R. C. [Richard Carew]. London, 1607. STC 10553.

Fabyan, Robert. *The Chronicle of Fabyan.* London, 1559. Vol. 2. STC 10664.

Grafton, Richard. *The Chronicle and History of the Affairs of England.* London, 1569. Vol. 2. STC 12147.

Holinshed, Raphael. *The Third Volume of Chronicles.* London, 1587. STC 13569.

Homily against Disobedience and Willful Rebellion. London, 1570. STC 13680.6.

Machiavelli, Niccolò. *Selected Political Writings.* Translated by David Wootton. Indianapolis: Hackett Publishing, 1994.

Montaigne, Michel de. *The Essays of Montaigne.* Translated by John Florio. London, 1603. STC 18041.

Ovid. *Metamorphoses.* Translated by Arthur Golding. 1567. Edited by Madeleine Forey. Baltimore: John Hopkins University Press, 2001.

Plato, *Symposium.* Translated by Alexander Nehamas and Paul Woodruff. Indianapolis: Hackett Publishing, 1989.

Plato, *Complete Works.* Edited by John M. Cooper and D. S. Hutchinson. Indianapolis: Hackett Publishing, 1997.

Ponet, John. *A Short Treatise of Politic Power.* Strasburg, 1556. STC 20178.

Shakespeare, William. *Complete Works of Shakespeare.* Edited by David Bevington. 6th ed. New York: Pearson Longman, 2009.

Stow, John. *Annals of England.* London, 1592. STC 23334.

Vindiciae contra Tyrannos: A Defense of Liberty against Tyrants. 1579. Translated into English. London, 1648. Wing L415.

Virgil, *Eclogues of Virgil.* Translated by David Ferry. New York: Farrar, Straus & Giroux, 2000.

Secondary Sources

Bartels, Emily C. *Spectacles of Strangeness: Imperialism, Alienation, and Marlowe.* Philadelphia: University of Pennsylvania Press, 1993.

Bevington, David M. *From Mankind to Marlowe.* Cambridge, MA: Harvard University Press, 1962.

Bianco, Marcie. "To Sodomize a Nation: *Edward II*, Ireland, and the Threat of Penetration." *Early Modern Literary Studies* 16 (2007): 1–21.

Borris, Kenneth. *Same-Sex Desire in the English Renaissance: A Sourcebook of Texts, 1470–1650*. New York: Routledge, 2003.

Bray, Alan. *Homosexuality in Renaissance England*. New York: Columbia University Press, 1982.

Brown, Georgia E. "Tampering with the Records: Engendering the Political Community and Marlowe's Appropriation of the Past in *Edward II*." *Marlowe's Empery: Expanding His Critical Contexts*. Edited by Sara Munson Deats and Robert A. Logan. Newark: University of Delaware Press, 2002. 164–87.

Burnett, Mark Thornton. "*Edward II* and Elizabethan Politics." *Marlowe, History, and Sexuality*. Edited by Paul Whitfield White. New York: American Studies Press, 1998. 91–107.

Cartelli, Thomas. "*Edward II*." *The Cambridge Companion to Christopher Marlowe*. Edited by Patrick Cheney. Cambridge: Cambridge University Press, 2004. 158–73.

Cheney, Patrick. *Marlowe's Republican Authorship: Lucan, Liberty, and the Sublime*. New York: Palgrave Macmillan, 2009.

Cole, Douglas. *Christopher Marlowe and the Renaissance of Tragedy*. Westport, CT: Greenwood Press, 1995.

Crewe, Jonathan. "Disorderly Love: Sodomy Revisited in Marlowe's *Edward II*." *Criticism* 51 (2009): 385–99.

Danson, Lawrence. "Continuity and Character in Shakespeare and Marlowe." *Studies in English Literature* 26 (1986): 217–34.

Deats, Sara Munson. *Sex, Gender, and Desire in the Plays of Christopher Marlowe*. Newark: University of Delaware Press, 1998.

Dessen, Alan C. "*Edward II* and Residual Allegory." *Christopher Marlowe the Craftsman: Lives, Stage, and Page*. Edited by Sarah K. Scott and Michael L. Stapleton. Aldershot, UK: Ashgate, 2010. 63–78.

Geckle, George L. *'Tamburlaine' and 'Edward II': Text and Performance*. Basingstoke, UK: Macmillan, 1988.

Goldberg, Jonathan. *Sodometries: Renaissance Texts, Modern Sensibilities*. Stanford, CA: Stanford University Press, 1992.

Honan, Park. *Christopher Marlowe: Poet and Spy*. Oxford: Oxford University Press, 2005.

Hopkins, Lisa. "Christopher Marlowe and the Succession to the English Crown." *Yearbook of English Studies* 38 (2008): 183–98.

Johnson, Paul. *A History of Christianity*. New York: Simon & Schuster, 1976.

Kuriyama, Constance B. *Christopher Marlowe: A Renaissance Life*. Ithaca, NY: Cornell University Press, 2002.

Levin, Harry. *The Overreacher: A Study of Marlowe.* 1952. Gloucester, MA: Peter Smith, 1974.

Logan, Robert A. *Shakespeare's Marlowe: The Influence of Christopher Marlowe on Shakespeare's Artistry.* Aldershot, UK: Ashgate, 2007.

Lunney, Ruth. *Marlowe and the Popular Tradition: Innovation in the English Drama before 1595.* Manchester: Manchester University Press, 2002.

Martin, Matthew. "Plays of Passion: Pain, History, and Theater in *Edward II.*" *The Sacred and Profane in English Renaissance Literature.* Edited by Mary A. Papazian. Newark: University of Delaware Press, 2008. 84–107.

McAdam, Ian. *The Irony of Identity: Self and Imagination in the Drama of Christopher Marlowe.* Newark: University of Delaware Press, 1999.

Orgel, Stephen. *Impersonations: The Performance of Gender in Shakespeare's England.* Cambridge: Cambridge University Press, 1996.

Parks, Joan. "History, Tragedy, and Truth in Christopher Marlowe's *Edward II.*" *Studies in English Literature* 39 (1999): 275–90.

Pearson, Meg F. "Audience as Witness in *Edward II.*" *Imagining the Audience in Early Modern Drama, 1558–1642.* Edited by Jennifer A. Low and Nova Myhill. New York: Palgrave Macmillan, 2011. 93–111.

Pettitt, Tom. "Categorical Transgression in Marlovian Death and Damnation." *Orbis Litterarum* 65 (2010): 292–317.

Riggs, David. *The World of Christopher Marlowe.* London: Faber, 2004.

Rutkoski, Marie. "Breeching the Boy in Marlowe's *Edward II.*" *Studies in English Literature* 46 (2006): 281–304.

Ryan, Patrick. "Marlowe's *Edward II* and the Medieval Passion Play." *Comparative Drama* 32 (1998–99): 465–95.

Sanders, Wilbur. *The Dramatist and the Received Idea.* Cambridge: Cambridge University Press, 1968.

Sirluck, Katherine A. "Marlowe's *Edward II* and the Pleasure of Outrage." *Modern Language Studies* 22 (1992): 15–24.

Smith, Bruce R. *Homosexual Desire in Shakespeare's England.* Chicago: University of Chicago Press, 1991.

Stewart, Alan. "Edward II and Male Same-Sex Desire." *Early Modern English Drama.* Edited by Garrett A. Sullivan, Patrick Cheney, and Andrew Hadfield. New York: Oxford University Press, 2006. 82–95.

Stymeist, David. "Status, Sodomy, and the Theater in Marlowe's *Edward II.*" *Studies in English Literature* 44 (2004): 233–53.

Thurn, David H. "Sovereignty, Disorder, and Fetishism in Marlowe's *Edward II.*" *Renaissance Drama* 21 (1990): 115–41.

Tromly, Fred B. *Playing with Desire: Christopher Marlowe and the Art of Tantalization.* Toronto: University of Toronto Press, 1998.

Tyler, Sharon. "Bedfellows Make Strange Politics: Christopher Marlowe's *Edward II.*" *Drama, Sex and Politics.* Edited by James Redmond. Cambridge: Cambridge University Press, 1985. 55–68.

DATE AND NOTE ON THE TEXT

No evidence survives to date *Edward II* with certainty, though 1592 seems plausible. The title page of the first quarto edition claims that the play "was sundry times publicly acted in the honorable city of London by the right honorable the Earl of Pembroke's Servants." The earliest records for Pembroke's acting company date from the last three months of 1592, though earlier performances were possible. Internal evidence also suggests the play was written late in Marlowe's career—perhaps his last play. Unlike his other plays (with dominating figures such as Tamburlaine, Barabas, and Faustus), *Edward II* develops a range of subtle and complex characters, with a central figure who is more of a misfit king than a bold overachiever. Aesthetically, the play seems an effort on Marlowe's part to break new ground.

The first edition of the play—*The troublesome raigne and lamentable death of Edward the second, King of England: with the tragicall fall of proud Mortimer . . . Written by Chri. Marlo, Gent.*—was printed in London in 1594. The text survives in two copies, one in Zurich, Switzerland (on which this edition is based), and another in Erlangen, Germany. A third copy survived into the twentieth century in Cassel, Germany, but was lost or destroyed during World War II (though all textual variants in the lost Cassel copy had been carefully noted by W. W. Greg in his facsimile edition). Differences among the three copies are slight—merely adjustments in punctuation and spelling—which indicate that the text was carefully proofread and some minor revisions were made while in press. The text was printed in an octavo edition, but with the size and shape of a quarto (and thus has traditionally been referred to as the first quarto or the "Q text").

The Q text does not include a list of *dramatis personae*, and the text is not divided into acts or scenes. Stage directions are often incomplete and sometimes not precisely located, and speech prefixes are inconsistent (*Kent/ Edmund, Isabella/Queen*) and sometimes vague (merely *Bishop* or *Lady* or *Lord*). The lack of full and precise stage directions suggests that the copy text was Marlowe's manuscript (and not the playhouse copy that would have been used for actual productions).

I have added act and scene divisions according to modern conventions (although there is no evidence that Marlowe thought of the play in terms of five acts, and an Elizabethan audience would never be aware of such divisions). Speech prefixes have been made consistent (always *Kent* and *Queen*), spelled out (*Lan* and *Qu* are expanded to *Lancaster* and *Queen*), and made more specific (*Lady* is adjusted to *Margaret*, and *Bishop* is specified as *Canterbury* or *Coventry* or *Winchester*). Misprinted verse lines have also been silently emended.

I have conserved the stage directions of the Q text, with the exception of silently translating occasional Latin terms and abbreviating the redundant *Exeunt omnes* to *Exeunt*. The Q text does not indicate any *Asides*, and thus all *Asides* are editorial conjectures based on dialogue and context. All editorial stage directions are enclosed in brackets.

The most substantive textual problem in the Q text is the confusion in the names *Arundel* and *Matrevis*. *Arundel* first appears in 2.5, and all references to him are consistent, until the end of the scene when he is suddenly referred to as *Matrevis* in the stage direction after line 97 and the speech prefix at line 103. In 3.2, the name *Matrevis* appears consistently, and yet the content of his speech at 3.2.96–100 clearly indicates that he is the *Arundel* who served as messenger for the king in 2.5.32–40. In 4.3, *Matrevis* appears in the opening stage direction and his single speech prefix at line 9, but he is called "lord of Arundel" in the dialogue. Thereafter, the confusion subsides, and only *Matrevis* appears in act 5. Some editors have concluded that he is one character, with Matrevis as his proper name and Earl of Arundel as his title (see Wiggins edition). Most editors, however, treat them as two distinct characters: the Earl of Arundel in acts 2–4, and Matrevis in act 5. The confusion may be the result of doubling of the roles. Marlowe may have planned for both roles to be played by the same actor, and thus he may have carelessly confused the names in the manuscript. In this edition, I have treated them as two distinct characters for the following reasons: first, the Arundel-Matrevis figure who appears in acts 2–4 consistently acts as a supporter and ally of the king, while the Matrevis figure in act 5 serves as a jailer of the king, and his actions toward Edward are entirely hostile; second, the Arundel-Matrevis figure in acts 2–4 is repeatedly called a "lord" (2.5.32, 2.5.80, 3.2.89, 4.3.7), while Matrevis in act 5 is never called a lord; and third, in Holinshed's *Chronicles* (the major source text), Arundel and Matrevis are clearly two different characters (Arundel is among the supporters of King Edward, and Matrevis is one of his jailers).

I have modernized spelling and punctuation throughout the text, and silently corrected all minor typesetting errors. All significant changes to the Q text are listed below:

1.1.22 fawn (Q: fanne)
1.1.36 SP *3 Poor Man* (speech prefix in Q is *Sold.* [Soldier])
1.1.39 porcupine (Q: porpintine)
1.1.46, 48 SP *Poor Men* (speech prefix in Q is *Omnes* [Latin for "All"])
1.1.126 Welshry (Q: Wilshere)

1.2.29 We'll (Q: Weele)

1.2.76–78 In Q these three lines are assigned to Mortimer, but the bishop of Canterbury is more likely the speaker since Lambeth Palace was his residence.

1.4.102 make (Q: may)

1.4.115 ne'er (Q: neare)

1.4.347 embroidery (Q: imbrotherie)

1.4.393 Hercules (Q: Hector)

2.1.73 In Q the stage direction (*Exit*) appears one line earlier.

2.2.81–82 In Q both lines are assigned to Pembroke: "Heere here King: convey hence Gaveston, thaile murder him." Most likely "King" was intended as a speech prefix but the compositors of Q mistook it as part of the dialogue.

2.2.218 In Q the stage direction (*Exit*) appears one line earlier.

2.4.0, 3 In Q these two stage directions are combined at the start of scene.

2.4.69 *Exit* (Q: *Exeunt*)

2.5.18 King (Q: Kind)

2.5.36 that (Q: yet)

2.5.97 SD *Arundel* (stage direction in Q has *Mat.* [Matrevis])

2.5.103 SP *Arundel* (speech prefix in Q is *Mat.* [Matrevis])

3.2.88–115 Q has *Matre.* (Matrevis) in the stage direction, speech prefixes, and dialogue in these lines. All have been amended to *Arundel* (since it is clear in lines 96–100 that this lord is the same as the lord of Arundel who served as messenger for the king in 2.5.32–40).

3.2.120 Struck (Q: Strake)

3.2.127 *Edward kneels* (Q: *Edward kneeles, and saith*)

3.2.151, 156 Q has *Messen.* (Messenger) as the speech prefixes for these two lines. Both have been amended to *Herald* (in keeping with *Herald* in the preceding stage direction).

3.3.18 Thou'd (Q: Th'ad), them (Q: thee)

4.2.7 He (Q: A). "A" is an unstressed form of "he."

4.2.81 lords (Q: lord)

4.3.0, 9 Q has *Matr.* (Matrevis) in the stage direction at the start of the scene and as the speech prefix for line 9, but the character is called "lord of Arundel" in the dialogue at line 7. I have amended both the stage direction and speech prefix to *Arundel*.

4.3.20 He (Q: A)

4.3.28 premised (Q: promised)

4.6.5 Vile (Q: Vilde)

4.6.62 Unhappy (Q: Unhappies)
4.7.30 He (Q: A)
4.7.63 lour (Q: lowre)
4.7.101 Rend (Q: Rent)

5.1.13 And, highly (Q: Highly)
5.1.47 vine (Q: Vines)
5.1.111 Q has the stage direction *Enter Bartley* (Berkeley) after line 111.
The dialogue, however, suggests that Bishop Berkeley enters later in the
scene. I have relocated the stage direction to line 127.
5.1.112 SP *Winchester* (Q: *Bartley*)
5.1.140 rend (Q: rent)
5.2.10 us (Q: as)
5.2.30 ere (Q: or)
5.2.60 Till (Q: And)
5.2.94 'tis his (Q: it his)
5.3.22 rends (Q: rents)
5.4.59 Puritan (Q: parentaine)
5.4.83 He (Q: A)
5.5.13 In Q the stage direction (*Enter Lightborn*) appears one line later.
5.5.77 That even (Q: That and even)
5.6.24, 38, 77, 89, 91, 93 In Q the speech prefixes for each of these lines
is simply *Lords*. I have emended them to *1 Lord* and *2 Lord* according
to the indications in the dialogue.
5.6.39 think it scorn (Q: think scorn)

EDWARD II

DRAMATIS PERSONAE[1]

EDWARD II, *King of England*
ISABELLA, *Queen of England and sister to the King of France*
PRINCE EDWARD, *their son, later King Edward III*
EDMUND, EARL OF KENT, *brother of the king*
GAVESTON, *favorite of the king*
SPENCER, *later favorite of the king*
SPENCER SENIOR, *his father*
LADY MARGARET, *niece of the king, betrothed to Gaveston*
BALDOCK, *her tutor*

MORTIMER
MORTIMER SENIOR, *his uncle*
EARL OF WARWICK
EARL OF LANCASTER
EARL OF PEMBROKE
EARL OF ARUNDEL
EARL OF LEICESTER
LORD BERKELEY
LORD BEAUMONT

ARCHBISHOP OF CANTERBURY
BISHOP OF COVENTRY
BISHOP OF WINCHESTER

MATREVIS
GURNEY
LIGHTBORN
LEVUNE
SIR JOHN OF HAINAULT
RICE AP HOWELL
MAYOR OF BRISTOL
TRUSSEL

Three Poor Men, Pembroke's Men, James, Horse-boy, Abbot, Monks, Mower, Champion, Ladies, Herald, Messenger, Posts, Guards, Soldiers, and Attendants.

---

1. No list of *dramatis personae* appears in the Q text.

ACT 1, SCENE 1

Enter Gaveston, reading on a letter that was
brought him from the King.

Gaveston. "My father is deceased. Come Gaveston,
 And share the kingdom with thy dearest friend."[2]
 Ah, words that make me surfeit° with delight!   *overflow*
 What greater bliss can hap° to Gaveston   *happen*
 Than live and be the favorite of a king?
 Sweet prince, I come! These, these thy amorous lines
 Might have enforced me to have swum from France,
 And, like Leander, gasped upon the sand,
 So thou wouldst smile, and take me in thy arms.[3]
 The sight of London to my exiled eyes   10
 Is as Elysium[4] to a new-come soul;
 Not that I love the city or the men,
 But that it harbors him I hold so dear,
 The king, upon whose bosom let me die,[5]
 And with the world be still at enmity.
 What need the arctic people love starlight,
 To whom the sun shines both by day and night?[6]
 Farewell base stooping to the lordly peers,
 My knee shall bow to none but to the king.
 As for the multitude, that are but sparks   20

2. The historical Gaveston was banished from England by Edward I but called back by Edward II at the start of his reign in 1307. Gaveston and Edward II were childhood friends before Gaveston was exiled to France.

3. In the Greek myth, *Leander* swam across the Hellespont every night to meet his beloved Hero. The affair ended tragically, however, when one night Leander drowned, and in grief Hero commits suicide. The story is retold by Marlowe in his unfinished narrative poem *Hero and Leander*. (In all footnotes, words in italics are direct quotations from the play, except for titles and foreign words, which are also italicized.)

4. *Elysium*: a place in the underworld reserved for the blessed (a Greek and Roman version of heaven).

5. To *die* can mean "to expire" or "to swoon," but the term also carried sexual connotations—"to have an orgasm." It was a common medical belief in the sixteenth century that each orgasm would shorten one's life.

6. In the *arctic* region, the sun would never set in the summer months, and thus the inhabitants would have no need of starlight. Analogously, Gaveston only needs the king (the sun) and has no need for the nobles (the stars).

Raked up in embers of their poverty,
Tanti![7] I'll fawn first on the wind[8]
That glanceth at my lips, and flieth away.
But how now, what are these?

> *Enter three Poor Men.*

Poor Men. Such as desire your worship's service.
Gaveston. What canst thou do?
1 Poor Man. I can ride.
Gaveston. But I have no horses. What art thou?
2 Poor Man. A traveler.
Gaveston. Let me see. Thou wouldst do well to wait at my   30
    trencher,° and tell me lies at dinner-time; and, as° I like   *wooden plate / if*
    your discoursing, I'll have you. And what art thou?
3 Poor Man. A soldier, that hath served against the Scot.[9]
Gaveston. Why, there are hospitals[10] for such as you.
    I have no war, and therefore, sir, begone.
3 Poor Man. Farewell, and perish by a soldier's hand,
    That wouldst reward them with an hospital!
      [The Poor Men start to leave.]
Gaveston. [Aside] Ay, ay, these words of his move me as much
    As if a goose should play the porcupine
    And dart her plumes, thinking to pierce my breast.[11]   40
    But yet it is no pain° to speak men fair;   *difficulty*
    I'll flatter these, and make them live in hope.
    [To Them] You know that I came lately out of France,
    And yet I have not viewed my lord the king.
    If I speed° well, I'll entertain° you all.   *succeed / employ*
Poor Men. We thank your worship.

---

7. *Tanti*: a term of contempt—"I care not for them."

8. "I'll first flatter the wind" (before I'll flatter low-born commoners). Gaveston expresses contempt for his social inferiors even though, ironically, he resents the way the barons (later in the play) express contempt for him as merely a member of the gentry class.

9. England fought a series of wars against Scotland during the reigns of Edward I and Edward II.

10. *hospitals*: charitable institutions that provided care for disabled soldiers as well as the poor and sick.

11. *Porcupines* were thought capable of shooting their quills in defense. The *plumes* of a goose would of course be harmless.

Gaveston. I have some business; leave me to myself.
Poor Men. We will wait here about the court.
    Exeunt [the three Poor Men].
Gaveston. Do. These are not men for me.

    I must have wanton° poets, pleasant wits,   *amorous*
    Musicians, that with touching of a string   51
    May draw the pliant king which way I please.
    Music and poetry is his delight;
    Therefore I'll have Italian masques[12] by night,
    Sweet speeches, comedies, and pleasing shows;
    And in the day, when he shall walk abroad,°   *outside*
    Like sylvan nymphs[13] my pages shall be clad.
    My men, like satyrs[14] grazing on the lawns,
    Shall with their goat feet dance an antic hay.[15]
    Sometime a lovely boy in Dian's shape,[16]   60
    With hair that gilds° the water as it glides,   *covers in gold*
    Crownets° of pearl about his naked arms,   *bracelets*
    And in his sportful° hands an olive tree,   *playful*
    To hide those parts which men delight to see,
    Shall bathe him in a spring. And there, hard by,°   *nearby*
    One like Actaeon,[17] peeping through the grove,
    Shall by the angry goddess be transformed,
    And running in the likeness of an hart,
    By yelping hounds pulled down and seem to die.

12. *Italian masques*: short elaborate plays. (The term is anachronistic since the genre of the masque was not invented until the sixteenth century and thus would not have been known in the time of Edward II.)

13. *sylvan nymphs*: female forest spirits.

14. *satyrs*: creatures with the body of a goat and upper torso of a man. Satyrs were notoriously lecherous and were also followers of Bacchus, god of wine and merrymaking.

15. *antic hay*: antique or old-fashioned dance (though *antic* also suggests grotesque and deranged).

16. In an Elizabethan masque or play, *Diana* (goddess of chastity) would have been played by a boy actor.

17. In the Greek myth, *Actaeon* spies Diana bathing naked in a spring. The goddess takes revenge by turning him into a stag, and then Actaeon is attacked and killed by his own hunting dogs. (The myth ironically anticipates the overall plot of the play: like Actaeon, King Edward falls for the charms of Gaveston, and Gaveston inadvertently provokes the nobles to act like hounds and hunt down the king.) For the Greek myth, see Ovid, *Metamorphoses*, III, 150–304 (Golding translation).

Such things as these best please his majesty,   70
    My lord. Here comes the king and the nobles
    From the parliament. I'll stand aside.

> *Enter the King, Lancaster, Mortimer Senior, Mortimer Junior,*
> *Edmund Earl of Kent, Guy Earl of Warwick, [and Attendants].*
> *[Gaveston conceals himself.]*

Edward. Lancaster!
Lancaster. My lord.
Gaveston. [Aside] That Earl of Lancaster do I abhor.
Edward. Will you not grant me this? *[Aside]* In spite of them
    I'll have my will, and these two Mortimers,
    That cross° me thus, shall know I am displeased.   *obstruct*
Mort. Senior. If you love us, my lord, hate Gaveston.
Gaveston. [Aside] That villain Mortimer! I'll be his death.   80
Mortimer. Mine uncle here, this earl, and I myself,
    Were sworn unto your father at his death
    That he should ne'er return into the realm;
    And know, my lord, ere° I will break my oath,   *before*
    This sword of mine, that should offend° your foes,   *fight off*
    Shall sleep within the scabbard at thy need,
    And underneath thy banners march who will,
    For Mortimer will hang his armor up.[18]
Gaveston. [Aside] Mort Dieu![19]
Edward. Well, Mortimer, I'll make thee rue° these words!   *regret*
    Beseems it thee to contradict thy king?[20]   91
    Frown'st thou thereat, aspiring Lancaster?
    The sword shall plane the furrows of thy brows,
    And hew these knees that now are grown so stiff.
    I will have Gaveston, and you shall know
    What danger 'tis to stand against your king.

---

18. Mortimer threatens to put his sword away and no longer fight for the king.

19. *Mort Dieu*: an oath meaning "death of God" (referring to Christ on the cross). The French expression would remind the audience that Gaveston is a Frenchman and thus a source of alien corruption in the English court. (Technically, however, Gaveston was an English subject from Gascon—a region of France under the control of the English king.) *Mort Dieu* may also be a pun "Mortimer" (and thus Gaveston may be insinuating Mortimer's god-like ambitions for power).

20. "Is it fitting for you to contradict the king?"

Gaveston. *[Aside]* Well done, Ned![21]

Lancaster. My lord, why do you thus incense your peers,
 That naturally would love and honor you,
 But for that base and obscure Gaveston?[22]   100
 Four earldoms have I besides Lancaster:
 Derby, Salisbury, Lincoln, Leicester.
 These will I sell to give my soldiers pay,
 Ere° Gaveston shall stay within the realm.   *before*
 Therefore, if he be come, expel him straight.

Kent. Barons and earls, your pride hath made me mute,
 But now I'll speak, and to the proof° I hope.   *irrefutably*
 I do remember, in my father's days,
 Lord Percy of the North, being highly moved,°   *angered*
 Braved° Mowbery in presence of the king;   *challenged*
 For which, had not his highness loved him well,   111
 He should have lost his head, but with his look
 The undaunted spirit of Percy was appeased,°   *pacified*
 And Mowbery and he were reconciled.[23]
 Yet dare you brave° the king unto his face?   *oppose*
 Brother,[24] revenge it, and let these their heads
 Preach upon poles for trespass of their tongues.[25]

Warwick. O, our heads!

Edward. Ay, yours; and therefore I would wish you grant.[26]

Warwick. Bridle thy anger, gentle Mortimer.   120

---

21. *Ned*: nickname for Edward. (Gaveston's use of the term indicates his intimacy with the king.)

22. Though Lancaster refers to Gaveston as *base and obscure*, and later the Mortimers denounce Gaveston as a *peasant* (see 1.2.30, 1.4.7, 1.4.14), the nobles clearly exaggerate Gaveston's low social status. The historical Gaveston was the son of a French knight of the gentry class, and thus he was legally a "gentleman." Later in the play, Mortimer contemptuously acknowledges Gaveston's gentry status when he describes Gaveston as "hardly . . . a gentleman by birth" (1.4.28–29).

23. This incident has no precedent in Holinshed's *Chronicles* or the other historical sources; it is apparently the invention of Marlowe.

24. Edmund, Earl of Kent, was actually the half brother of the king. He was also far too young to be involved in the Gaveston controversy. Born in 1301, Edmund was only six years old when Gaveston returned from exile in 1307.

25. The *heads* of traitors were put on *poles* and displayed as a warning to others. (In London, the heads of traitors were placed high on London Bridge and were thus visible to all as they entered the city.)

26. "I wish you would consent" (to allow Gaveston to return from exile).

Mortimer. I cannot, nor I will not. I must speak!
    Cousin,[27] our hands I hope shall fence° our heads,   *defend*
    And strike off his° that makes you threaten us.   *(Gaveston's head)*
    Come, uncle, let us leave the brainsick king,
    And henceforth parley° with our naked swords.   *negotiate*
Mort. Senior. Welshry[28] hath men enough to save our heads.
Warwick. All Warwickshire will love him for my sake.
Lancaster. And northward Gaveston hath many friends.[29]
    Adieu, my lord, and either change your mind,
    Or look to see the throne, where you should sit,   130
    To float in blood, and at thy wanton° head   *lovesick*
    The glozing° head of thy base minion[30] thrown.   *flattering*
        Exeunt Nobles [except Kent].
Edward. I cannot brook° these haughty menaces.°   *tolerate / threats*
    Am I a king, and must be overruled?
    Brother, display my ensigns° in the field;   *banners*
    I'll bandy° with the barons and the earls,   *fight*
    And either die or live with Gaveston.
Gaveston. [Approaching] I can no longer keep me from my lord.
        [Gaveston kneels before the King.]
Edward. What, Gaveston, welcome! Kiss not my hand;
    Embrace me, Gaveston, as I do thee.   140
    Why shouldst thou kneel? Knowest thou not who I am?
    Thy friend, thy self, another Gaveston![31]
    Not Hylas was more mourned of Hercules[32]
    Than thou hast been of me since thy exile.

27. *Cousin* could refer to any relative beyond the immediate family. Like most of the nobles, Mortimer was a distant relative of King Edward.

28. The Q text reads "Wilshere," perhaps a variant spelling of "Wiltshire," but the emendation to *Welshry* is more plausible since the historical Mortimer Senior held lands in Wales but had no connection to Wiltshire in England.

29. Warwick and Lancaster speak sarcastically. (Gaveston is apparently hated in Warwick and the north.)

30. *minion:* a male favorite (from the French *mignon*, meaning "charming or pretty"). The term often, but not always, suggested homosexual lover.

31. To refer to a close friend as another *self* was a proverbial Elizabethan expression, but Marlowe may also have in mind the myth of the double selves told by Aristophanes in Plato's *Symposium* as well as Cicero's description in *Of Friendship* of an intimate friend as a second self. See appendix of Related Texts.

32. *Hylas* was a young boy loved by Hercules. Hercules mourned his loss after the boy was stolen away by water nymphs during the voyage of the Argonaut.

Gaveston. And since I went from hence,° no soul in hell   *here*
    Hath felt more torment than poor Gaveston.
Edward. I know it. *[To Kent]* Brother, welcome home my friend.
    Now let the treacherous Mortimers conspire,
    And that high-minded Earl of Lancaster.
    I have my wish, in that I joy° thy sight,   *enjoy*
    And sooner shall the sea o'erwhelm my land   151
    Than bear the ship that shall transport thee hence.
    I here create thee Lord High Chamberlain,
    Chief Secretary to the state and me,
    Earl of Cornwall, King and Lord of Man.[33]
Gaveston. My lord, these titles far exceed my worth.
Kent. Brother, the least of these may well suffice
    For one of greater birth than Gaveston.[34]
Edward. Cease, brother, for I cannot brook° these words.   *tolerate*
    [To Gav.] Thy worth, sweet friend, is far above my gifts;   160
    Therefore, to equal it, receive my heart.
    If for these dignities thou be envied,
    I'll give thee more, for but to honor thee
    Is Edward pleased with kingly regiment.°   *rule*
    Fear'st thou thy person?[35] Thou shalt have a guard.
    Wants thou gold?[36] Go to my treasury.
    Wouldst thou be loved and feared? Receive my seal.[37]
    Save or condemn, and in our name command
    Whatso thy mind affects° or fancy likes.   *desires*
Gaveston. It shall suffice me to enjoy your love,   170
    Which whiles I have, I think myself as great
    As Caesar riding in the Roman street,
    With captive kings at his triumphant car.[38]

---

33. The *Lord of Man* (Isle of Man) was sometimes referred to as a *King* but was technically a subject of the king of England.

34. "These titles would be suitable for a nobleman but not for Gaveston."

35. "Do you fear your safety?"

36. "Do you lack gold?"

37. In the stage action, Edward may hand Gaveston the Great Seal of the Realm (used to stamp a royal image in wax to authenticate documents of the highest importance), or he may offer Gaveston a more modest symbol of royal authority, such as a ring. In any case, by granting Gaveston access to the Great Seal, Edward is, in effect, sharing royal authority with Gaveston.

38. Gaveston's comparison of himself to *Caesar* may be ironic in that Julius Caesar was assassinated for his political ambition to make himself king.

Enter the Bishop of Coventry.

Edward. Whither goes my lord of Coventry so fast?
Coventry. To celebrate your father's exequies.°   *funeral rites*
    But is that wicked Gaveston returned?
Edward. Ay, priest, and lives to be revenged on thee
    That wert the only cause of his exile.
Gaveston. 'Tis true, and but for reverence of these robes,
    Thou shouldst not plod° one foot beyond this place.   *step*
Coventry. I did no more than I was bound to do;   181
    And, Gaveston, unless thou be reclaimed,°   *morally reformed*
    As then I did incense° the Parliament,   *incite*
    So will I now, and thou shalt back to France.
Gaveston. Saving your reverence,[39] you must pardon me.
    [Gaveston takes hold of Coventry.]
Edward. Throw off his golden mitre, rend his stole,°   *tear his priestly garment*
    And in the channel° christen him anew.   *open sewer*
Kent. Ah, brother, lay not violent hands on him,
    For he'll complain unto the see of Rome.°   *(the Pope)*
Gaveston. Let him complain unto the see of Hell!   190
    I'll be revenged on him for my exile.
Edward. No, spare his life, but seize upon his goods.
    Be thou lord bishop, and receive his rents,°   *income from taxes*
    And make him serve thee as thy chaplain.
    I give him thee; here, use him as thou wilt.
Gaveston. He shall to prison, and there die in bolts.°   *leg irons or chains*
Edward. Ay, to the Tower, the Fleet, or where thou wilt.[40]
Coventry. For this offense be thou accurst of God.°   *excommunicated*
Edward. Who's there?
    [Enter Guards]
        Convey this priest to the Tower.
Coventry. True, true.[41]   200
    [Exit Bishop of Coventry, guarded.]

39. *Saving your reverence*: an expression of respect for a social superior (but spoken
sarcastically by Gaveston).

40. The *Tower* (Tower of London) was an expansive castle complex, part of which
was used to house political prisoners; the *Fleet* was a prison in London primarily
for debtors. The historical bishop of Coventry was sent to the Tower.

41. Coventry's response, *True, true*, is spoken ironically in reaction to Edward's
command that the guards *convey* him to the *Tower. Convey* meant "to transport" but
also "to steal," and thus the bishop is calling the king a thief.

Edward. But in the meantime, Gaveston, away,
    And take possession of his house and goods.
    Come, follow me, and thou shalt have my guard
    To see it done, and bring thee safe again.°   *back again*
Gaveston. What should a priest do with so fair a house?
    A prison may beseem° his holiness.   *better suit*
    [Exeunt.]

ACT 1, SCENE 2

    Enter both the Mortimers [from one side],
    Warwick and Lancaster [from the other side].

Warwick. 'Tis true, the bishop is in the Tower,
    And goods and body given to Gaveston.
Lancaster. What! Will they tyrannize upon the church?
    Ah, wicked king! Accursèd Gaveston!
    This ground, which is corrupted with their steps,
    Shall be their timeless sepulcher[42] or mine.
Mortimer. Well, let that peevish° Frenchman guard him° sure;   *troublesome / himself*
    Unless his breast be swordproof, he shall die.

    [The Mortimers approach Warwick and Lancaster.]

Mort. Senior. How now, why droops the Earl of Lancaster?
Mortimer. Wherefore is Guy of Warwick discontent?   10
Lancaster. That villain[43] Gaveston is made an earl.
Mort. Senior. An earl!
Warwick. Ay, and besides° Lord Chamberlain of the realm,   *also*
    And Secretary too, and Lord of Man.
Mort. Senior. We may not, nor we will not suffer this.
Mortimer. Why post we not from hence to levy men?[44]
Lancaster. "My Lord of Cornwall,"° now at every word!   *(Gaveston)*
    And happy is the man whom he vouchsafes,°   *grants*
    For vailing° of his bonnet, one good look.   *doffing*
    Thus, arm in arm, the king and he doth march;   20

---

42. *timeless sepulcher*: early grave (by dying in an "untimely" and premature way), and perhaps with the double sense of "eternal grave."

43. *villain*: rascal or scoundrel (but the term also retained the medieval meaning of "peasant"—and thus once again the nobles object to the lowly status of Gaveston).

44. "Why not travel from here to raise an army?"

Nay, more, the guard upon his lordship waits,
   And all the court begins to flatter him.
Warwick. Thus leaning on the shoulder of the king,
   He nods, and scorns, and smiles at those that pass.
Mort. Senior. Doth no man take exceptions at the slave?[45]
Lancaster. All stomach[46] him, but none dare speak a word.
Mortimer. Ah, that bewrays° their baseness, Lancaster!   *reveals*
   Were all the earls and barons of my mind,
   We'll hale° him from the bosom of the king,   *drag*
   And at the court gate hang the peasant up,   30
   Who, swoll'n with venom of ambitious pride,
   Will be the ruin of the realm and us.

   Enter the Bishop of Canterbury[47] [with an Attendant].

Warwick. Here comes my lord of Canterbury's grace.
Lancaster. His countenance bewrays° he is displeased.   *his expression reveals*
Canterbury. [To his Attendant] First were his° sacred   *(Bishop of Coventry's)*
   garments rent and torn,
   Then laid they violent hands upon him, next
   Himself imprisoned and his goods asseized.°   *seized*
   This certify° the Pope. Away, take horse.   *inform*
   [Exit Attendant.]
Lancaster. My lord, will you take arms against the king?
Canterbury. What need I? God himself is up in arms   40
   When violence is offered to the church.
Mortimer. Then will you join with us that be his peers
   To banish or behead that Gaveston?
Canterbury. What else, my lords? For it concerns me near;°   *deeply*
   The bishopric of Coventry is his.

   Enter the Queen [Isabella].[48]

Mortimer. Madam, whither walks your majesty so fast?

---

45. *slave*: the term could refer to any low-level servant, but it was also used as a derogatory insult.

46. *stomach*: resent (the stomach was considered the source of choler, the body humor that caused anger).

47. Though the Q text uses the title *Bishop of Canterbury*, the more proper title would be "Archbishop of Canterbury."

48. Historically, Queen Isabella (daughter of King Philip the Fair of France) was not married to Edward until 1308, the year after Gaveston's return to England.

Queen. Unto the forest, gentle Mortimer,
    To live in grief and baleful° discontent;   *sorrowful*
    For now my lord the king regards me not,
    But dotes upon the love of Gaveston.   50
    He claps° his cheeks and hangs about his neck,   *pats*
    Smiles in his face and whispers in his ears,
    And when I come he frowns, as who should say,
    "Go whither thou wilt, seeing I have Gaveston."
Mort. Senior. Is it not strange that he is thus bewitched?
Mortimer. Madam, return unto the court again.
    That sly inveigling° Frenchman we'll exile,   *deceiving*
    Or lose our lives; and yet, ere° that day come,   *before*
    The king shall lose his crown, for we have power,
    And courage too, to be revenged at full.   60
Canterbury. But yet lift not your swords against the king.
Lancaster. No, but we'll lift Gaveston from hence.
Warwick. And war must be the means, or he'll stay still.° *remain (with the king)*
Queen. Then let him stay; for rather than my lord
    Shall be oppressed by civil mutinies,
    I will endure a melancholy life,
    And let him frolic with his minion.[49]
Canterbury. My lords, to ease all this, but° hear me speak: *only*
    We and the rest that are his counselors
    Will meet, and with a general consent   70
    Confirm his banishment with our hands and seals.
Lancaster. What we confirm the king will frustrate.°   *resist*
Mortimer. Then may we lawfully revolt from him.
Warwick. But say, my lord, where shall this meeting be?
Canterbury. At the New Temple.[50]
Mortimer. Content.
Canterbury. And in the meantime, I'll entreat you all
    To cross to Lambeth,[51] and there stay with me.
Lancaster. Come then, let's away.
Mortimer. Madam, farewell.   80
Queen. Farewell, sweet Mortimer, and for my sake
    Forbear to levy arms° against the king.   *do not raise arms*

---

49. *Frolic* meant "play or sport" but could also carry sexual connotations; *minion* meant "favorite" (see note at 1.1.132).

50. *New Temple*: a church in London founded by the Knights Templar.

51. *Lambeth*: palace of the archbishop of Canterbury on the south bank of the Thames.

Mortimer. Ay, if words will serve; if not, I must.
    [Exeunt, the Queen one way, the rest the other.]

ACT 1, SCENE 3

Enter Gaveston and the Earl of Kent [Edmund].

Gaveston. Edmund,[52] the mighty prince of Lancaster,
    That hath more earldoms than an ass can bear,
    And both the Mortimers, two goodly men,
    With Guy of Warwick, that redoubted° knight,   *fearsome*
    Are gone towards Lambeth. There let them remain.
    Exeunt.

ACT 1, SCENE 4

*Enter Nobles [Lancaster, Warwick, Pembroke, both
Mortimers, Archbishop of Canterbury, and Attendants].*

Lancaster. *[Presenting a document]*
    Here is the form of Gaveston's exile.
    May it please your lordship to subscribe your name.
Canterbury. Give me the paper.
    [Canterbury signs.]
Lancaster. Quick, quick, my lord; I long to write my name.
    [Lancaster and the other Nobles sign.]
Warwick. But I long more to see him banished hence.
Mortimer. The name of Mortimer shall fright the king,
    Unless he be declined° from that base peasant.   *turn away*

    Enter the King and Gaveston [and Kent].
    [Edward sits on the throne with Gaveston beside him.]

Edward. What? Are you moved° that Gaveston sits here?   *angered*
    It is our pleasure; we will have it so.[53]

---

52. Gaveston addresses Edmund informally by his personal name, not his formal
title, Kent—an indication of Gaveston's boldness and ambition. The speech that
follows is clearly spoken with ironic contempt for the nobles.

53. The nobles are angered because Gaveston occupies the place of the queen
(beside the king on the throne)—suggesting Gaveston's political power as well as
his amorous relationship with the king.

Lancaster. Your grace doth well to place him by your side,   10
    For nowhere else the new earl is so safe.
Mort. Senior. What man of noble birth can brook° this sight?   endure
    Quam male conveniunt![54]
    See what a scornful look the peasant casts.
Pembroke. Can kingly lions fawn on creeping ants?
Warwick. Ignoble vassal, that like Phaethon
    Aspir'st unto the guidance of the sun.[55]
Mortimer. Their downfall is at hand, their forces down.
    We will not thus be faced and over-peered.[56]
Edward. Lay hands on that traitor Mortimer!   20
Mort. Senior. Lay hands on that traitor Gaveston!

    [The Nobles seize Gaveston.]

Kent. Is this the duty that you owe your king?
Warwick. We know our duties; let him know his peers.
Edward. Whither will you bear him? Stay, or ye shall die.
Mort. Senior. We are no traitors; therefore threaten not.
Gaveston. No, threaten not, my lord, but pay them home.
    Were I a king—
Mortimer. Thou, villain!° Wherefore talks thou of a king,   peasant
    That hardly art a gentleman by birth?
Edward. Were he a peasant, being my minion,   30
    I'll make the proudest of you stoop to him.
Lancaster. My lord, you may not thus disparage° us.   degrade
    Away, I say, with hateful Gaveston!
Mort. Senior. And with the Earl of Kent that favors him.
    [Exeunt Attendants with Kent and Gaveston.]
Edward. Nay, then lay violent hands upon your king!
    Here, Mortimer, sit thou in Edward's throne;
    Warwick and Lancaster, wear you my crown.
    Was ever king thus overruled as I?
Lancaster. Learn then to rule us better, and the realm.

---

54. "How badly suited they are together" (Latin). Mortimer Senior's objection to Gaveston is primarily social and political. Though Gaveston is of gentry status, he is far below the social rank of the barons (see note at 1.1.100).

55. *Phaethon* attempted to drive his father Apollo's sun chariot across the sky. But as an inexperienced youth, he could not control the horses. Flying too low, he scorched the ground, creating the Sahara desert. In fear the earth would be destroyed, Jove killed Phaethon with a thunderbolt. See Ovid, *Metamorphoses*, II, 1–415.

56. "We will not be intimidated and looked down upon" (by this social inferior).

Mortimer. What we have done, our heart-blood shall maintain.   40
Warwick. Think you that we can brook° this upstart pride?   *endure*
Edward. Anger and wrathful fury stops my speech.
Canterbury. Why are you moved? Be patient, my lord,
 And see what we your counselors have done.
Mortimer. My lords, now let us all be resolute,
 And either have our wills or lose our lives.
Edward. Meet you for this, proud overdaring peers?
 Ere° my sweet Gaveston shall part from me,   *before*
 This isle shall fleet° upon the ocean,   *float*
 And wander to the unfrequented Inde.°   *India*
Canterbury. You know that I am legate to the Pope;[57]   51
 On your allegiance to the see of Rome,
 Subscribe as we have done to his exile.
Mortimer. Curse him if he refuse, and then may we
 Depose him and elect another king.[58]
Edward. Ay, there it goes! But yet I will not yield;
 Curse me, depose me, do the worst you can.[59]
Lancaster. Then linger not, my lord, but do it straight.
Canterbury. Remember how the bishop was abused.
 Either banish him that was the cause thereof,   60
 Or I will presently° discharge these lords   *immediately*
 Of duty and allegiance due to thee.
Edward. [Aside] It boots° me not to threat; I must speak fair;   *avails or helps*
 The legate of the Pope will be obeyed.—
 My lord, you° shall be Chancellor of the realm;   *(Canterbury)*
 Thou, Lancaster, High Admiral of our fleet;
 Young Mortimer and his uncle shall be earls;
 And you, Lord Warwick, President of the North;
 And thou° of Wales. If this content you not,   *(Pembroke)*
 Make several kingdoms of this monarchy,   70

57. The archbishop of Canterbury was the leading bishop in England, but he was not *legate to the Pope* during the reign of Edward II.

58. If the king is *cursed* (excommunicated) his subjects would no longer owe him obedience. The nobles (by way of Parliament) could then depose him and elect a new king.

59. Edward's defiance against the Church of Rome would certainly evoke the defiance of Queen Elizabeth, who was excommunicated by Pope Pius V in 1570 but continued to rule until her death in 1603. Likewise, her father, King Henry VIII, was excommunicated by Pope Clement VII in 1533 but ruled until his death in 1547.

And share it equally amongst you all,
So I may have some nook or corner left
To frolic with my dearest Gaveston.
Canterbury. Nothing shall alter us; we are resolved.
Lancaster. Come, come, subscribe.
Mortimer. Why should you love him whom the world hates so?
Edward. Because he loves me more than all the world.
    Ah, none but rude and savage-minded men
    Would seek the ruin of my Gaveston.
    You that be noble born should pity him.   80
Warwick. You that are princely born should shake him off.
    For shame subscribe and let the lown° depart.   *peasant*
Mort. Senior. Urge him, my lord.
Canterbury. Are you content to banish him the realm?
Edward. I see I must, and therefore am content.
    Instead of ink, I'll write it with my tears.
        [Edward signs.]
Mortimer. The king is lovesick for his minion.
Edward. 'Tis done, and now, accursèd hand, fall off!
Lancaster. Give it me; I'll have it published in the streets.
Mortimer. I'll see him presently dispatched away.   90
Canterbury. Now is my heart at ease.
Warwick.   And so is mine.
Pembroke. This will be good news to the common sort.°   *common people*
Mort. Senior. Be it or no, he shall not linger here.
        Exeunt Nobles.
Edward. How fast they run to banish him I love.
    They would not stir, were it to do me good.
    Why should a king be subject to a priest?
    Proud Rome, that hatchest such imperial grooms,°   *servants*
    For these thy superstitious taper-lights,°   *candles*
    Wherewith thy antichristian churches blaze,
    I'll fire thy crazèd° buildings, and enforce   *cracked or decayed*
    The papal towers to kiss the lowly ground,   101
    With slaughtered priests make Tiber's channel° swell,   *Tiber River (in Rome)*
    And banks raised higher with their sepulchers!
    As for the peers that back the clergy thus,
    If I be king, not one of them shall live.

        Enter Gaveston.

Gaveston. My lord, I hear it whispered everywhere
    That I am banished and must fly the land.

Edward. 'Tis true, sweet Gaveston. O were it false!
    The legate of the Pope will have it so,
    And thou must hence, or I shall be deposed.   110
    But I will reign to be revenged of° them,   *on*
    And therefore, sweet friend, take it patiently.
    Live where thou wilt; I'll send thee gold enough.
    And long thou shalt not stay, or if thou dost,
    I'll come to thee. My love shall ne'er decline.
Gaveston. Is all my hope turned to this hell of grief?
Edward. Rend° not my heart with thy too piercing words.   *tear*
    Thou from this land, I from myself am banished.
Gaveston. To go from hence grieves not poor Gaveston,
    But to forsake you, in whose gracious looks   120
    The blessedness of Gaveston remains,
    For nowhere else seeks he felicity.
Edward. And only this torments my wretched soul,
    That whether I will or no, thou must depart.
    Be Governor of Ireland in my stead,
    And there abide till fortune call thee home.[60]
    Here, take my picture, and let me wear thine.
       [They exchange pictures.]
    O might I keep thee here, as I do this,
    Happy were I. But now most miserable.
Gaveston. 'Tis something to be pitied of a king.   130
Edward. Thou shalt not hence;° I'll hide thee, Gaveston.   *go away*
Gaveston. I shall be found, and then 'twill grieve me more.
Edward. Kind words and mutual talk makes our grief greater.
    Therefore, with dumb° embracement, let us part.   *silent*
       [They embrace.]
    Stay, Gaveston, I cannot leave thee thus.
Gaveston. For every look, my lord, drops down a tear;
    Seeing I must go, do not renew my sorrow.
Edward. The time is little that thou hast to stay,
    And therefore give me leave to look my fill.
    But come, sweet friend, I'll bear° thee on thy way.   *accompany*
Gaveston. The peers will frown.   141
Edward. I pass° not for their anger. Come, let's go.   *care*
    O that we might as well return as go!

    Enter Edmund and Queen Isabella.

---

60. The historical Gaveston was made governor of Ireland from 1308 to 1309.

Queen. Whither goes my lord?

Edward. Fawn not on me, French strumpet.° Get thee gone.   *prostitute*

Queen. On whom but on my husband should I fawn?

Gaveston. On Mortimer, with whom, ungentle queen—

    I say no more; judge you the rest, my lord.

Queen. In saying this, thou wrong'st me, Gaveston.

    Is't not enough that thou corrupts my lord,   150

    And art a bawd° to his affections,   *pander*

    But thou must call mine honor thus in question?

Gaveston. I mean not so; your grace must pardon me.

Edward. Thou art too familiar with that Mortimer,

    And by thy means is Gaveston exiled;

    But I would wish thee reconcile the lords,

    Or thou shalt ne'er be reconciled to me.

Queen. Your highness knows, it lies not in my power.

Edward. Away then, touch me not! Come, Gaveston.

Queen. Villain, 'tis thou that robb'st me of my lord.   160

Gaveston. Madam, 'tis you that rob me of my lord.

Edward. Speak not unto her; let her droop and pine.

Queen. Wherein, my lord, have I deserved these words?

    Witness the tears that Isabella sheds,

    Witness this heart, that sighing for thee breaks,

    How dear my lord is to poor Isabel!

Edward. And witness heaven how dear thou art to me.

    [Edward embraces Gaveston.]

    There weep; for till my Gaveston be repealed,

    Assure thyself thou com'st not in my sight.

    Exeunt Edward and Gaveston [and Kent].[61]

Queen. O miserable and distressèd queen!   170

    Would when I left sweet France and was embarked,

    That charming Circe, walking on the waves,

    Had changed my shape,[62] or at the marriage day

61. Kent's exit at this point is an editorial conjecture. The Q text does not indicate any exit for Kent in the scene. Perhaps Kent remains on stage while the queen bemoans her rejection by Edward in the lines that follow.

62. The allusion to *Circe, walking on the waves,* is from Ovid's *Metamorphoses.* Ovid describes Circe running over the surface of the ocean to pour poison into a pool in which the young virgin Scylla liked to bathe. Entering the pool, Scylla was transformed into a ravenous dog-monster (who then perched herself above the whirlpool of Charybdis). The allusion may ironically foreshadow the fate of Isabella, who begins the play as an innocent and faithful wife but gradually transforms into

The cup of Hymen[63] had been full of poison,
Or with those arms° that twined about my neck   *(Edward's arms)*
I had been stifled, and not lived to see
The king my lord thus to abandon me.
Like frantic Juno will I fill the earth
With ghastly murmur° of my sighs and cries,   *horrifying complaints*
For never doted Jove on Ganymede   180
So much as he on cursèd Gaveston.[64]
But that will more exasperate° his wrath;   *intensify*
I must entreat° him, I must speak him fair,   *plead with*
And be a means to call home Gaveston.
And yet he'll ever° dote on Gaveston,   *forever*
And so am I for ever miserable.

> *Enter the Nobles [Lancaster, Warwick, Pembroke,*
> *and both Mortimers] to the Queen.*

Lancaster. Look where the sister of the king of France
    Sits wringing of her hands and beats her breast.
Warwick. The king, I fear, hath ill entreated° her.   *treated*
Pembroke. Hard is the heart that injures such a saint.   190
Mortimer. I know 'tis 'long of° Gaveston she weeps.   *because of*
Mort. Senior. Why? He is gone.
Mortimer.   Madam, how fares your grace?
Queen. Ah, Mortimer! Now breaks the king's hate forth,
    And he confesseth that he loves me not.
Mortimer. Cry quittance,[65] madam, then, and love not him.
Queen. No, rather will I die a thousand deaths,
    And yet I love in vain; he'll ne'er love me.

---

a figure of ruthless power. Circe is also famous for using her magic charms to turn Ulysses's men into swine. See Ovid, *Metamorphoses*, XIV, 1–79, 285–498. (Circe is also a major figure in book 10 of Homer's *Odyssey*, but Ovid was the primary source of mythology for Renaissance poets and playwrights.)

63. *Hymen*: Greek god of marriage.

64. The goddess Juno grew frantic with jealousy after Jove fell in love with the young boy Ganymede and made the boy his cupbearer. See Ovid, *Metamorphoses*, X, 157–67. In sixteenth-century England, the terms "Ganymede" and "catamite" (from the Latin word for Ganymede, *Catamitus*) were sometimes used to describe a young homosexual lover.

65. *Cry quittance* means "quit him and leave him" but can also mean "requite" or "get even with him" (and thus Mortimer could be tempting Isabella into adultery).

Lancaster. Fear ye not, madam; now his minion's gone,
    His wanton humor° will be quickly left.   *amorous mood*
Queen. O never, Lancaster! I am enjoined°   *obligated*
    To sue° unto you all for his repeal.   *plead*
    This wills my lord, and this must I perform,   202
    Or else be banished from his highness' presence.
Lancaster. For his repeal, madam? He comes not back,
    Unless the sea cast up his shipwreck body.
Warwick. And to behold so sweet a sight as that,
    There's none here but would run his horse to death.[66]
Mortimer. But madam, would you have us call him home?
Queen. Ay, Mortimer, for till he be restored,
    The angry king hath banished me the court;   210
    And therefore, as thou lov'st and tender'st° me,   *care for*
    Be thou my advocate unto these peers.
Mortimer. What, would ye have me plead for Gaveston?
Mort. Senior. Plead for him he that will, I am resolved.
Lancaster. And so am I, my lord. Dissuade the queen.
Queen. O Lancaster, let him° dissuade the king,   *(Mortimer Senior)*
    For 'tis against my will he should return.
Warwick. Then speak not for him; let the peasant go.
Queen. 'Tis for myself I speak, and not for him.
Pembroke. No speaking will prevail, and therefore cease.   220
Mortimer. Fair queen, forbear to angle for the fish
    Which, being caught, strikes him that takes it dead.
    I mean that vile torpedo,[67] Gaveston,
    That now, I hope, floats on the Irish seas.
Queen. Sweet Mortimer, sit down by me a while,
    And I will tell thee reasons of such weight
    As thou wilt soon subscribe to his repeal.
Mortimer. It is impossible; but speak your mind.
Queen. Then thus, but none shall hear it but ourselves.
    [The Queen and Mortimer speak privately.]
Lancaster. My lords, albeit the queen win Mortimer,   230
    Will you be resolute and hold with me?
Mort. Senior. Not I, against my nephew.
Pembroke. Fear not, the queen's words cannot alter him.

---

66. "All of us would go to extremes to see the dead body of Gaveston."

67. A *torpedo* was an electric ray, a fish capable of numbing its prey. (The modern meaning of torpedo evolved in the nineteenth century to describe a variety of underwater mines and projectiles.)

Warwick. No? Do but mark° how earnestly she pleads.   observe
Lancaster. And see how coldly his looks make denial.
Warwick. She smiles; now, for my life, his mind is changed.
Lancaster. I'll rather lose his friendship, I, than grant.°   consent
   [Mortimer approaches the Nobles.]
Mortimer. Well, of necessity it must be so.
  My lords, that I abhor base Gaveston,
  I hope your honors make no question;   240
  And therefore, though I plead for his repeal,
  'Tis not for his sake, but for our avail;°   advantage
  Nay, for the realm's behoof,° and for the king's.   benefit
Lancaster. Fie, Mortimer, dishonor not thyself!
  Can this be true, 'twas good to banish him?
  And is this true, to call him home again?
  Such reasons make white black, and dark night day.
Mortimer. My lord of Lancaster, mark the respect.°   consider the circumstances
Lancaster. In no respect can contraries be true.
Queen. Yet, good my lord, hear what he can allege.°   argue
Warwick. All that he speaks is nothing; we are resolved.   251
Mortimer. Do you not wish that Gaveston were dead?
Pembroke. I would he were.
Mortimer. Why then, my lord, give me but leave to speak.
Mort. Senior. But nephew, do not play the sophister.[68]
Mortimer. This which I urge is of a burning zeal
  To mend° the king and do our country good.   reform
  Know you not Gaveston hath store of gold,
  Which may in Ireland purchase him such friends
  As he will front° the mightiest of us all?   confront or oppose
  And whereas° he shall live and be beloved,   while
  'Tis hard for us to work his overthrow.   262
Warwick. Mark you but that, my lord of Lancaster.
Mortimer. But were he here, detested as he is,
  How easily might some base slave be suborned°   bribed
  To greet his lordship with a poniard,°   dagger
  And none so much as blame the murderer,
  But rather praise him for that brave attempt,
  And in the chronicle enroll his name
  For purging of the realm of such a plague.   270

---

68. *sophister*: someone who uses clever arguments to defend any side of a question. The term was also used to describe second- and third-year university students, trained in the arts of debate and disputation.

Pembroke. He saith true.

Lancaster. Ay, but how chance this was not done before?

Mortimer. Because, my lords, it was not thought upon.
    Nay, more, when he shall know it lies in us
    To banish him, and then to call him home,
    'Twill make him vail° the top flag of his pride,   *lower*
    And fear to offend the meanest nobleman.

Mort. Senior. But how if he do not, nephew?

Mortimer. Then may we with some color° rise in arms;   *excuse*
    For howsoever we have borne it out,   280
    'Tis treason to be up against the king.
    So shall we have the people of° our side,   *on*
    Which, for his father's sake, lean to the king
    But cannot brook a night-grown mushrump°—   *mushroom*
    Such a one as my lord of Cornwall is—
    Should bear us down of the nobility.
    And when the commons and the nobles join,
    'Tis not the king can buckler° Gaveston.   *shield or protect*
    We'll pull him from the strongest hold he hath.
    My lords, if to perform this I be slack,   290
    Think me as base a groom° as Gaveston.   *servant*

Lancaster. On that condition, Lancaster will grant.

Warwick. And so will Pembroke and I.[69]

Mort. Senior. And I.

Mortimer. In this I count me highly gratified,
    And Mortimer will rest at your command.

Queen. And when this favor Isabel forgets,
    Then let her live abandoned and forlorn.
    But see, in happy time, my lord the king,
    Having brought the Earl of Cornwall on his way,   300
    Is new returned. This news will glad him much,
    Yet not so much as me. I love him more
    Than he can Gaveston. Would he loved me
    But half so much, then were I treble° blest.   *triple*

    Enter King Edward mourning,
    [with Beaumont and Attendants].

---

69. Some editors emend this line so that Pembroke speaks the first part ("And so will Pembroke"), followed by Warwick ("And I"). Marlowe may have intended for each lord to speak for himself, but the Q text could be accurate if Marlowe wanted to convey strong unanimity among the barons.

Edward. He's gone, and for his absence thus I mourn.
  Did never sorrow go so near my heart
  As doth the want° of my sweet Gaveston?   *absence*
  And could my crown's revenue bring him back,
  I would freely give it to his enemies,
  And think I gained, having bought so dear a friend.   310
Queen. Hark, how he harps upon his minion!
Edward. My heart is as an anvil unto sorrow,
  Which beats upon it like the Cyclops' hammers,[70]
  And with the noise turns up my giddy brain,
  And makes me frantic for my Gaveston.
  Ah, had some bloodless Fury rose from hell,[71]
  And with my kingly sceptre struck me dead,
  When I was forced to leave my Gaveston!
Lancaster. Diabolo!° What passions call you these?   *Devil (Spanish)*
Queen. My gracious lord, I come to bring you news.   320
Edward. That you have parlied° with your Mortimer?   *met*
Queen. That Gaveston, my lord, shall be repealed.
Edward. Repealed! The news is too sweet to be true.
Queen. But will you love me, if you find it so?
Edward. If it be so, what will not Edward do?
Queen. For Gaveston, but not for Isabel.
Edward. For thee, fair queen, if thou lovest Gaveston,
  I'll hang a golden tongue about thy neck,
  Seeing thou hast pleaded with so good success.
    [He embraces the Queen.]
Queen. No other jewels hang about my neck   330
  Than these,° my lord; nor let me have more wealth   *(Edward's arms)*
  Than I may fetch from this rich treasury.
    [They kiss.]
  O how a kiss revives poor Isabel!
Edward. Once more receive my hand, and let this be
  A second marriage 'twixt thyself and me.
Queen. And may it prove more happy than the first!
  My gentle lord, bespeak° these nobles fair   *speak to*
  That wait attendance for a gracious look,
  And on their knees salute your majesty.

---

70. The *Cyclops* worked with *hammers* in Vulcan's forge, making thunderbolts for Jove (see Virgil, *Aeneid*, VIII, 418ff.).

71. "If only some bloodless Fury had risen from hell." (Furies were goddesses of revenge in the classical underworld.)

[The Nobles kneel.]

Edward. Courageous Lancaster, embrace thy king, 340
 And as gross vapors° perish by the sun,   *heavy fog*
 Even so let hatred with thy sovereign's smile.
 Live thou with me as my companion.
  [The King and Lancaster embrace.]
Lancaster. This salutation overjoys my heart.
Edward. Warwick shall be my chiefest counselor.
 These silver hairs will more adorn my court
 Than gaudy° silks or rich embroidery.   *extravagant*
 Chide me, sweet Warwick, if I go astray.
Warwick. Slay me, my lord, when I offend your grace.[72]
Edward. In solemn triumphs° and in public shows   *processions*
 Pembroke shall bear the sword before the king. 351
Pembroke. And with this sword Pembroke will fight for you.
Edward. But wherefore walks young Mortimer aside?
 Be thou commander of our royal fleet,
 Or if that lofty office like° thee not,   *please*
 I make thee here Lord Marshal of the realm.
Mortimer. My lord, I'll marshal so your enemies,
 As England shall be quiet and you safe.
Edward. And as for you, Lord Mortimer of Chirk,[73]
 Whose great achievements in our foreign war 360
 Deserves no common place nor mean reward,
 Be you the general of the levied troops
 That now are ready to assail the Scots.
Mort. Senior. In this your grace hath highly honored me,
 For with my nature war doth best agree.
Queen. Now is the king of England rich and strong,
 Having the love of his renownèd peers.
Edward. Ay, Isabel, ne'er was my heart so light.°   *carefree*
 [To Beaumont] Clerk of the Crown, direct our warrant forth
 For Gaveston to Ireland. Beaumont, fly 370
 As fast as Iris or Jove's Mercury.[74]
Beaumont. It shall be done, my gracious lord.

---

72. Ironically the king will indeed *slay* Warwick later in the play (see 3.4.25–28).

73. *Chirk*: a region in Wales (along the English border) over which Mortimer Senior was lord.

74. Some editors treat the *Clerk of the Crown* and *Beaumont* as two separate characters (the Q text does not clarify the issue). *Iris* was the messenger god for Juno, and *Mercury* the messenger for Jove.

[Exit Beaumont and Attendants].
Edward. Lord Mortimer, we leave you to your charge.
    Now let us in and feast it royally.
    Against our friend the Earl of Cornwall comes,[75]
    We'll have a general tilt° and tournament,   *jousting contest*
    And then his marriage shall be solemnized,
    For wot° you not that I have made him sure°   *know / betrothed*
    Unto our cousin, the Earl of Gloucester's heir?[76]
Lancaster. Such news we hear, my lord.   380
Edward. That day, if not for him, yet for my sake,
    Who in the triumph° will be challenger,   *tournament*
    Spare for no cost; we will requite your love.
Warwick. In this or aught your highness shall command us.
Edward. Thanks, gentle Warwick. Come, let's in and revel.
    Exeunt [all except the Mortimers].
Mort. Senior. Nephew, I must to Scotland; thou stayest here.
    Leave° now to oppose thyself against the king.   *cease*
    Thou seest by nature he is mild and calm,
    And seeing his mind so dotes on Gaveston,
    Let him without controlment° have his will.   *restraint*
    The mightiest kings have had their minions: 391
    Great Alexander loved Hephaestion,
    The conquering Hercules for Hylas wept,
    And for Patroclus stern Achilles drooped.[77]
    And not kings only, but the wisest men:
    The Roman Tully loved Octavius,

75. "In preparation for the time when Gaveston arrives."

76. The historical Gaveston was married to Lady Margaret de Clare (daughter of the Earl of Gloucester and niece of King Edward) on November 1, 1307, three months before Edward's marriage to Isabella on January 25, 1308.

77. *Hephaestion* was the friend of *Alexander* the Great; *Hylas* was a young boy loved by *Hercules* but stolen away by water nymphs; *Patroclus* was the friend of *Achilles* in Homer's *Iliad*. None of the ancient historians described Hephaestion and Alexander as lovers, nor did Homer explicitly describe Patroclus and Achilles as such (though in Homer, Achilles is inconsolable with grief after the death of Patroclus, and the ancient historian Arrian describes Alexander as similarly inconsolable after the death of Hephaestion). Renaissance writers often assumed these relationships were homoerotic. In Shakespeare's *Troilus and Cressida*, for example, Patroclus is described as Achilles's "masculine whore" (5.1.17).

Grave Socrates, wild Alcibiades.[78]
Then let his grace, whose youth is flexible,
And promiseth as much as we can wish,
Freely enjoy that vain lightheaded earl,   400
For riper years will wean him from such toys.°   *trifles*
Mortimer. Uncle, his wanton humor grieves not me,
But this I scorn, that one so basely born
Should by his sovereign's favor grow so pert,°   *bold*
And riot it with the treasure of the realm,
While soldiers mutiny for want° of pay.   *lack*
He wears a lord's revenue on his back,[79]
And Midas-like[80] he jets it° in the court   *struts about*
With base outlandish cullions[81] at his heels,
Whose proud fantastic liveries[82] make such show   410
As if that Proteus, god of shapes,[83] appeared.
I have not seen a dapper jack so brisk.°   *dandy so well dressed*
He wears a short Italian hooded cloak,
Larded° with pearl, and in his Tuscan cap   *covered*
A jewel of more value than the crown.[84]
Whiles other[85] walk below, the king and he
From out a window laugh at such as we,

78. *Tully* (Marcus Tullius Cicero [106–43 BC]) was a famous Roman philosopher and statesman. No evidence survives to indicate that he was intimate with *Octavius* (who became Emperor Octavius Augustus in 27 BC after the death of Cicero). *Alcibiades* was a notoriously handsome and reckless Greek nobleman and close friend of *Socrates*. Their relationship is described at length in Plato's *Symposium* (see Related Texts).

79. "He (Gaveston) wears extraordinarily expensive clothing."

80. *Midas* was the king of Phrygia who turned everything he touched into gold. See Ovid, *Metamorphoses*, XI, 100–216.

81. *Outlandish* means "foreign" (out of this land), and *cullions* means "scoundrels" (literally, testicles).

82. *Liveries* were distinct costumes or badges worn by the servants of a nobleman.

83. *Proteus* was a sea god who could change his form at will. See Ovid, *Metamorphoses*, VIII, 913–23; XI, 251–92.

84. Gaveston's attire suggests Elizabethan stereotypes about Italians (from Tuscany and elsewhere) who were notorious for overly elaborate dress. Italy was also the center of Roman Catholicism, the homeland of Machiavelli, and reputedly a land where sodomy was commonplace. See Henri Estienne's *A World of Wonders* in Related Texts.

85. *other*: the term in the sixteenth century could imply plurality.

And flout our train° and jest at our attire.   *mock our attendants*
    Uncle, 'tis this that makes me impatient.
Mort. Senior. But nephew, now you see the king is changed.   420
Mortimer. Then so am I, and live to do him service;
    But while I have a sword, a hand, a heart,
    I will not yield to any such upstart.
    You know my mind. Come, uncle, let's away.
        Exeunt.

ACT 2, SCENE 1

Enter Spencer and Baldock.

Baldock. Spencer,
    Seeing that our lord th' Earl of Gloucester's dead,
    Which of the nobles dost thou mean to serve?
Spencer. Not Mortimer, nor any of his side,
    Because the king and he are enemies.
    Baldock, learn this of me: a factious° lord   *seditious*
    Shall hardly do himself good, much less us,
    But he that hath the favor of a king
    May with one word advance us while we live.
    The liberal[86] Earl of Cornwall is the man   10
    On whose good fortune Spencer's hope depends.
Baldock. What, mean you then to be his follower?
Spencer No, his companion, for he loves me well,
    And would have once preferred me to the king.[87]
Baldock. But he is banished; there's small hope of him.
Spencer. Ay, for a while; but Baldock, mark the end:°   *conclusion*
    A friend of mine told me in secrecy
    That he's repealed and sent for back again,
    And even now a post came from the court
    With letters to our lady° from the king,   *(Lady Margaret)*
    And as she read, she smiled, which makes me think   21
    It is about her lover Gaveston.

86. *Liberal* means "generous" but can also imply "extravagant and unrestrained" (as Gaveston is exceedingly generous in spending the king's money).

87. Gaveston would have *preferred* (recommended) Spencer for employment by the king. (Historically, Gaveston and Spencer were never allies, and Spencer and Baldock were never servants of the Earl of Gloucester.)

Baldock. 'Tis like enough, for since he was exiled,
    She neither walks abroad nor comes in sight.
    But I had thought the match had been broke off,
    And that his banishment had changed her mind.
Spencer. Our lady's first love is not wavering.
    My life for thine,[88] she will have Gaveston.
Baldock. Then hope I by her means to be preferred,
    Having read unto her since she was a child.[89]   30
Spencer. Then, Baldock, you must cast the scholar off,
    And learn to court it like a gentleman.[90]
    'Tis not a black coat and a little band,°   *collar*
    A velvet-caped cloak, faced before with serge,°   *cheap wool*
    And smelling to a nosegay° all the day,   *bouquet of flowers*
    Or holding of a napkin in your hand,
    Or saying a long grace at a table's end,
    Or making low legs° to a nobleman,   *low bows*
    Or looking downward, with your eyelids close,
    And saying, "truly, an't° may please your honor,"   *if it*
    Can get you any favor with great men.   41
    You must be proud, bold, pleasant,° resolute,   *witty*
    And now and then stab, as occasion serves.
Baldock. Spencer, thou knowest I hate such formal toys,°   *trivial conventions*
    And use them but of mere hypocrisy.
    Mine old lord, whiles he lived, was so precise°   *puritanical*
    That he would take exceptions at my buttons,
    And, being like pins' heads, blame me for the bigness,
    Which made me curate-like in mine attire,
    Though inwardly licentious enough,   50
    And apt° for any kind of villainy.   *prepared*
    I am none of these common pedants,° I,   *tutors or teachers*
    That cannot speak without *propterea quod.*

---

88. *My life for thine*: proverbial expression meaning "I assure you."

89. Baldock claims to have served as Lady Margaret's tutor. (The historical Baldock had no connection to Lady Margaret.)

90. In the lines that follow, Spencer mockingly describes the attire of a poor *scholar* (or university student) and the traditional behavior expected from such scholars. Spencer's conclusion is that submissive and well-mannered young scholars are no longer valued at court; *great men* (line 41) now employ only bold and ruthless Machiavellians.

Spencer. But one of those that saith *quandoquidem*
　　hath a special gift to form a verb.[91]
Baldock. Leave off this jesting; here my lady comes.

　　　　Enter the Lady [Margaret, with letters].
　　　　[Spencer and Baldock draw aside].

Margaret. The grief for his exile was not so much
　　As is the joy of his returning home.
　　This letter came from my sweet Gaveston.
　　What needst thou, love, thus to excuse thyself?   60
　　I know thou couldst not come and visit me.
　　[She reads] "I will not long be from thee, though I die."
　　This argues the entire love of my lord.
　　[She reads] "When I forsake thee, death seize on my heart."
　　But rest thee here where Gaveston shall sleep.
　　　　[She places the letter in her bosom.]
　　Now to the letter of my lord the king.
　　　　[She reads another letter.]
　　He wills me to repair° unto the court   come
　　And meet my Gaveston. Why do I stay,
　　Seeing that he talks thus of my marriage day?
　　Who's there? Baldock!   70
　　　　[Baldock and Spencer approach.]
　　See that my coach[92] be ready; I must hence.
Baldock. It shall be done, madam.
Margaret. And meet me at the park pale° presently.   fence or border
　　　　Exit [Baldock].
　　Spencer, stay you and bear° me company,   keep
　　For I have joyful news to tell thee of:
　　My lord of Cornwall is a-coming over
　　And will be at the court as soon as we.
Spencer. I knew the king would have him home again.
Margaret. If all things sort out as I hope they will,
　　Thy service, Spencer, shall be thought upon.   80
Spencer. I humbly thank your ladyship.

---

91. Both Latin expressions mean the same thing: "because." The second version
was apparently considered more fashionable. *To form a verb* means "to conjugate
a verb" or, more generally, "to speak with eloquence." University students were
expected to converse in Latin.

92. An anachronism—coaches were not used in England until the mid-sixteenth
century.

Margaret. Come lead the way; I long° till I am there.   *pine (for Gaveston)*
        [Exeunt.]

ACT 2, SCENE 2

Enter Edward, the Queen, Lancaster, Mortimer, Warwick,
Pembroke, Kent, Attendants. [The Lords, or their Attendants,
carry shields painted with heraldic emblems and mottos.]

Edward. The wind is good. I wonder why he stays.
        I fear me he is wracked° upon the sea.   *shipwrecked*
Queen. Look, Lancaster, how passionate he is,
        And still his mind runs° on his minion.   *dwells*
Lancaster. My lord—
Edward. How now, what news? Is Gaveston arrived?
Mortimer. Nothing but "Gaveston"! What means your grace?
        You have matters of more weight to think upon;
        The king of France sets foot in Normandy.[93]
Edward. A trifle! We'll expel him when we please.   10
        But tell me, Mortimer, what's thy device[94]
        Against the stately triumph° we decreed?   *prepared for the pageant*
Mortimer. A homely° one, my lord, not worth the telling.   *simple*
Edward. Prithee let me know it.
Mortimer. But seeing you are so desirous, thus it is:
        A lofty cedar tree, fair flourishing,
        On whose top branches kingly eagles perch,
        And by the bark a canker° creeps me up   *caterpillar*
        And gets unto the highest bough of all;
        The motto: *Aeque tandem.*°   *equal in height (Latin)*
Edward. And what is yours, my lord of Lancaster?   21
Lancaster. My lord, mine's more obscure than Mortimer's.
        Pliny reports there is a flying fish[95]

---

93. In Holinshed's *Chronicles*, King Charles IV of France did not invade Normandy but did invade English territories in Guienne (in southwestern France) in reprisal for Edward's failure to pay homage to him in person (see Related Texts). King Edward held lands in France as a vassal to the French king and thus was obligated to pay homage, but he feared leaving England in the midst of political turmoil.

94. *device*: heraldic emblem painted on a shield.

95. *Pliny* was the author of *Natural History* (c. 79 AD), an ancient encyclopedia of human knowledge. Pliny includes descriptions of all sorts of creatures (many of them fantastical) but does not actually mention flying fish.

Which all the other fishes deadly hate,
And therefore, being pursued, it takes the air;
No sooner is it up, but there's a fowl
That seizeth it. This fish, my lord, I bear;
The motto this: *Undique mors est.*°   *death is on all sides (Latin)*
Edward. Proud Mortimer! Ungentle Lancaster!
    Is this the love you bear your sovereign?   30
    Is this the fruit your reconcilement bears?
    Can you in words make show of amity,
    And in your shields display your rancorous minds?
    What call you this but private libeling°   *defamation*
    Against the Earl of Cornwall and my brother?[96]
Queen. Sweet husband, be content; they all love you.
Edward. They love me not that hate my Gaveston.
    I am that cedar; shake me not too much.
    And you the eagles, soar ye ne'er so high,
    I have the jesses[97] that will pull you down,   40
    And *Aeque tandem*° shall that canker cry   *equal in height*
    Unto the proudest peer of Britainy.°   *England*
    Though thou compar'st him to a flying fish,
    And threatenest death whether he rise or fall,
    'Tis not the hugest monster of the sea
    Nor foulest harpy[98] that shall swallow him.
Mortimer. *[To the Nobles]* If in his absence thus he favors him,
    What will he do whenas° he shall be present?   *when*
Lancaster. That shall we see. Look where his lordship comes.

        Enter Gaveston.

Edward. My Gaveston!   50
    Welcome to Tynemouth, welcome to thy friend!
    Thy absence made me droop and pine away;
    For as the lovers of fair Danaë,[99]
    When she was locked up in a brazen tower,
    Desired her more and waxed outrageous,°   *grew immoderate*
    So did it sure with me; and now thy sight

96. *my brother* refers not to Edward's half brother Kent but to his beloved friend
Gaveston, the Earl of Cornwall.

97. *jesses*: straps tied to the legs of trained falcons.

98. *harpy*: a ravenous birdlike creature with the upper torso of a woman.

99. *Danaë* was locked in a tower by her father. Jove fell in love with her and seduced
her in the form of a shower of gold.

Is sweeter far than was thy parting hence
Bitter and irksome to my sobbing heart.
Gaveston. Sweet lord and king, your speech preventeth° mine,   *anticipates*
    Yet have I words left to express my joy.   60
    The shepherd, nipped with biting winter's rage,
    Frolics not more to see the painted° spring   *colorful (with flowers)*
    Than I do to behold your majesty.
Edward. Will none of you salute my Gaveston?
Lancaster. Salute him? Yes. Welcome, Lord Chamberlain.[100]
Mortimer. Welcome is the good Earl of Cornwall.
Warwick. Welcome, Lord Governor of the Isle of Man.
Pembroke. Welcome, Master Secretary.
Kent. Brother, do you hear them?
Edward. Still will these earls and barons use me thus?   70
Gaveston. My lord, I cannot brook these injuries.
Queen. [Aside] Ay me, poor soul, when these begin to jar.°   *quarrel*
Edward. Return it to their throats; I'll be thy warrant.[101]
Gaveston. Base, leaden earls,[102] that glory in your birth,
    Go sit at home, and eat your tenants' beef,
    And come not here to scoff at Gaveston,
    Whose mounting thoughts did never creep so low
    As to bestow a look on such as you.
Lancaster. Yet I disdain not to do this for you.
    [Lancaster draws his sword, followed by
    the other Nobles and Gaveston.]
Edward. Treason, treason![103] Where's the traitor?   80
Pembroke. [Pointing to Gaveston] Here, here!
Edward. [To Attendants]
    Convey hence Gaveston! They'll murder him.
Gaveston. [To Mortimer]
    The life of thee shall salve° this foul disgrace.   *pay for*
Mortimer. Villain, thy life, unless I miss mine aim.
    [Gaveston and Mortimer fight. Gaveston is wounded.]

---

100. The greetings offered to Gaveston by Lancaster and the nobles (in the lines
that follow) are spoken sarcastically (as becomes evident by the reactions of Kent,
Edward, and Gaveston).

101. "Return their insults; I'll protect you."

102. Gaveston's insult, *leaden earls*, suggests that the nobles are dull and weighed
down with earthly desires, unlike the spirited Gaveston who has "mounting
thoughts" (line 77).

103. It was an act of *treason* to draw a weapon in the presence of the king.

Queen. Ah, furious Mortimer, what hast thou done?

Mortimer. No more than I would answer° were he slain.   *publicly justify*
    [Exit Gaveston with Attendants.]

Edward. Yes, more than thou canst answer, though he live.
    Dear shall you both aby this riotous deed.[104]
    Out of my presence! Come not near the court!

Mortimer. I'll not be barred the court for° Gaveston.   *because of*

Lancaster. We'll hale° him by the ears unto the block.   *drag*

Edward. Look to your own heads; his is sure° enough.   *safe*

Warwick. Look to your own crown,[105] if you back him thus.   93

Kent. Warwick, these words do ill beseem thy years.[106]

Edward. Nay, all of them conspire to cross° me thus;   *torment*
    But if I live, I'll tread upon their heads
    That think with high looks thus to tread me down.
    Come Edmund, let's away and levy men.°   *raise an army*
    'Tis war that must abate these barons' pride.
    Exit the King, [Kent, and the Queen].

Warwick. Let's to our castles, for the king is moved.°   *angry*

Mortimer. Moved may he be,[107] and perish in his wrath!   101

Lancaster. Cousin, it is no dealing with him now.
    He means to make us stoop° by force of arms,   *submit*
    And therefore let us jointly here protest°   *vow*
    To prosecute that Gaveston to the death.

Mortimer. By heaven, the abject villain° shall not live!   *base peasant*

Warwick. I'll have his blood, or die in seeking it.

Pembroke. The like oath Pembroke takes.

Lancaster. And so doth Lancaster.
    Now send our heralds to defy° the king,   *renounce allegiance to*
    And make the people swear to put him down.   110

    Enter a Post.

Mortimer. Letters? From whence?

Post. From Scotland, my lord.
    [Mortimer takes the letters and reads.]

---

104. "You both (Mortimer and Lancaster) shall pay dearly for this deed."

105. Warwick threatens to seize the *crown* from the king, or perhaps to cut off his "crown" (his head).

106. "These rash words are unbecoming for one your age" (who should be more wise).

107. Mortimer's retort implies a double sense: the king is *moved* (angry), but also the king may be *moved* off this throne by the nobles.

Lancaster. Why, how now, cousin, how fares all our friends?
Mortimer. My uncle's taken prisoner by the Scots.
Lancaster. We'll have him ransomed, man; be of good cheer.
Mortimer. They rate his ransom at five thousand pound.
    Who should defray° the money but the king,   *pay*
    Seeing he is taken prisoner in his wars?
    I'll to the king.[108]
Lancaster. Do, cousin, and I'll bear thee company.   120
Warwick. Meantime, my lord of Pembroke and myself
    Will to Newcastle here and gather head.°   *raise an army*
Mortimer. About it then, and we will follow you.
Lancaster. Be resolute and full of secrecy.
Warwick. I warrant you.°   *I assure you*
    [Exeunt all except Mortimer and Lancaster.]
Mortimer. Cousin, an if he will not ransom him,
    I'll thunder such a peal into his ears
    As never subject did unto his king.
Lancaster. Content,° I'll bear my part. Holla! Who's there?   *agreed*

    [Enter a Guard.]

Mortimer. Ay, marry,° such a guard as this doth well.   *certainly*
Lancaster. Lead on the way.   131
Guard. Whither will your lordships?
Mortimer. Whither else but to the king?
Guard. His highness is disposed to be alone.
Lancaster. Why, so he may, but we will speak to him.
Guard. You may not in,° my lord.   *enter*
Mortimer. May we not?

    [Enter Edward and Kent.]

Edward. How now, what noise is this?
    Who have we there? Is't you?
    [Edward and Kent begin to exit.]
Mortimer. Nay, stay, my lord; I come to bring you news: 140
    Mine uncle's taken prisoner by the Scots.

108. There is no mention in the historical sources of Mortimer Senior being captured and held for ransom by the Scots. Marlowe invents this turn of events, which (later in the scene) will put Edward in an ignoble light when he refuses to fulfill the traditional feudal obligation of the king to pay ransom for a lord captured while in his service. (The historical Mortimer Senior was actually taken prisoner by King Edward and died in the Tower of London.)

Edward. Then ransom him.

Lancaster. 'Twas in your wars. You should ransom him.

Mortimer. And you shall ransom him, or else—

Kent. What, Mortimer, you will not threaten him?

Edward. Quiet yourself. You shall have the broad seal

    To gather for him throughout the realm.[109]

Lancaster. Your minion Gaveston hath taught you this.

Mortimer. My lord, the family of the Mortimers

    Are not so poor but, would they sell their land,   150

    'Twould levy men° enough to anger you.   *raise an army*

    We never beg, but use such prayers as these.

    [Mortimer grasps his sword.]

Edward. Shall I still be haunted° thus?   *tormented*

Mortimer. Nay, now you are here alone, I'll speak my mind.

Lancaster. And so will I, and then, my lord, farewell.

Mortimer. The idle° triumphs, masks, lascivious shows,   *worthless*

    And prodigal° gifts bestowed on Gaveston   *extravagant*

    Have drawn thy treasure dry, and made thee weak;

    The murmuring commons overstretchèd hath.[110]

Lancaster. Look for rebellion; look to be deposed.   160

    Thy garrisons are beaten out of France,

    And, lame and poor, lie groaning at the gates.

    The wild O'Neil, with swarms of Irish kerns,

    Lives uncontrolled within the English pale.[111]

    Unto the walls of York the Scots made road,°   *raided*

    And, unresisted, drave° away rich spoils.   *carried*

Mortimer. The haughty Dane commands the narrow seas,[112]

    While in the harbor ride thy ships unrigged.°   *unprepared*

Lancaster. What foreign prince sends thee ambassadors?

Mortimer. Who loves thee but a sort° of flatterers?   *group*

---

109. The *broad seal* is a document with an official wax imprint from the Great Seal (see note at 1.1.167) that would enable a person to collect alms or charity for a special purpose. As the lines that follow indicate, Edward insultingly offers the broad seal because his treasury is overspent, and he lacks the funds to pay the ransom.

110. "The disgruntled common people have been overburdened with taxes."

111. There is no mention of *O'Neil* in Holinshed's account of the reign of Edward II, but the O'Neils were a powerful Irish clan who fought against the English during the reign of Queen Elizabeth I. *Irish kerns* were foot soldiers. *The English pale* was the region around Dublin colonized by the English.

112. There is no mention in Holinshed or the other historical sources of the Danes taking control of the English Channel.

Lancaster. Thy gentle queen, sole sister to Valois,[113]   171
    Complains that thou hast left her all forlorn.
Mortimer. Thy court is naked, being bereft° of those   *emptied*
    That make a king seem glorious to the world:
    I mean the peers, whom thou shouldst dearly love.
    Libels° are cast against thee in the street;   *defamatory pamphlets*
    Ballads and rhymes made of thy overthrow.
Lancaster. The northern borderers, seeing their houses burnt,
    Their wives and children slain, run up and down,
    Cursing the name of thee and Gaveston.   180
Mortimer. When wert thou in the field with banner spread?
    But once,[114] and then thy soldiers marched like players,°   *stage actors*
    With garish robes, not armor; and thyself,
    Bedaubed with gold, rode laughing at the rest,
    Nodding and shaking of thy spangled crest,
    Where women's favors hung like labels down.[115]
Lancaster. And thereof came it that the fleering° Scots,   *jeering*
    To England's high disgrace, have made this jig:°   *song*
    "Maids of England, sore may you mourn,
    For your lemans° you have lost at Bannockburn,   *lovers*
        With a heave and a ho!   191
    What weeneth° the king of England,   *hopes*
    So soon to have won Scotland?
        With a rumbelow!"[116]

---

113. Queen Isabella's three brothers (who reigned in succession as kings of France) were of the house of Capet, not the house of Valois. Philip of Valois, however, was her cousin, and he later became king of France.

114. Edward actually fought several minor battles against the Scots (beginning with his role as the Prince of Wales under his father, King Edward I), but his one major engagement with the Scots (to which Mortimer and Lancaster refer in the lines that follow) was the battle of Bannockburn in 1314, a disastrous loss for the English. According to Holinshed, Edward's army was woefully unprepared: the king went to battle "with a mighty army bravely furnished and gorgeously appareled, more seemly for a triumph than meet to encounter with the cruel enemy in the field" (see Related Texts).

115. Medieval knights would attach gifts from ladies (such as ribbons or gloves) on the crests of their helmets. Edward is described as an excessively vain knight with many tokens hanging from his helmet like *labels* (strips of parchment used to attach seals to a document).

116. The song—which Marlowe took almost verbatim from Fabyan's *Chronicle* (1559)—was composed by the Scots in celebration of their victory at Bannockburn. *With a rumbelow* is a nonsense phrase used to fill out the meter and rhyme.

Mortimer. Wigmore shall fly to set my uncle free.[117]

Lancaster. And when 'tis gone, our swords shall purchase° more.   *win*

    If ye be moved, revenge it as you can.

    Look next to see us with our ensigns° spread.   *banners*

       Exeunt Nobles [Mortimer and Lancaster].

Edward. My swelling heart for very anger breaks.

    How oft have I been baited by these peers,   200

    And dare not be revenged, for their power is great.

    Yet shall the crowing of these cockerels°   *young roosters*

    Affright a lion? Edward, unfold thy paws,

    And let their lives' blood slake° thy fury's hunger.   *quench*

    If I be cruel and grow tyrannous,

    Now let them thank themselves, and rue° too late.   *regret*

Kent. My lord, I see your love to Gaveston

    Will be the ruin of the realm and you,

    For now the wrathful nobles threaten wars,

    And therefore, brother, banish him forever.   210

Edward. Art thou an enemy to my Gaveston?

Kent. Ay, and it grieves me that I favored him.

Edward. Traitor, begone! Whine thou with Mortimer.

Kent. So will I, rather than with Gaveston.

Edward. Out of my sight, and trouble me no more!

Kent. No marvel though thou scorn thy noble peers,

    When I thy brother am rejected thus.[118]

Edward. Away!

      Exit [Kent].

    Poor Gaveston, that hast no friend but me.

    Do what they can, we'll live in Tynemouth here,   220

    And, so I walk with him about the walls,

    What care I though the earls begirt° us round?   *enclose*

    Here comes she that's cause of all these jars.

      Enter the Queen, three Ladies [Margaret and two
      others], Baldock and Spencer [and Gaveston].

Queen. My lord, 'tis thought the earls are up in arms.

Edward. Ay, and 'tis likewise thought you favor him.°   *(Mortimer)*

Queen. Thus do you still suspect me without cause.

---

117. "Wigmore (Mortimer's estate) will be sold to pay the ransom for my uncle."
118. The historical Kent was not banished by the king, nor did he join the rebel lords, as Marlowe's Kent will do in the following scene. The historical Kent, however, did join the queen's rebellion in 1326 (depicted later in the play in 4.4).

Margaret. Sweet uncle, speak more kindly to the queen.
Gaveston. *[Aside to Edward]*
    My lord, dissemble with her,° speak her fair.   *deceive her*
Edward. Pardon me, sweet, I forgot myself.
Queen. Your pardon is quickly got of Isabel.   230
Edward. The younger Mortimer is grown so brave°   *defiant*
    That to my face he threatens civil wars.
Gaveston. Why do you not commit him to the Tower?
Edward. I dare not, for the people love him well.
Gaveston. Why then, we'll have him privily made away.°   *secretly murdered*
Edward. Would Lancaster and he had both caroused°   *drunk*
    A bowl of poison to each other's health!
    But let them go,° and tell me what are these.   *enough talk of them*
Margaret. Two of my father's servants whilst he lived.
    May't please your grace to entertain° them now.   *employ*
Edward. Tell me, where wast thou born? What is thine arms?°   *coat of arms*
Baldock. My name is Baldock, and my gentry   242
    I fetched from Oxford, not from heraldry.[119]
Edward. The fitter art thou, Baldock, for my turn.
    Wait on me, and I'll see thou shalt not want.°   *lack employment*
Baldock. I humbly thank your majesty.
Edward. Knowest thou him, Gaveston?
Gaveston.   Ay, my lord,
    His name is Spencer; he is well allied.°   *socially connected*
    For my sake, let him wait upon your grace.
    Scarce shall you find a man of more desert.   250
Edward. Then, Spencer, wait upon me; for his sake
    I'll grace thee with a higher style ere long.[120]
Spencer. No greater titles happen unto me
    Than to be favored of° your majesty.   *by*
Edward. *[To Margaret and then to Gaveston]*
    Cousin, this day shall be your marriage feast.
    And, Gaveston, think that I love thee well
    To wed thee to our niece, the only heir
    Unto the Earl of Gloucester late deceased.

119. Baldock gained *gentry* status not from *heraldry* (family lineage) but by earning a degree at Oxford University. (Similarly, Christopher Marlowe was born a commoner—the son of a Canterbury shoemaker—but became a "gentleman" by earning a degree at Cambridge.)

120. "I will reward you with a higher status soon."

Gaveston. I know, my lord, many will stomach° me,   resent
    But I respect neither their love nor hate.   260
Edward. The headstrong barons shall not limit me;
    He that I list° to favor shall be great.   choose
    Come, let's away; and when the marriage ends,
    Have at the rebels and their complices!°   accomplices
      Exeunt.

ACT 2, SCENE 3

Enter Lancaster, Mortimer, Warwick, Pembroke,
Kent, [and Attendants].

Kent. My lords, of love to this our native land
    I come to join with you and leave the king,
    And in your quarrel and the realm's behoof°   benefit
    Will be the first that shall adventure° life.   risk
Lancaster. I fear me you are sent of policy,[121]
    To undermine us with a show of love.
Warwick. He is your brother; therefore have we cause
    To cast° the worst, and doubt of your revolt.   fear
Kent. Mine honor shall be hostage of my truth.
    If that will not suffice, farewell my lords.   10
Mortimer. Stay, Edmund. Never was Plantagenet
    False of his word, and therefore trust we thee.[122]
Pembroke. But what's the reason you should leave him now?
Kent. I have informed the Earl of Lancaster.
Lancaster. And it sufficeth. Now, my lords, know this,
    That Gaveston is secretly arrived,
    And here in Tynemouth frolics with the king.
    Let us with these our followers scale the walls,
    And suddenly surprise them unawares.
Mortimer. I'll give the onset.°   lead the attack
Warwick.   And I'll follow thee.   20

---

121. The term *policy* in Elizabethan England often evoked associations with the trickery and deception advocated in Machiavelli's *The Prince*. Marlowe used the term fourteen times in *The Jew of Malta*, a play introduced by "Machevil."

122. *Plantagenet* was the family name of the royal dynasty that ruled medieval England from 1126 to 1485. The logic of Mortimer's comment to Kent is obscure since King Edward is also a Plantagenet (but the nobles do not trust him).

Mortimer. This tattered ensign° of my ancestors,   *banner*
  Which swept the desert shore of that Dead Sea
  Whereof we got the name of Mortimer,[123]
  Will I advance upon these castle walls.
  Drums, strike alarum! Raise them from their sport,°   *idleness*
  And ring aloud the knell° of Gaveston!   *death knell*
Lancaster. None be so hardy° as to touch the king,   *bold*
  But neither spare you Gaveston nor his friends.
   Exeunt.

ACT 2, SCENE 4

Enter the King and Spencer.

Edward. O tell me, Spencer, where is Gaveston?
Spencer. I fear me he is slain, my gracious lord.
Edward. No, here he comes! Now let them spoil° and kill.   *plunder*

  [Enter] to them Gaveston, [the Queen,
  Margaret, and Attendants].

  Fly, fly, my lords! The earls have got the hold.°   *captured the fort*
  Take shipping° and away to Scarborough.   *go by ship*
  Spencer and I will post away by land.
Gaveston. O stay, my lord; they will not injure you.
Edward. I will not trust them. Gaveston, away!
Gaveston. Farewell, my lord.
Edward. Lady, farewell.   10
Margaret. Farewell, sweet uncle, till we meet again.
Edward. Farewell, sweet Gaveston, and farewell, niece.
Queen. No farewell to poor Isabel, thy queen?
Edward. Yes, yes, for Mortimer, your lover's sake.
Queen. Heavens can witness I love none but you.
  Exeunt all except Isabella.
  From my embracements thus he breaks away.
  O that mine arms could close this isle about,
  That I might pull him to me where I would,

123. The name *Mortimer* did not originate from the Latin *Mortuum Mare* (Dead Sea) but instead from their ancestral homeland, Mortemer (in Normandy). Though the name had no connection to the exploits of crusaders in the Holy Land, the false etymology was widely believed in Elizabethan England.

Or that these tears that drizzle from mine eyes
Had power to mollify his stony heart,   20
That when I had him we might never part!

Enter the Barons [Lancaster, Mortimer,
Warwick, and Attendants]. Alarums.[124]

Lancaster. I wonder how he 'scaped?
Mortimer.   Who's this? The queen?
Queen. Ay, Mortimer, the miserable queen,
    Whose pining heart her inward sighs have blasted,
    And body with continual mourning wasted.
    These hands are tired with haling° of my lord   *dragging*
    From Gaveston, from wicked Gaveston,
    And all in vain, for when I speak him fair,
    He turns away, and smiles upon his minion.
Mortimer. Cease to lament, and tell us where's the king?   30
Queen. What would you with the king? Is't him you seek?
Lancaster. No, madam, but that cursèd Gaveston.
    Far be it from the thought of Lancaster
    To offer violence to his sovereign;
    We would but rid the realm of Gaveston.
    Tell us where he remains, and he shall die.
Queen. He's gone by water unto Scarborough.
    Pursue him quickly, and he cannot 'scape.
    The king hath left him, and his train° is small.   *retinue*
Warwick. Forslow° no time, sweet Lancaster; let's march.   *waste*
Mortimer. How comes it that the king and he is parted?   41
Queen. That this your army, going several ways,
    Might be of lesser force, and with the power°   *army*
    That he intendeth presently to raise
    Be easily suppressed; and therefore begone.
Mortimer. Here in the river rides a Flemish hoy.°   *fishing boat*
    Let's all aboard and follow him amain.°   *quickly*
Lancaster. The wind that bears him hence will fill our sails.
    Come, come, aboard; 'tis but an hour's sailing.
Mortimer. Madam, stay you within this castle here.   50
Queen. No, Mortimer, I'll to my lord the king.
Mortimer. Nay, rather sail with us to Scarborough.
Queen. You know the king is so suspicious
    As, if he hear I have but talked with you,

---

124. *Alarums:* military trumpet or drum signals (sometimes sounded off stage).

Mine honor will be called in question;
    And therefore, gentle Mortimer, begone.
Mortimer. Madam, I cannot stay to answer you;
    But think of Mortimer as he deserves.
        [Exeunt all except the Queen.]
Queen. So well hast thou deserved, sweet Mortimer,
    As Isabel could live with thee forever.   60
    In vain I look for love at Edward's hand,
    Whose eyes are fixed on none but Gaveston.
    Yet once more I'll importune him with prayers.
    If he be strange° and not regard my words,   *standoffish*
    My son and I will over into France,
    And to the king my brother there complain
    How Gaveston hath robbed me of his love.
    But yet I hope my sorrows will have end,
    And Gaveston this blessèd day be slain.[125]
        [Exit.]

ACT 2, SCENE 5

Enter Gaveston, pursued.

Gaveston. Yet, lusty lords, I have escaped your hands,
    Your threats, your 'larums,° and your hot pursuits;   *alarums*
    And though divorcèd from King Edward's eyes,
    Yet liveth Piers of Gaveston unsurprised,°   *uncaptured*
    Breathing in hope—*malgrado*° all your beards   *in spite of (Italian)*
    That muster rebels thus against your king—
    To see his royal sovereign once again.

        Enter the Nobles [Warwick, Mortimer, Lancaster,
        Pembroke, with Attendants, Soldiers, James,
        and Horse-boy].

Warwick. Upon him, soldiers; take away his weapons!
Mortimer. Thou proud disturber of thy country's peace,
    Corrupter of thy king, cause of these broils,°   *quarrels*
    Base flatterer, yield! And were it not for shame,   11

---

125. In Holinshed, Isabella did not go to France to complain about Gaveston; instead, she was sent by Edward on a diplomatic mission after the French king seized English territories in Guienne.

Shame and dishonor to a soldier's name,
    Upon my weapon's point here shouldst thou fall,
    And welter° in thy gore.   *roll*
Lancaster.   Monster of men,
    That, like the Greekish strumpet, trained to arms
    And bloody wars so many valiant knights,[126]
    Look for no other fortune, wretch, than death!
    King Edward is not here to buckler° thee.   *protect*
Warwick. Lancaster, why talk'st thou to the slave?
    Go, soldiers, take him hence, for by my sword,   20
    His head shall off. Gaveston, short warning
    Shall serve thy turn.[127] It is our country's cause
    That here severely we will execute
    Upon thy person. Hang him at a bough.
Gaveston. My lord—
Warwick. Soldiers, have him away.
    But for° thou wert the favorite of a king,   *because*
    Thou shalt have so much honor at our hands.[128]
Gaveston. I thank you all, my lords. Then I perceive
    That heading is one, and hanging is the other,   30
    And death is all.

        Enter Earl of Arundel.

Lancaster. How now, my lord of Arundel?
Arundel. My lords, King Edward greets you all by me.
Warwick. Arundel, say your message.
Arundel.   His majesty,
    Hearing that you had taken Gaveston,
    Entreateth you by me, that but he may
    See him before he dies; for why,° he says,   *for this reason*
    And sends you word, he knows that die he shall.
    And if you gratify his grace so far,
    He will be mindful° of the courtesy.   *grateful*

---

126. "Like Helen of Troy who lured into battle so many valiant knights" (in Homer's *Iliad*).

127. Warwick gives *short warning* (little time) for Gaveston to prepare for death (by prayer and repentance), thus increasing the likelihood that Gaveston's soul would be damned to hell.

128. After ordering Gaveston to be hanged, Warwick says, sardonically, that Gaveston shall receive the *honor* of death by beheading. (Common criminals were hanged; gentry and nobles were granted the privilege of beheading.)

Warwick. How now?   41

Gaveston.   *[Aside]* Renownèd Edward, how thy name
    Revives poor Gaveston!

Warwick.   No, it needeth not.°   *no need to allow it*
    Arundel, we will gratify the king
    In other matters; he must pardon us in this.
    Soldiers, away with him.

Gaveston.   Why, my lord of Warwick,
    Will not these delays beget my hopes?
    I know it, lords, it is this life you aim at;
    Yet grant King Edward this.[129]

Mortimer.   Shalt thou appoint°   *decide*
    What we shall grant? Soldiers, away with him.
    Thus we'll gratify the king: 50
    We'll send his head by thee. Let him bestow
    His tears on that, for that is all he gets
    Of Gaveston, or else his senseless trunk.

Lancaster. Not so, my lord, lest he bestow more cost
    In burying him than he hath ever earned.[130]

Arundel. My lords, it is his majesty's request,
    And in the honor of a king he swears,
    He will but talk with him and send him back.

Warwick. When, can you tell?[131] Arundel, no.
    We wot,° he that the care of realm remits,°   *know / abandons*
    And drives his nobles to these exigents°   *extremes*
    For Gaveston, will, if he seize him once,   62
    Violate any promise to possess him.[132]

Arundel. Then if you will not trust his grace in keep,
    My lords, I will be pledge for his return.[133]

Mortimer. It is honorable in thee to offer this,
    But for we know thou art a noble gentleman,

---

129. "Warwick, do you really think this delay would inspire my hope to live? I know you (lords) intend to kill me; yet grant Edward this request."

130. "No, we will not send his dead body to the king, for the king might spend lavishly on the funeral."

131. An expression of doubt: "When would that be?"

132. "If the king takes possession of Gaveston, the king will violate his promise" (and not return him).

133. "If you do not trust the king in taking custody of Gaveston, I will offer myself as a hostage to guarantee Gaveston's return."

We will not wrong thee so,
To make away a true man for a thief.[134]

Gaveston. How mean'st thou, Mortimer? That is over-base!   70

Mortimer. Away, base groom, robber of kings' renown!
Question° with thy companions and thy mates.[135]   *dispute*

Pembroke. My lord Mortimer, and you my lords each one,
To gratify the king's request therein
Touching the sending of this Gaveston,
Because his majesty so earnestly
Desires to see the man before his death,
I will upon mine honor undertake
To carry him and bring him back again,
Provided this: that you, my lord of Arundel,   80
Will join with me.

Warwick.   Pembroke, what wilt thou do?
Cause yet more bloodshed? Is it not enough
That we have taken him, but must we now
Leave him on "had-I-wist"[136] and let him go?

Pembroke. My lords, I will not over-woo° your honors,   *plead too much*
But if you dare trust Pembroke with the prisoner,
Upon mine oath, I will return him back.

Arundel. My lord of Lancaster, what say you in this?

Lancaster. Why, I say let him go on Pembroke's word.

Pembroke. And you, lord Mortimer?   90

Mortimer. How say you, my lord of Warwick?

Warwick. Nay, do your pleasures. I know how 'twill prove.[137]

Pembroke. Then give him me.

Gaveston.   Sweet sovereign, yet I come
To see thee ere° I die!   *before*

Warwick.   [*Aside*]Yet not, perhaps,
If Warwick's wit and policy prevail.[138]

Mortimer. My lord of Pembroke, we deliver him you;
Return him on your honor. Sound away!

---

134. "To execute a true man (Arundel) in place of a thief (Gaveston)."

135. The connotations of *companions* and *mates* were derogatory, suggesting low-life scoundrels.

136. *had-I-wist*: a proverbial expression of regret, meaning "if only I'd known."

137. "Do as you want. I know how it will turn out." (The line suggests that Warwick has a secret plan.)

138. The term *policy* suggests Machiavellian cunning and trickery (see note at 2.3.5).

[Trumpets sound.] Exeunt all except Pembroke,
Arundel, Gaveston, and Pembroke's men: four
Soldiers [including James and a Horse-boy].
Pembroke. *[To Arundel]* My lord, you shall go with me.
    My house is not far hence, out of the way
    A little, but our men shall go along.   100
    We that have pretty wenches to° our wives,   *as*
    Sir, must not come so near and balk° their lips.   *refuse*
Arundel. 'Tis very kindly spoke, my lord of Pembroke.
    Your honor hath an adamant° of power   *magnet*
    To draw a prince.
Pembroke.   So, my lord. Come hither, James.
    I do commit this Gaveston to thee.
    Be thou this night his keeper; in the morning
    We will discharge thee of thy charge. Begone.
Gaveston. Unhappy° Gaveston, whither goest thou now? *unlucky*
Horse-boy. My lord, we'll quickly be at Cobham.[139]   110
    Exeunt [Pembroke, Arundel, and Horse-boy].

ACT 3, SCENE 1

Enter Gaveston mourning, and the Earl of
Pembroke's men [James and three Soldiers].

Gaveston. O treacherous Warwick, thus to wrong thy friend!° *(Pembroke)*
James. I see it is your life these arms° pursue.   *soldiers*
Gaveston. Weaponless must I fall, and die in bands?°   *bondage*
    O, must this day be period° of my life?   *the end*
    Center of all my bliss![140] An° ye be men,   *if*
    Speed to the king.

    Enter Warwick and his company [of Soldiers].

Warwick.   My lord of Pembroke's men,
    Strive° you no longer. I will have that Gaveston. *struggle*

---

139. *Cobham*: town in Kent.

140. The phrase *Center of all my bliss* is obscure. *Center* may refer to *this day* (in which Gaveston hopes for a moment of bliss in meeting Edward for the last time), or *center* could refer to Edward (the source of his bliss), or *center* could refer to the earth as the center of the universe in the traditional cosmology (as the term is used in 4.7.62).

James. Your lordship doth dishonor to yourself,
    And wrong our lord, your honorable friend.
Warwick. No, James, it is my country's cause I follow.   10
    Go, take the villain.
        [Warwick's soldiers seize Gaveston.]
                              Soldiers, come away.
    We'll make quick work. *[To James]* Commend me
        to your master,
    My friend, and tell him that I watched it well.[141]
    [To Gav.] Come, let thy shadow° parley with King Edward.   *ghost*
Gaveston. Treacherous earl! Shall I not see the king?
Warwick. The king of heaven perhaps, no other king.
    Away!
        Exeunt Warwick and his men, with Gaveston.
        James remains with the others.
James. Come, fellows, it booted not° for us to strive.   *was useless*
    We will in haste go certify° our lord.   *inform*
        Exeunt.

ACT 3, SCENE 2

Enter King Edward and Spencer [and Baldock],
with drums and fifes.

Edward. I long to hear an answer from the barons
    Touching my friend, my dearest Gaveston.
    Ah Spencer, not the riches of my realm
    Can ransom him; ah, he is marked to die.
    I know the malice of the younger Mortimer;
    Warwick, I know, is rough, and Lancaster
    Inexorable; and I shall never see
    My lovely Piers, my Gaveston, again.
    The barons overbear me with their pride.
Spencer. Were I King Edward, England's sovereign,   10
    Son to the lovely Eleanor of Spain,
    Great Edward Longshanks' issue,[142] would I bear

141. Warwick speaks sarcastically: "Tell Pembroke that I guarded Gaveston well" (while leading him to his execution).

142. Edward was the son of Eleanor of Castile and King Edward I (nicknamed "Longshanks" because of his height and long legs).

These braves,° this rage, and suffer° uncontrolled   *insults / tolerate*
These barons thus to beard[143] me in my land,
In mine own realm? My lord, pardon my speech.
Did you retain your father's magnanimity,°   *greatness*
Did you regard the honor of your name,
You would not suffer thus your majesty
Be counterbuffed of° your nobility.   *rebuffed by*
Strike off their heads, and let them preach on poles.[144]   20
No doubt such lessons they° will teach the rest,   *(executed rebels)*
As by their preachments° they will profit much   *sermons*
And learn obedience to their lawful king.
Edward. Yea, gentle Spencer, we have been too mild,
    Too kind to them, but now have drawn our sword,
    And if they send me not my Gaveston,
    We'll steel it on their crest and poll their tops.[145]
Baldock. This haught° resolve becomes your majesty,   *brave*
    Not to be tied to their affection[146]
    As though your highness were a schoolboy still   30
    And must be awed and governed like a child.

    Enter Hugh Spencer, an old man, father to the young
    Spencer, with his truncheon,[147] *and Soldiers.*

Spencer Senior. Long live my sovereign, the noble Edward,
    In peace triumphant, fortunate in wars!
Edward. Welcome, old man. Com'st thou in Edward's aid?
    Then tell thy prince of whence° and what thou art.   *from where*
Spencer Senior. Lo, with a band of bowmen and of pikes,
    Brown bills and targeteers,[148] four hundred strong,
    Sworn to defend King Edward's royal right,
    I come in person to your majesty:
    Spencer, the father of Hugh Spencer there,   40

143. *to beard*: to defy or offend (it was a grave insult to pull a man's beard).

144. The heads of traitors were put on poles and displayed as a warning to others (see note at 1.1.117).

145. "We will strike their helmets (with steel swords) and cut off their heads."

146. "Not to be subjected to the nobles' desires."

147. *truncheon*: a staff or club.

148. Spencer Senior leads an army of men carrying bows, *pikes* (spears), *brown bills* (spears with bronzed axe-shaped heads), and targets (shields).

Bound to you highness everlastingly
For favors done in him unto us all.[149]

Edward. Thy father, Spencer?

Spencer.   True, an it like° your grace,   *if it pleases*
That pours, in lieu of° all your goodness shown,   *in return for*
His life, my lord, before your princely feet.

Edward. Welcome ten thousand times, old man, again!
[*To Spencer Jr.*] Spencer, this love, this kindness to thy king
Argues° thy noble mind and disposition.   *proves*
Spencer, I here create thee Earl of Wiltshire,[150]
And daily will enrich thee with our favor,   50
That, as the sunshine, shall reflect o'er thee.
Besides, the more to manifest our love,
Because we hear Lord Bruce doth sell his land,
And that the Mortimers are in hand withal,°   *ready to buy*
Thou shalt have crowns of us t' outbid the barons.[151]
And, Spencer, spare them not, but lay it on.°   *be generous*
Soldiers, a largess,° and thrice welcome all!   *extra pay*

Spencer. My lord, here comes the queen.

        *Enter the Queen [reading a letter] and her
        son [Prince Edward], and Levune, a Frenchman.*[152]

Edward.   Madam, what news?

Queen. News of dishonor, lord, and discontent.
Our friend Levune, faithful and full of trust,
Informeth us, by letters and by words,°   60
That Lord Valois our brother, king of France,   *oral reports*
Because your highness hath been slack in homage,
Hath seizèd Normandy into his hands.[153]
These be the letters, this the messenger.

149. "For favors done to him (Spencer Junior) and thus to all of us."

150. There is no mention in Holinshed or the other historical sources of Edward granting the title *Earl of Wiltshire* to Spencer Junior. Holinshed does mention, however, that Spencer Senior owned a manor in Wiltshire.

151. According to Holinshed, in 1321 Lord William Bruce offered some of his lands in the marches (borderlands) of Wales for sale to cover his debts. The two Mortimers attempted to buy the lands, but Spencer Junior (with the help of King Edward) succeeded in making the purchase.

152. *Levune*: an invented character with no historical basis.

153. Historically, King Charles IV was a Capet, not a Valois, and he seized English territories in Guienne, not Normandy (see note at 2.2.9).

Edward. Welcome, Levune. Tush, Sib,[154] if this be all,
    Valois and I will soon be friends again.
    But to my Gaveston: shall I never see,
    Never behold thee now? Madam, in this matter
    We will employ you and your little son;   70
    You shall go parley with the king of France.
    Boy, see you bear you bravely° to the king   *with dignity*
    And do your message with a majesty.
Prince Edward. Commit not to my youth things of more weight
    Than fits a prince so young as I to bear.
    And fear not, lord and father; heaven's great beams
    On Atlas' shoulder[155] shall not lie more safe
    Than shall your charge committed to my trust.
Queen. Ah boy, this towardness° makes thy mother fear   *boldness*
    Thou are not marked to many days on earth.[156]   80
Edward. Madam, we will that you with speed be shipped,
    And this our son. Levune shall follow you
    With all the haste we can dispatch him hence.
    Choose of our lords to bear you company,
    And go in peace; leave us in wars at home.
Queen. Unnatural wars, where subjects brave° their king;   *oppose*
    God end them once!° My lord, I take my leave   *at one stroke*
    To make my preparation for France.
    [Exeunt the Queen and Prince Edward.]

    Enter Lord Arundel.

Edward. What, lord Arundel, dost thou come alone?
Arundel. Yea, my good lord, for Gaveston is dead.   90
Edward. Ah traitors! Have they put my friend to death?
    Tell me, Arundel, died he ere° thou cam'st,   *before*
    Or didst thou see my friend to take his death?
Arundel. Neither, my lord, for as he was surprised,
    Begirt° with weapons and with enemies round,   *encircled*
    I did your highness' message to them all,
    Demanding him of them, entreating rather,

154. *Sib* apparently means kinswoman or relative (derived from "sibling"), or it may
be a diminutive form of "Isabel."

155. In Greek mythology, Atlas was a Titan who bore the weight of the heavens
on his shoulders.

156. Despite Isabella's fears in the play, the historical Edward III enjoyed a long life
and ruled England for fifty years (1327–77).

And said, upon the honor of my name,
That I would undertake to carry him
Unto your highness, and to bring him back.   100
Edward. And tell me, would the rebels deny me that?
Spencer. Proud recreants!°   *traitors*
Edward.   Yea, Spencer, traitors all!
Arundel. I found them at the first inexorable.°   *unyielding*
     The Earl of Warwick would not bide° the hearing;   *abide*
     Mortimer hardly; Pembroke and Lancaster   •
     Spake least. And when they flatly had denied,
     Refusing to receive me pledge for him,
     The Earl of Pembroke mildly thus bespake:
     "My lords, because our sovereign sends for him,
     And promiseth he shall be safe returned,   110
     I will this undertake: to have him hence
     And see him re-delivered to your hands."
Edward. Well, and how fortunes that he came not?
Spencer. Some treason or some villainy was cause.
Arundel. The Earl of Warwick seized him on his way,
     For, being delivered unto Pembroke's men,
     Their lord rode home thinking his prisoner safe;
     But ere he came, Warwick in ambush lay,
     And bare him to his death, and in a trench
     Struck off his head, and marched unto the camp.   120
Spencer. A bloody part,° flatly against law of arms.°   *act / code of chivalry*
Edward. O, shall I speak, or shall I sigh and die?
Spencer. My lord, refer° your vengeance to the sword   *direct*
     Upon these barons; hearten up your men;
     Let them° not unrevenged murder your friends.   *(the barons)*
     Advance your standard,° Edward, in the field,   *banner*
     And march to fire them from their starting holes.[157]
          Edward kneels.
Edward. By earth, the common mother of us all,
     By heaven, and all the moving orbs° thereof,   *planets*
     By this right hand, and by my father's sword,   130
     And all the honors 'longing° to my crown,   *belonging*
     I will have heads and lives for him, as many
     As I have manors, castles, towns, and towers.
     Treacherous Warwick! Traitorous Mortimer!

157. A hunting metaphor—hunters used *fire* and smoke to drive animals out of
their *holes* or hiding places.

If I be England's king, in lakes of gore
Your headless trunks, your bodies will I trail,°   *drag*
That you may drink your fill and quaff in blood,
And stain my royal standard with the same,
That so my bloody colors may suggest
Remembrance of revenge immortally   140
On your accursèd traitorous progeny,°   *lineage*
You villains that have slain my Gaveston.
 [The King rises.]
And in this place of honor and of trust,
Spencer, sweet Spencer, I adopt thee here,
And merely° of our love we do create thee   *simply*
Earl of Gloucester and Lord Chamberlain,
Despite of times, despite of enemies.[158]
Spencer. My lord, here is a messenger from the barons
 Desires access unto your majesty.
Edward. Admit him near.   150

 Enter the Herald from the Barons, with his
 coat of arms.[159]

Herald. Long live King Edward, England's lawful lord!
Edward. So wish not they, I wis,° that sent thee hither.   *I know*
 Thou com'st from Mortimer and his complices.°   *accomplices*
 A ranker rout° of rebels never was.   *unruly group*
 Well, say thy message.
Herald. The barons up in arms by me salute
 Your highness with long life and happiness,
 And bid me say, as plainer[160] to your grace,
 That if without effusion of blood
 You will this grief have ease and remedy,[161]   160
 That from your princely person you remove
 This Spencer, as a putrefying branch

---

158. As with Gaveston, Edward elevates the social status of his new favorite, Spencer Junior. Though Holinshed repeatedly refers to Spencer as the Earl of Gloucester, the historical Spencer never actually gained the title (though he was married to the sister of the earl). The historical Spencers were also members of the minor nobility even before their close alliance with the king.

159. *coat of arms*: a shield decorated with family symbols, or a coat worn by a herald with similar decorations.

160. *plainer*: one who delivers an official complaint or accusation.

161. "If without bloodshed you want to find a remedy for this turmoil."

That deads° the royal vine whose golden leaves   *deadens*
Empale your princely head, your diadem,[162]
Whose brightness such pernicious upstarts dim,
Say they, and lovingly advise your grace
To cherish virtue and nobility,
And have old servitors° in high esteem,   *advisers*
And shake off smooth dissembling° flatterers.   *deceiving*
This granted, they, their honors, and their lives   170
Are to your highness vowed and consecrate.°   *solemnly dedicated*
Spencer. Ah, traitors, will they still display their pride?
Edward. Away! Tarry° no answer, but begone!   *wait for*
     Rebels, will they appoint° their sovereign   *decide for*
     His sports,° his pleasures, and his company?   *pastimes*
     Yet ere° thou go, see how I do divorce   *before*
     Spencer from me.
        [The King] embraces Spencer.
                  Now get thee to thy lords,
     And tell them I will come to chastise them
     For murdering Gaveston. Hie° thee, get thee gone!   *hurry*
     Edward with fire and sword follows at thy heels.   180
        [Exit Herald.]
     My lords, perceive you how these rebels swell?°   *(with pride)*
     Soldiers, good hearts, defend your sovereign's right,
     For now, even now, we march to make them stoop.°   *submit*
     Away!
        Exeunt.

ACT 3, SCENE 3

Alarums, excursions, a great fight, and a retreat.
Enter the King, Spencer the father, Spencer the son,
and the noblemen of the King's side.

Edward. Why do we sound retreat? Upon them, lords!
     This day I shall pour vengeance with my sword
     On those proud rebels that are up in arms
     And do confront and countermand° their king.   *oppose*

---

162. The *diadem* (crown of England) that *empales* (encircles) the head of the king
was decorated with vines and strawberry leaves.

Spencer. I doubt it not, my lord; right will prevail.

Spencer Senior. 'Tis not amiss, my liege,° for either part°   lord / side
    To breathe a while. Our men, with sweat and dust
    All choked well near, begin to faint for heat,
    And this retire° refresheth horse and man.   retreat

Spencer. Here come the rebels.   10

      Enter the Barons: Mortimer, Lancaster, Warwick,
      Pembroke, and others.

Mortimer. Look, Lancaster,
    Yonder is Edward among his flatterers.

Lancaster. And there let him be,
    Till he pay dearly for their company.

Warwick. And shall, or Warwick's sword shall smite in vain.

Edward. What, rebels, do you shrink and sound retreat?

Mortimer. No, Edward, no. Thy flatterers faint and fly.

Lancaster. Thou'd best betimes° forsake them and their trains,°   soon / intrigues
    For they'll betray thee, traitors as they are.

Spencer. Traitor on thy face, rebellious Lancaster!   20

Pembroke. Away, base upstart! Brav'st thou nobles thus?

Spencer Senior. A noble attempt and honorable deed
    Is it not, trow ye,° to assemble aid   think you
    And levy arms against your lawful king?

Edward. For which ere° long their heads shall satisfy,   before
    T' appease the wrath of their offended king.

Mortimer. Then, Edward, thou wilt fight it to the last,
    And rather bathe thy sword in subjects' blood
    Than banish that pernicious company?

Edward. Ay, traitors all! Rather than thus be braved,°   opposed (by rebels)
    Make England's civil towns huge heaps of stones,   31
    And ploughs to go about our palace gates.

Warwick. A desperate and unnatural resolution.
    Alarum to the fight!
    Saint George for England, and the barons' right!

Edward. Saint George for England,[163] and King Edward's right!
    [Alarums. Exeunt both parties on different sides.]

163. *Saint George* was the patron saint of England (though not until the reign of
Edward III).

ACT 3, SCENE 4

Enter Edward, [both Spencers, Baldock, Levune,
and Soldiers,] with the Barons [Mortimer, Lancaster,
Warwick, and Kent as] captives.[164]

Edward. Now, lusty lords, now, not by chance of war,
    But justice of the quarrel and the cause,
    Vailed° is your pride. Methinks you hang the heads,   *lowered*
    But we'll advance them, traitors.[165] Now 'tis time
    To be avenged on you for all your braves°   *insults*
    And for the murder of my dearest friend,
    To whom right well you knew our soul was knit,
    Good Piers of Gaveston, my sweet favorite.
    Ah rebels, recreants,° you made him away!°   *traitors / killed him*
Kent. Brother, in regard of° thee and of thy land   *concern for*
    Did they remove that flatterer from thy throne.   11
Edward. So, sir, you have spoke. Away, avoid our presence!
    [Exit Kent.]
    Accursèd wretches, was't in regard of us,
    When we had sent our messenger to request
    He might be spared to come to speak with us,
    And Pembroke undertook for his return,
    That thou, proud Warwick, watched° the prisoner,   *guarded*
    Poor Piers, and headed° him against law of arms?   *beheaded*
    For which thy head shall overlook the rest
    As much as thou in rage outwent'st the rest.[166]   20
Warwick. Tyrant, I scorn thy threats and menaces;
    'Tis but temporal° that thou canst inflict.   *bodily harm*
Lancaster. The worst is death, and better die to live[167]
    Than live in infamy under such a king.

164. Pembroke is apparently not among the captive barons. Though insulted when Mortimer seized Gaveston from his men in 2.5, Pembroke continued in alliance with the barons in 3.3, but he never appears again in the play. (The historical Pembroke sided with the king during the revolt of the barons in 1322. Later, the king accused Pembroke of aiding the barons, but he was released after paying a fine.)

165. The heads of the traitors will indeed be advanced when they are beheaded and their heads are raised on poles for public display.

166. "Your head shall be raised on a higher pole than the others since you exceeded them in rebellion."

167. *better die to live*: proverbial expression meaning "it is better to die in this world and live eternally in the afterlife."

Edward. Away with them, my lord of Winchester,[168]
  These lusty leaders, Warwick and Lancaster.
  I charge you roundly: off with both their heads.
  Away!
Warwick. Farewell, vain world.
Lancaster.   Sweet Mortimer, farewell.
  *[Exeunt Warwick and Lancaster, guarded
  by Spencer Senior and Soldiers.]*
Mortimer. England, unkind to thy nobility,   30
  Groan for this grief; behold how thou art maimed.
Edward. Go, take that haughty Mortimer to the Tower.[169]
  There see him safe bestowed, and for the rest,
  Do speedy execution on them all.
  Begone!
Mortimer. What, Mortimer! Can ragged° stony walls   *rough and uneven*
  Immure thy virtue[170] that aspires to heaven?
  No, Edward, England's scourge, it may not be;
  Mortimer's hope surmounts° his fortune far.   *surpasses*
  [Exit Mortimer, guarded.]
Edward. Sound drums and trumpets! March with me, my friends.   40
  Edward this day hath crowned him° king anew.   *himself*
  [Drums and trumpets sound.]
  Exit all except Spencer, Levune, and Baldock.
Spencer. Levune, the trust that we repose° in thee   *place*
  Begets° the quiet of King Edward's land.   *will produce*
  Therefore begone in haste, and with advice°   *judicious care*

---

168. Spencer Senior was made Earl of Winchester in 1322, according to Holinshed.

169. Edward gives no reason for sparing the life of Mortimer while ordering the execution of the other rebellious barons. The action makes sense, however, in light of the historical events. In Holinshed, Mortimer takes no part in the revolt of the barons at the battle of Boroughbridge in 1322. Earlier that year, the two Mortimers had already surrendered to the king and were imprisoned in the Tower of London (for offenses that Holinshed never specifies). Marlowe needs to keep Mortimer alive in the play because of Mortimer's key role in later events. Four years later, Mortimer escapes from the Tower of London, travels to France, and joins Isabella's revolt and invasion of England in 1326. (Marlowe also freely altered the historical facts concerning Warwick, who likewise had no part in the rebellion of 1322. The historical Warwick had died in his bed from natural causes seven years earlier.)

170. *Virtue*, as Mortimer uses the term, does not mean moral excellence but "manliness and force of character" (as in the Italian *virtù*, a favorite term in Machiavelli's *The Prince*).

Bestow that treasure on the lords of France,
That therewith all enchanted, like the guard
That suffered Jove to pass in showers of gold
To Danaë, all aid may be denied
To Isabel the queen—that now in France
Makes friends—to cross the seas with her young son,   50
And step into his father's regiment.[171]

Levune. That's it these barons and the subtle queen
Long leveled° at.   *aimed*

Baldock.   Yea, but Levune, thou seest
These barons lay their heads on blocks together.
What they intend, the hangman frustrates clean.[172]

Levune. Have you no doubts, my lords. I'll clap so close°   *deal so secretly*
Among the lords of France with England's gold,
That Isabel shall make her plaints° in vain,   *complaints*
And France shall be obdurate° with her tears.   *unyielding*

Spencer. Then make for France amain,° Levune, away!   *at once*
Proclaim King Edward's wars and victories.   61
    Exeunt.

ACT 4, SCENE 1

Enter Edmund [Earl of Kent].

Kent. Fair blows the wind for France. Blow, gentle gale,
Till Edmund be arrived for England's good.[173]
Nature, yield to my country's cause in this!
A brother, no, a butcher of thy friends,
Proud Edward, dost thou banish me thy presence?

---

171. Spencer wants Levune to bribe the lords of France so that they will refuse to aid Queen Isabella in her plan to return to England with an army to set her son on the throne. Marlowe invents an added dimension to the *Danaë* myth, claiming that the *guard* who defended Danaë's tower was *enchanted* and in effect bribed by Jove's shower of gold. (For an earlier allusion to the Danaë, see 2.2.53.)

172. Baldock speaks sardonically: the rebel lords will put their heads together, as though conspiring a plot, but all their heads will be chopped off by the hangman. (The term *hangman* could refer to any executioner, regardless of the method of execution.)

173. Kent is not yet on board a ship but is waiting for Mortimer near the Tower of London.

But I'll to France, and cheer the wrongèd queen,
And certify what Edward's looseness[174] is.
Unnatural king, to slaughter noblemen
And cherish flatterers!
Mortimer, I stay° thy sweet escape;   *await*
Stand gracious, gloomy night, to his device.°   *plot*

    Enter Mortimer, disguised.

Mortimer. Holla! Who walketh there? Is't you my lord?   12
Kent. Mortimer, 'tis I.
    But hath thy potion wrought so happily?[175]
Mortimer. It hath, my lord. The warders all asleep,
    I thank them, gave me leave to pass in peace.
    But hath your grace got shipping unto France?
Kent. Fear it not.
      Exeunt.

ACT 4, SCENE 2

    Enter the Queen and her son [Prince Edward].

Queen. Ah boy, our friends do fail us all in France.
    The lords are cruel, and the king unkind.[176]
    What shall we do?
Prince Edward.   Madam, return to England
    And please my father well, and then a fig[177]
    For all my uncle's° friendship here in France.   *(Kent's)*
    I warrant° you, I'll win his highness quickly;   *assure*
    He loves me better than a thousand Spencers.
Queen. Ah boy, thou art deceived, at least in this,
    To think that we can yet be tuned together.
    No, no, we jar too far.[178] Unkind Valois!°   *(king of France)*

---

174. The term *looseness* implies both political and sexual transgressions.

175. "Has the sleep potion succeeded?"

176. The king of France is *unkind* in a double sense: he is uncharitable, and he is not acting like a "kin" or relative to Isabella.

177. *a fig:* an expression of contempt, sometimes accompanied by an obscene gesture (the thumb thrust between the index and middle finger).

178. "We are too discordant." Isabella follows her musical metaphor from the previous line: she and Edward cannot be *tuned together.*

Unhappy° Isabel! When France rejects,   *unlucky*
Whither, O whither dost thou bend thy steps?[179]   12

    Enter Sir John of Hainault.

Sir John. Madam, what cheer?°   *why this mood*
Queen.   Ah, good Sir John of Hainault,
  Never so cheerless, nor so far distressed.
Sir John. I hear, sweet lady, of the king's unkindness.
  But droop not, madam; noble minds contemn°   *reject*
  Despair. Will your grace with me to Hainault,
  And there stay time's advantage with your son?[180]
  [To Prince Ed.] How say you, my lord, will you go with
    your friends,
  And shake off all our fortunes equally?[181]   20
Prince Edward. So° pleaseth the queen my mother, me it likes.   *as it*
  The king of England, nor the court of France,
  Shall have° me from my gracious mother's side,   *move*
  Till I be strong enough to break a staff,°   *lance*
  And then have at° the proudest Spencer's head.   *strike at*
Sir John. Well said, my lord.
Queen. O my sweet heart, how do I moan° thy wrongs,   *lament*
  Yet triumph in the hope of thee, my joy.
  Ah, sweet Sir John, even to the utmost verge
  Of Europe, or the shore of Tanais,[182]   30
  Will we with thee to Hainault, so we will.
  The Marquis[183] is a noble gentleman;
  His grace, I dare presume, will welcome me.
  But who are these?

    Enter Edmund [Earl of Kent] and Mortimer.

179. "O where can I go to now?"

180. "Will you come with me to *Hainault* (a county in the Netherlands) and there
wait for an opportune time with your son?"

181. "And cast aside all our disappointments?" (from not receiving help from the
French king).

182. *Tanais*: Latin name for the River Don in Russia, considered the border
between Europe and Asia.

183. *Marquis* of Hainault, brother of Sir John.

Kent.   Madam, long may you live
        Much happier than your friends in England do.
Queen. Lord Edmund and Lord Mortimer alive!
        Welcome to France. *[To Mort.]* The news was here, my lord,
        That you were dead or very near your death.
Mortimer. Lady, the last was truest of the twain,
        But Mortimer, reserved for better hap,°   *fortune*
        Hath shaken off the thralldom° of the Tower,   *captivity*
        [To Prince Ed.] And lives t' advance your standard,[184]   42
            good my lord.
Prince Edward. How mean you, an° the king my father lives?   *if*
        No, my lord Mortimer, not I, I trow.°   *know*
Queen. Not, son? Why not? I would it were no worse.[185]
        But gentle lords, friendless we are in France.
Mortimer. Monsieur le Grand,[186] a noble friend of yours,
        Told us at our arrival all the news:
        How hard the nobles, how unkind the king°   *(of France)*
        Hath showed himself. But madam, right makes room   50
        Where weapons want.° And though a many friends   *are lacking*
        Are made away°—as Warwick, Lancaster,   *dead*
        And others of our part and faction—
        Yet have we friends, assure your grace, in England
        Would cast up caps and clap their hands for joy
        To see us there appointed for° our foes.   *prepared to battle*
Kent. Would all were well, and Edward well reclaimed,°   *reformed*
        For England's honor, peace, and quietness.
Mortimer. But by the sword, my lord, it must be deserved.°   *earned*
        The king will ne'er forsake his flatterers.   60
Sir John. My lords of England, sith° the ungentle king   *since*
        Of France refuseth to give aid of arms
        To this distressèd queen his sister here,
        Go you with her to Hainault. Doubt ye not
        We will find comfort, money, men, and friends

184. *advance your standard*: raise your banner (and thus support your claim to the throne of England).

185. "I hope we do not need to resort to a worse or lesser option" (than putting you on the throne).

186. *Monsieur le Grand*: an invented character with no historical basis.

Ere long to bid the English king a base.[187]
How say, young prince, what think you of the match?
Prince Edward. I think King Edward will outrun us all.
Queen. Nay, son, not so, and you must not discourage
    Your friends that are so forward in your aid.   70
Kent. Sir John of Hainault, pardon us, I pray.
    These comforts that you give our woeful queen
    Bind us in kindness all at your command.
Queen. Yea, gentle brother, and the God of heaven
    Prosper your happy motion,° good Sir John.   *proposal*
Mortimer. This noble gentleman, forward in arms,°   *eager to fight*
    Was born, I see, to be our anchor-hold.
    Sir John of Hainault, be it thy renown
    That England's queen and nobles in distress
    Have been by thee restored and comforted.   80
Sir John. Madam, along, and you, my lords, with me,
    That England's peers may Hainault's welcome see.
      Exeunt.

ACT 4, SCENE 3

Enter the King, Arundel, the two Spencers, with others.

Edward. Thus, after many threats of wrathful war,
    Triumpheth England's Edward with his friends;
    And triumph Edward with his friends uncontrolled.[188]
    My lord of Gloucester, do you hear the news?
Spencer. What news, my lord?
Edward. Why man, they say there is great execution
    Done through the realm. My lord of Arundel,
    You have the note,° have you not?   *list of names*
Arundel. From the Lieutenant of the Tower, my lord.

187. "Before long to challenge the English king." The allusion is to the children's game "prisoner's base" in which a contestant would "bid a base" by challenging an opponent to a running race from one base to another. The game metaphor is continued in the two lines that follow.

188. "May Edward and his friends triumph without restraint or interference" (from the king's enemies).

Edward. I pray, let us see it. What have we there?   10
    Read it, Spencer.
       Spencer reads their names.[189]
    Why so, they barked apace a month ago;[190]
    Now, on my life, they'll neither bark nor bite.
    Now, sirs, the news from France. Gloucester, I trow°   *know*
    The lords of France love England's gold so well
    As Isabella gets no aid from thence.
    What now remains? Have you proclaimed, my lord,
    Reward for them can bring in Mortimer?
Spencer. My lord, we have, and if he be in England,
    He will be had ere long,° I doubt it not.   *captured soon*
Edward. "If," dost thou say? Spencer, as true as death,[191]   21
    He is in England's ground. Our port-masters
    Are not so careless of their king's command.[192]

    Enter a Post [with letters].

    How now, what news with thee? From whence come these?
Post. Letters, my lord, and tidings forth of France;
    To you, my lord of Gloucester, from Levune.
    [He gives the letters to Spencer.]

---

189. The names of the executed do not appear in the Q text, most likely because Marlowe would have provided a separate sheet with the names to be read on stage. The following list appears in Holinshed and is likely similar to what would have been read on stage: "the Lord William Tuchet, the Lord William Fitzwilliam, the Lord Warren de Lisle, the Lord Henry Bradborne, and the Lord William Chenie, barons, with John Page, an esquire, were drawn and hanged at Pomfret . . . and then shortly after, Roger Lord Clifford, John Lord Mowbray, and Sir Gosein d'Eivill, barons, were drawn and hanged at York. At Bristol in like manner were executed Sir Henry de Willington and Sir Henry Montfort, baronets; and at Gloucester, the Lord John Gifford and Sir William Elmebridge, knight; and at London, the Lord Henry Teies, baron; at Winchelsea, Sir Thomas Culpepper, knight; at Windsor, the Lord Francis de Aldham, baron; and at Canterbury, the Lord Bartholomew de Badlesmere and the Lord Bartholomew de Ashburnham, barons. Also, at Cardiff in Wales, Sir William Fleming, knight, was executed; diverse were executed in their countries, as Sir Thomas Mandit and others" (see Holinshed, *Chronicles* 331).

190. "They barked rapidly (like dogs) a month ago," but also suggesting, "they embarked quickly (for the afterlife) a month ago."

191. *as true as death*: proverbial expression meaning "with absolute certainty."

192. Edward claims (wrongly) that Mortimer could not possibly have escaped from England after fleeing from the Tower.

Edward. Read.

    Spencer reads the letter.

Spencer. "My duty to your honor premised,° etcetera.   *stated first*
    I have, according to instructions in that behalf, dealt with
    the king of France his lords, and effected that the queen,   30
    all discontented and discomforted, is gone; whither, if you
    ask, with Sir John of Hainault, brother to the Marquis, into
    Flanders. With them are gone Lord Edmund and the Lord
    Mortimer, having in their company divers° of your nation   *several*
    and others; and, as constant° report goeth, they intend to   *reliable*
    give King Edward battle in England sooner than he can
    look for them.° This is all the news of import.   *before he is ready*
              Your honor's in all service, Levune."

Edward. Ah, villains, hath that Mortimer escaped?
    With him is Edmund gone associate?   40
    And will Sir John of Hainault lead the round?°   *dance*
    Welcome, i' God's name, madam, and your son;
    England shall welcome you and all your rout.°   *unruly group*
    Gallop apace, bright Phoebus,° through the sky,   *Apollo (sun god)*
    And dusky night, in rusty iron car,
    Between you both shorten the time, I pray,
    That I may see that most desirèd day
    When we may meet these traitors in the field.
    Ah, nothing grieves me but my little boy
    Is thus misled to countenance their ills.°   *approve their evils*
    Come, friends, to Bristol, there to make us strong;   51
    And, winds, as equal be to bring them in
    As you injurious were to bear them forth.[193]

    [Exeunt.]

---

193. "And, winds, may you act justly in returning our enemies to England, as you were unjust in bearing them away."

ACT 4, SCENE 4

Enter the Queen, her son [Prince Edward], Edmund
[Earl of Kent], Mortimer, and Sir John [of Hainault].

Queen. Now lords, our loving friends and countrymen,
    Welcome to England all. With prosperous° winds   *favorable*
    Our kindest friends in Belgia° have we left,   *the Netherlands*
    To cope° with friends at home. A heavy case,°   *deal / sad affair*
    When force to force is knit,° and sword and glaive° *brought together / spear*
    In civil broils make kin and countrymen
    Slaughter themselves in others, and their sides
    With their own weapons gored.[194] But what's the help?°   *remedy*
    Misgoverned kings are cause of all this wrack;°   *destruction*
    And Edward, thou art one among them all   10
    Whose looseness[195] hath betrayed thy land to spoil
    And made the channels° overflow with blood.   *street gutters*
    Of thine own people patron° shouldst thou be,   *father figure*
    But thou—
Mortimer. Nay, madam, if you be a warrior,
    You must not grow so passionate in speeches.[196]
    Lords, sith° that we are by sufferance° of heaven   *since / permission*
    Arrived and armèd in this prince's right,
    Here for our country's cause swear we to him
    All homage, fealty, and forwardness.°   *loyalty and eagerness*
    And for the open wrongs and injuries   21
    Edward hath done to us, his queen, and land,
    We come in arms to wreck° it with the sword,   *avenge*
    That England's queen in peace may repossess
    Her dignities and honors, and withal
    We may remove these flatterers from the king,
    That havocs° England's wealth and treasury.   *destroys*
Sir John. Sound trumpets, my lord, and forward let us march.
    Edward will think we come to flatter him.
Kent. I would he never had been flattered more.   30
    [Trumpets sound. Exeunt.]

194. "In civil wars, men kill their own countrymen, and thus (metaphorically) they stab themselves."

195. As in 4.1.7, *looseness* implies both political and sexual irresponsibility.

196. Mortimer's sudden interruption of the queen's speech may suggest his secret desire to usurp power for himself—even though, ironically, in the lines that follow he professes complete submission to the young prince and the queen.

ACT 4, SCENE 5

Enter the King, Baldock, and Spencer the son,
flying about the stage.

Spencer. Fly, fly, my lord! The queen is over-strong;
　　Her friends do multiply, and yours do fail.[197]
　　Shape we our course to Ireland, there to breathe.
Edward. What, was I born to fly and run away,
　　And leave the Mortimers conquerors behind?
　　Give me my horse, and let's r'enforce° our troops,　　　　*encourage*
　　And in this bed of honor die with fame.
Baldock. O no, my lord, this princely resolution
　　Fits not the time. Away, we are pursued!
　　　　[Exeunt.]

ACT 4, SCENE 6

[Enter] Edmund [Earl of Kent] alone, with a
sword and target.[198]

Kent. This way he fled, but I am come too late.
　　Edward, alas, my heart relents for thee.
　　Proud traitor, Mortimer, why dost thou chase
　　Thy lawful king, thy sovereign, with thy sword?
　　Vile wretch, and why hast thou, of all unkind,[199]
　　Borne arms against thy brother and thy king?
　　Rain showers of vengeance on my cursèd head,
　　Thou God, to whom in justice it belongs
　　To punish this unnatural revolt.
　　Edward, this Mortimer aims at thy life;　　　　　　　　　10
　　O fly him then! But Edmund, calm this rage;
　　Dissemble or thou diest, for Mortimer
　　And Isabel do kiss while they conspire;

197. The term *fail* suggests that Edward's forces are not only being defeated but also refusing to fight.

198. *target*: shield.

199. Kent calls himself *unkind*, meaning "cruel" but also "un-kin-like" (or unbrotherly).

And yet she bears a face of love forsooth.[200]
Fie on that love that hatcheth death and hate!
Edmund, away! Bristol to Longshanks' blood
Is false.[201] Be not found single for suspect;
Proud Mortimer pries near into thy walks.[202]

> *Enter the Queen, Mortimer, the young Prince,*
> *and Sir John of Hainault [and Soldiers].*

Queen. Successful battles gives the God of kings
  To them that fight in right and fear his wrath.[203]   20
  Since then successfully we have prevailed,
  Thanks be heaven's great architect and you.
  Ere farther we proceed, my noble lords,
  We here create our well-belovèd son,
  Of° love and care unto his royal person,   *out of*
  Lord Warden of the realm.[204] And sith the Fates°   *goddesses of Fate*
  Have made his father so infortunate,
  Deal you, my lords, in this, my loving lords,
  As to your wisdoms fittest seems in all.[205]
Kent. Madam, without offense if I may ask,   30
  How will you deal with Edward in his fall?
Prince Edward. Tell me, good uncle, what Edward do you mean?
Kent. Nephew, your father; I dare not call him king.
Mortimer. My lord of Kent, what needs these questions?
  'Tis not in her controlment,° nor in ours,   *power*
  But as the realm and Parliament shall please,
  So shall your brother be disposèd of.
  [Aside to Queen] I like not this relenting mood in Edmund.
  Madam, 'tis good to look to him betimes.°   *keep an eye on him*

---

200. *Forsooth* means "in truth," but Kent uses the term ironically since Isabella's love for Kent is entirely untrue.

201. "The town of Bristol has proven false to the son of Longshanks." Longshanks was the nickname of King Edward I (see 3.2.12).

202. "Be not found alone, for that will provoke suspicion; Mortimer spies into all your movements."

203. "God gives success in battle to those who fight for the right cause."

204. Prince Edward is made *Lord Warden* (Viceroy) of England. Normally, a viceroy is appointed only when the king is a minor or absent from the realm (neither is the case for King Edward).

205. "As seems most suitable in your judgments."

Queen. [To Mortimer]
 My lord, the Mayor of Bristol knows our mind?°   *intentions*
Mortimer. [To Queen]
 Yea, madam, and they 'scape not easily   **41**
 That fled the field.[206]
Queen.   *[Aloud]* Baldock is with the king;
 A goodly chancellor,° is he not, my lord?[207]   *secretary*
Sir John. So are the Spencers, the father and the son.
Kent. [Aside] This Edward is the ruin of the realm.[208]

  Enter Rice ap Howell and the Mayor of Bristol, with
  Spencer the father [as prisoner, guarded by Soldiers].

Rice. God save Queen Isabel and her princely son!
 Madam, the mayor and citizens of Bristol,
 In sign of love and duty to this presence,°   *(Prince Edward)*
 Present by me this traitor to the state:
 Spencer, the father to that wanton Spencer,   **50**
 That, like the lawless Catiline of Rome,[209]
 Revelled in England's wealth and treasury.
Queen. We thank you all.
Mortimer.   Your loving care in this
 Deserveth princely favors and rewards.
 But where's the king and the other Spencer fled?
Rice. Spencer the son, created Earl of Gloucester,
 Is with that smooth-tongued scholar Baldock gone
 And shipped but late° for Ireland with the king.   *recently*
Mortimer. Some whirlwind fetch them back, or sink them all!
 They shall be started thence,° I doubt it not.   *chased from there*
Prince Edward. Shall I not see the king my father yet?   **61**
Kent. [Aside] Unhappy Edward, chased from England's bounds.° *borders*

---

206. "Yes, madam, and those who escaped the battlefield will be rounded up" (by the mayor of Bristol's men).

207. The queen's compliment of Baldock is either sarcastic or dissembling.

208. Kent's remark is ambiguous due to the unreliability of punctuation in early modern texts. Kent may be speaking to the absent King Edward—"This, Edward, is the ruin of the realm"—meaning that Mortimer and Isabel are the ruin of the realm. But the line could also mean that King Edward is to blame—"This Edward is the ruin of the realm." The line in the Q text does not include commas, but their absence is not a reliable guide to Marlowe's intentions.

209. *Catiline* (108–62 BC) was a Roman patrician who attempted to overthrow the Roman Republic. His name became synonymous with conspiracy and treason.

Sir John. Madam, what resteth? Why stand ye in a muse?[210]

Queen. I rue° my lord's ill fortune; but alas,   grieve over
    Care of my country called me to this war!

Mortimer. Madam, have done with care and sad complaint.
    Your king hath wronged your country and himself,
    And we must seek to right it as we may.
    Meanwhile, have hence° this rebel to the block.   take away
    [To Spencer Sen.] Your lordship cannot privilege your head.[211]   70

Spencer Senior. Rebel is he that fights against his prince;°   (King Edward)
    So fought not they that fought in Edward's right.

Mortimer. Take him away; he prates.
       [Exit Spencer Senior, guarded.]
               You, Rice ap Howell,
    Shall do good service to her majesty,
    Being of countenance° in your country here,   authority
    To follow these rebellious runagates.°   renegades
    We in meanwhile, madam, must take advice,°   carefully consider
    How Baldock, Spencer, and their complices,°   accomplices
    May in their fall be followed to their end.[212]
      Exeunt.

ACT 4, SCENE 7

Enter the Abbot, Monks, Edward, Spencer, and
Baldock [the last three disguised as monks or penitents].

Abbot. Have you no doubt, my lord, have you no fear.
    As silent and as careful will we be
    To keep your royal person safe with us,
    Free from suspect and fell invasion[213]
    Of such as have your majesty in chase—
    Yourself and those your chosen company—
    As danger of this stormy time requires.

Edward. Father, thy face should harbor no deceit.
    O hadst thou ever been a king, thy heart,

---

210. "Madam, what remains to be done? Why stand you in deep thought?"

211. "Your lordship (noble status) will not save you from death by beheading."
(According to Holinshed, Spencer Senior was actually hanged.)

212. "May in their fall from power be pursued and killed."

213. "Free from suspicion and fierce attack."

Piercèd deeply with sense of my distress,   10
Could not but take compassion of my state.
Stately and proud in riches and in train,°   *followers*
Whilom° I was, powerful and full of pomp;   *once*
But what is he whom rule and empery°   *empire*
Have not in life or death made miserable?
Come, Spencer, come, Baldock, come sit down by me;
Make trial now of that philosophy
That in our famous nurseries of arts[214]
Thou sucked'st from Plato and from Aristotle.
Father, this life contemplative is heaven;[215]   20
O that I might this life in quiet lead!
But we, alas, are chased, and you, my friends,
Your lives and my dishonor they pursue.
Yet, gentle monks, for treasure, gold, nor fee,
Do you betray us and our company.

Monk. Your grace may sit secure, if none but we
Do wot° of your abode.   *know*

Spencer. Not one alive; but shrewdly° I suspect   *fearfully*
A gloomy fellow in a mead below.[216]
He gave a long look after us, my lord,   30
And all the land, I know, is up in arms,
Arms that pursue our lives with deadly hate.

Baldock. We were embarked for Ireland, wretched we,
With awkward winds and sore° tempests driven   *rough*
To fall on shore and here to pine in fear
Of Mortimer and his confederates.[217]

Edward. Mortimer! Who talks of Mortimer?
Who wounds me with the name of Mortimer,
That bloody man? Good father, on thy lap
Lay I this head, laden with mickle° care.   *much*
     [He rests his head on the Abbot's lap.]

214. The *nurseries of arts* were the universities of Oxford and Cambridge.

215. King Edward now seeks the *life contemplative* of religious study and prayer, as opposed to the "active" secular life of kings and nobles.

216. The *gloomy fellow* in the *mead* or meadow is the Mower who enters the scene at line 45. He appears *gloomy* because he would carry a scythe and thus resemble the allegorical figure of Death.

217. According to Holinshed, King Edward and his followers attempted to escape to Ireland or the Isle of Lundy but were driven back to Wales by contrary winds.

O might I never open these eyes again,   41
Never again lift up this drooping head,
O nevermore lift up this dying heart!
Spencer. Look up, my lord. Baldock, this drowsiness
Betides no good.[218] Here even we are betrayed.

> *Enter, with Welsh hooks,*[219] *Rice ap Howell [and Soldiers],*
> *a Mower, and the Earl of Leicester.*

Mower. Upon my life, those be the men ye seek.
Rice. Fellow, enough. *[To Leicester]* My lord, I pray be short;
A fair commission warrants what we do.[220]
Leicester. [Aside] The queen's commission, urged by Mortimer.
What cannot gallant Mortimer with the queen?   50
Alas, see where he sits, and hopes unseen
T' escape their hands that seek to reave° his life.   *take*
Too true it is, *quem dies vidit veniens superbum,*
Hunc dies vidit fugiens iacentem.[221]
But Leicester, leave to grow° so passionate.—   *stop growing*
[Aloud] Spencer and Baldock, by no other names,
I arrest you of high treason here.[222]
Stand not on titles, but obey th' arrest;
'Tis in the name of Isabel the queen.
[To Edward] My lord, why droop you thus?   60
Edward. O day, the last of all my bliss on earth,
Center of all misfortune![223] O my stars,
Why do you lour° unkindly on a king?   *frown*
Comes Leicester then in Isabella's name
To take my life, my company from me?

218. *Drowsiness* was considered an omen of bad fortune.

219. *Welsh hooks* may be weapons (poles with steel hooks or blades on top), or perhaps horticultural cutting tools (especially since the soldiers are accompanied by a *Mower*).

220. "A legal document authorizes our actions."

221. "He whom the dawning day has seen exalted and proud, the departing day has seen downfallen"—from Seneca's *Thyestes*, lines 613–14.

222. Leicester refuses to address them by the aristocratic *names* (titles) that King Edward had bestowed on them.

223. As in 3.1.5, the term *center* may refer to this unfortunate *day*, or it may refer to the *earth* as the *center* of the universe.

Here, man, rip up this panting breast of mine,
And take my heart in rescue of my friends.[224]
Rice. Away with them!
Spencer.   It may become thee yet
  To let us take our farewell of his grace.
Abbot. [Aside] My heart with pity earns° to see this sight: *grieves*
  A king to bear these words and proud commands.   71
Edward. Spencer, ah sweet Spencer, thus then must we part?
Spencer. We must, my lord; so will° the angry heavens.   *command*
Edward. Nay, so will hell and cruel Mortimer.
  The gentle heavens have not to do in this.
Baldock. My lord, it is in vain to grieve or storm.°   *protest*
  Here humbly of your grace we take our leaves.
  Our lots are cast; I fear me, so is thine.
Edward. In heaven we may, in earth never shall we meet.
  And Leicester, say, what shall become of us?   80
Leicester. Your majesty must go to Killingworth.[225]
Edward. Must! 'Tis somewhat hard when kings must go.
Leicester. Here is a litter[226] ready for your grace
  That waits your pleasure; and the day grows old.°   *it's getting late*
Rice. As good be gone, as stay and be benighted.[227]
Edward. A litter hast thou? Lay me in a hearse,
  And to the gates of hell convey me hence.
  Let Pluto's bells ring out my fatal knell,
  And hags howl for my death at Charon's shore,[228]

224. King Edward's offer of his heart as payment or ransom to free his friends may have been influenced by the similar offer of Arthur in the anonymous *Troublesome Reign of King John* (printed in 1591): "O, would she with her hands pull forth my heart, / I could afford it to appease these broils" (IV, 147–48).

225. *Killingworth* is an old-spelling variant of "Kenilworth." The old spelling appears in the Q text and has been retained in this edition in order to preserve the ironic association with "killing" and death. *Killingworth* also appears in the 1587 edition of Holinshed, and thus Marlowe may have simply followed his source text without any conscious irony.

226. *litter:* a coach on which the king would be carried by servants.

227. "Better to get going than to delay and get caught in darkness."

228. *Pluto* (or Hades) is the god of the underworld; the *hags* are apparently the Furies; and *Charon* is the ferryman who transports the souls of the dead across the river Styx.

For friends hath Edward none but these, and these,[229]   90
And these must die under a tyrant's sword.
Rice. My lord, be going. Care not for these,
   For we shall see them shorter by the heads.[230]
Edward. Well, that shall be shall be. Part we must,
   Sweet Spencer, gentle Baldock, part we must.
   Hence, feignèd weeds!
      [He removes his disguise.]
                           Unfeignèd are my woes.
   Father, farewell. Leicester, thou stay'st for me,
   And go I must. Life, farewell, with my friends!
      Exeunt Edward [guarded by Soldiers] and Leicester.
Spencer. O, is he gone? Is noble Edward gone,
   Parted from hence, never to see us more?   100
   Rend, sphere of heaven, and fire, forsake thy orb;
   Earth, melt to air![231] Gone is my sovereign,
   Gone, gone, alas, never to make return.
Baldock. Spencer, I see our souls are fleeted hence;°   *flown away*
   We are deprived the sunshine of our life.
   Make for a new life, man; throw up thy eyes
   And heart and hand to heaven's immortal throne;
   Pay nature's debt with cheerful countenance.
   Reduce we all our lessons unto this:
   To die, sweet Spencer, therefore live we all;   110
   Spencer, all live to die, and rise to fall.[232]

229. Edward apparently gestures to his two groups of loyal friends: Spencer and Baldock, and the Abbot and monks.

230. Spencer and Baldock will indeed be *shorter* after they are beheaded.

231. Spencer calls for the *sphere of heaven* (the sphere of the sun, or perhaps the stars, in the Ptolemaic universe) to be torn from the sky, and for the sphere of *fire* (located just above the earth's atmosphere) likewise to be torn from its place in the cosmos, and finally for the earth to fall into chaos. The passage echoes the apocalyptic vision in Revelation: "And I beheld when he had opened the sixth seal, and lo, there was a great earthquake, and the sun was as black as sackcloth of hair, and the moon was like blood. And the stars of heaven fell unto the earth. . . . And heaven departed away, as a scroll when it is rolled, and every mountain and isle were moved out of their places" (Rev. 6:12-14, Geneva Bible).

232. As a scholar, Baldock evokes the literary and philosophical tradition of Fortune's wheel, in which characters rise in power and prosperity, only to fall in disaster and disgrace.

Rice. Come, come, keep these preachments till you come
    to the place appointed.[233] You, and such as you are, have
    made wise work in England.[234] Will your lordships away?
Mower. Your worship, I trust, will remember me?
Rice. Remember thee, fellow? What else? Follow me
    to the town.[235]

      [Exeunt, with Spencer and Baldock, guarded.]

ACT 5, SCENE 1

Enter the King, Leicester, with a Bishop [of Winchester]
for the crown, Trussel, [and Attendants].[236]

Leicester. Be patient, good my lord; cease to lament.
    Imagine Killingworth Castle were your court,
    And that you lay° for pleasure here a space,°   *reside / a while*
    Not of compulsion or necessity.
Edward. Leicester, if gentle words might comfort me,
    Thy speeches long ago had eased my sorrows,
    For kind and loving hast thou always been.
    The griefs of private men are soon allayed,°   *relieved*
    But not of kings. The forest deer, being struck,
    Runs to an herb that closeth up the wounds;[237]   10
    But when the imperial lion's flesh is gored,
    He rends and tears it with his wrathful paw,
    And, highly scorning that the lowly earth
    Should drink his blood, mounts° up into the air.   *rises*
    And so it fares with me, whose dauntless mind

233. "Refrain from these philosophical comments until we arrive at the place of execution." (The condemned were traditionally permitted to speak their final words from the gallows.)

234. Rice speaks sarcastically: their *wise work* has corrupted England.

235. Rice assures the Mower that he will be *remembered* (rewarded) with payment for his services. The Mower's request—*remember me*—may also be ironic since the Mower appears as a figure of death.

236. The Q text does not specify which *Bishop* enters the scene *for the crown*, but it becomes clear in the next scene that it is bishop of Winchester (see 5.2.27-28).

237. *Deer* and other animals supposedly knew by instinct how to treat their own ailments. A deer wounded by an arrow would eat the dittany *herb*, which would help expel the arrow and heal the wound.

The ambitious Mortimer would seek to curb,
And that unnatural queen, false Isabel,
That thus hath pent and mewed[238] me in a prison;
For such outrageous passions cloy° my soul,   *overwhelm*
As with the wings of rancor and disdain   20
Full often am I soaring up to heaven
To plain° me to the gods against them both.   *complain or protest*
But when I call to mind I am a king,
Methinks I should revenge me of the wrongs
That Mortimer and Isabel have done.
But what are kings, when regiment° is gone,   *royal power*
But perfect shadows in a sunshine day?
My nobles rule; I bear the name of king.
I wear the crown, but am controlled by them,
By Mortimer and my unconstant queen,   30
Who spots my nuptial° bed with infamy,   *marriage*
Whilst I am lodged within this cave of care,
Where sorrow at my elbow still attends
To company° my heart with sad laments   *accompany*
That bleeds within me for this strange exchange.[239]
But tell me, must I now resign my crown
To make usurping Mortimer a king?
Winchester. Your grace mistakes; it is for England's good
And princely Edward's right we crave the crown.[240]
Edward. No, 'tis for Mortimer, not Edward's head,   40
For he's a lamb encompassèd by wolves,
Which in a moment will abridge his life.
But if proud Mortimer do wear this crown,
Heavens turn it to a blaze of quenchless fire,[241]

238. *Pent and mewed*: confined and caged. A *mew* was a small cage used to house a falcon (a royal bird). The falcon metaphor is continued in the lines that follow.

239. *strange exchange*: change of fortune from his former glory to his current loss of power.

240. In Holinshed, the bishops of Winchester and Lincoln urged Edward to give up his crown in order to ensure that his son would inherit the throne: they warned Edward that "if he refused so to do, the people . . . would not fail but proceed to the election of some other that should happily not touch him in lineage" (see Related Texts).

241. An allusion to Medea who in revenge gave Jason's new bride a golden crown that burned into her skull.

Or, like the snaky wreath of Tisiphon,[242]
Engirt° the temples of his hateful head;   *encircle*
So shall not England's vine be perishèd,
But Edward's name survive, though Edward dies.[243]
Leicester. My lord, why waste you thus the time away?
They stay° your answer. Will you yield your crown?   *await*
Edward. Ah Leicester, weigh° how hardly I can brook°   *consider / endure*
To lose my crown and kingdom without cause,   52
To give ambitious Mortimer my right,
That like a mountain overwhelms my bliss,
In which extreme my mind here murdered is.
But what the heavens appoint I must obey.
Here, take my crown, the life of Edward too.
     [He removes his crown.]
Two kings in England cannot reign at once.
But stay a while; let me be king till night,
That I may gaze upon this glittering crown;   60
So shall my eyes receive their last content,
My head, the latest honor due to it,
And jointly both yield up their wishèd° right.   *desired*
Continue ever, thou celestial sun;
Let never silent night possess this clime;°   *climate or region*
Stand still, you watches of the element;
All times and seasons, rest you at a stay,
That Edward may be still fair England's king.[244]
But day's bright beams doth vanish fast away,
And needs I must resign my wishèd crown.   70
Inhuman creatures, nursed with tiger's milk,
Why gape you for your sovereign's overthrow?
My diadem, I mean, and guiltless life.
See, monsters, see, I'll wear my crown again.
     [He places the crown back on his head.]

242. *Tisiphon*: one of the Furies (goddesses of revenge with writhing snakes for hair).

243. Edward alludes to the *vine* depicted on the English crown. The *vine* will not perish, metaphorically, if the line of royal descent continues with his son Edward.

244. Edward asks the sun and the planets (the *watches of the elements*) to remain motionless so that time will stop and he can remain king forever. (The planets look down and "watch" the earth from the *element* of heavenly ether above.) Contrast Edward's earlier desire for the heavenly bodies to speed up (see 4.3.44–48).

What, fear you not the fury of your king?
But hapless Edward, thou art fondly° led.   *foolishly*
They pass° not for thy frowns as late° they did,   *care / lately*
But seek to make a new-elected king,[245]
Which fills my mind with strange despairing thoughts,
Which thoughts are martyrèd with endless torments,   80
And in this torment comfort find I none
But that I feel the crown upon my head.
And therefore let me wear it yet a while.[246]

Trussel. My lord, the Parliament must have present news,
   And therefore say, will you resign or no?

    The King rageth.

Edward. I'll not resign, but whilst I live—[247]
   Traitors, begone, and join you with Mortimer!
   Elect, conspire, install,° do what you will;   *install in office*
   Their blood and yours shall seal these treacheries.

Winchester. This answer we'll return, and so farewell.   90
    [Bishop of Winchester and Trussel begin to exit.]

Leicester. Call them again, my lord, and speak them fair,
   For if they go, the prince shall lose his right.

Edward. Call thou them back. I have no power to speak.

Leicester. My lord, the king is willing to resign.
    [Winchester and Trussel return.]

Winchester. If he be not, let him choose.

Edward. O would I might! But heavens and earth conspire
   To make me miserable. Here, receive my crown.
    [He removes his crown.]
   Receive it? No, these innocent hands of mine
   Shall not be guilty of so foul a crime.
   He of you all that most desires my blood,   100
   And will be called the murderer of a king,
   Take it. What, are you moved? Pity you me?

245. Edward fears the nobles will choose a *new-elected king* by way of Parliament (not by a general election).

246. Shakespeare, in the deposition scene in *Richard II* 4.1, borrowed extensively from this speech by Edward.

247. This line is metrically short. Some editors suspect missing words in the Q text, and expand the phrase: "but whilst I live *be king.*" It seems equally possible, however, that Marlowe intended the line to break off, so that Edward pauses and emotionally breaks down and thus cannot complete the line.

Then send for unrelenting Mortimer,
And Isabel, whose eyes, being turned to steel,
Will sooner sparkle fire than shed a tear.
Yet stay, for rather than I will look on them,
Here, here!
    [He hands over the crown.]
            Now, sweet God of Heaven,
Make me despise this transitory pomp,
And sit for aye° enthronizèd in heaven.   *forever*
Come, death, and with thy fingers close my eyes,   110
Or if I live, let me forget myself.
Winchester. My lord—
Edward. Call me not lord. Away, out of my sight!
Ah, pardon me, grief makes me lunatic.
Let not that Mortimer protect° my son.   *(act as Protector over)*
More safety is there in a tiger's jaws
Than his embracements. Bear this to the queen,
Wet with my tears and dried again with sighs.
    [He hands over his handkerchief.]
If with the sight thereof she be not moved,
Return it back and dip it in my blood.[248]   120
Commend me to my son, and bid him rule
Better than I. Yet how have I transgressed,
Unless it be with too much clemency?
Trussel. And thus, most humbly do we take our leave.
    [Exeunt Bishop of Winchester and Trussel with
    the crown and handkerchief.]
Edward. Farewell. I know the next news that they bring
Will be my death, and welcome shall it be;
To wretched men death is felicity.

    [Enter Berkeley with a letter].

Leicester. Another post. What news brings he?
    [Leicester takes the letter and reads.]

---

248. Edward speaks of himself as though he were a saint or martyr, and his blood
could serve as a holy relic. The image of the blood-dipped handkerchief may have
been influenced by York in Shakespeare's *3 Henry VI*: "This cloth thou dipped'st in
blood of my sweet boy, / And I with tears do wash the blood away. / Keep thou
the napkin, and go boast of this" (1.4.157–59).

Edward. Such news as I expect. Come, Berkeley, come,
    And tell thy message to my naked breast.[249]   130
Berkeley. My lord, think not a thought so villainous
    Can harbor in a man of noble birth.
    To do your highness service and devoir,°   *duty*
    And save you from your foes, Berkeley would die.
Leicester. My lord, the council of the queen commands
    That I resign my charge.
Edward. And who must keep me now? Must you, my lord?
Berkeley. Ay, my most gracious lord, so 'tis decreed.
Edward. [*Taking the letter*]
    By Mortimer, whose name is written here.
    Well may I rend° his name that rends my heart!   *tear*
    [*He tears the letter.*]
    This poor revenge hath something eased my mind.   141
    So may his limbs be torn as is this paper!
    Hear me, immortal Jove, and grant it too.
Berkeley. Your grace must hence with me to
    Berkeley° straight.   *(Berkeley Castle)*
Edward. Whither° you will; all places are alike,   *wherever*
    And every earth is fit for burial.
Leicester. [*To Berkeley*]
    Favor him,° my lord, as much as lieth in you.   *treat him well*
Berkeley. Even so betide my soul as I use him.[250]
Edward. Mine enemy hath pitied my estate,°   *condition*
    And that's the cause that I am now removed.[251]   150
Berkeley. And thinks your grace that Berkeley will be cruel?
Edward. I know not, but of this am I assured:
    That death ends all, and I can die but once.
    Leicester, farewell.
Leicester. Not yet, my lord; I'll bear you on your way.
    Exeunt.

249. On stage Edward might expose his *naked breast* with the expectation that Berkeley has come with a dagger to murder him. Or perhaps Edward speaks metaphorically, expecting that the news Berkeley delivers will in effect kill him.

250. "Let happen to my soul (may it go to heaven or hell) according to the way I treat the king."

251. Edward speaks sarcastically, knowing full well that Mortimer has no pity for him.

ACT 5, SCENE 2

Enter Mortimer and Queen Isabella.

Mortimer. Fair Isabel, now have we our desire.
    The proud corrupters of the light-brained° king   *frivolous*
    Have done their homage to the lofty gallows,
    And he himself lies in captivity.
    Be ruled by me, and we will rule the realm.
    In any case, take heed of childish fear,
    For now we hold an old wolf by the ears
    That if he slip will seize upon us both,
    And grip the sorer, being gripped himself.[252]
    Think therefore, madam, that imports° us much   *it concern*
    To erect° your son with all the speed we may,   *place on the throne*
    And that I be Protector over him,[253]   12
    For our behoof will bear the greater sway
    Whenas a king's name shall be under writ.[254]
Queen. Sweet Mortimer, the life of Isabel,
    Be thou persuaded that I love thee well;
    And therefore, so° the prince my son be safe,   *provided*
    Whom I esteem as dear as these mine eyes,
    Conclude against his father what thou wilt,
    And I myself will willingly subscribe.   20
Mortimer. First would I hear news that he were deposed,
    And then let me alone to handle him.

Enter Messenger [with letter of the king's abdication].

Mortimer. Letters, from whence?
Messenger.   From Killingworth, my lord.
Queen. How fares my lord the king?
Messenger. In health, madam, but full of pensiveness.°   *sadness*
Queen. Alas, poor soul, would I could ease his grief.

[Enter Bishop of Winchester with the crown.]

---

252. "Now we hold an old wolf (Edward) by the ears, but if he escapes our grip he will bite us more viciously as we attempt to restrain him."

253. *Protector* was a legal title for a lord selected to rule on behalf of a young king. The title was actually not used until the reign of the boy-king Henry VI, a full century after Edward III took the throne.

254. "For our authority will be greater when a king's name appears on the document."

Thanks, gentle Winchester. *[To Messenger]* Sirrah, begone.[255]
   [Exit Messenger.]
Winchester. The king hath willingly resigned his crown.
Queen. O happy news! Send for the prince my son.
Winchester. Further, ere this letter was sealed, Lord
   Berkeley came,   30
   So that he° now is gone from Killingworth.   *(King Edward)*
   And we have heard that Edmund laid a plot
   To set his brother free; no more but so.
   The lord of Berkeley is so pitiful°   *full of pity*
   As Leicester that had charge of him before.
Queen. Then let some other be his guardian.
Mortimer. Let me alone. Here is the privy seal.
   [Exit Bishop of Winchester.][256]
   [Calls off stage] Who's there? Call hither Gurney and Matrevis.
   [To Queen] To dash the heavy-headed Edmund's drift,[257]
   Berkeley shall be discharged, the king removed,   40
   And none but we shall know where he lieth.
Queen. But Mortimer, as long as he survives
   What safety rests° for us or for my son?   *remains*
Mortimer. Speak, shall he presently be dispatched and die?
Queen. I would he were, so it were not by my means.

   Enter Matrevis and Gurney.

Mortimer. Enough.
   [Speaking privately to Matrevis and Gurney]
   Matrevis, write a letter presently
   Unto the Lord of Berkeley from ourself,
   That he resign° the king to thee and Gurney,   *turn over*
   And when 'tis done, we will subscribe our name.   50

---

255. *Sirrah*: a term of address to a male servant or boy, often expressing contempt. (*Sirrah* has evolved into "sir," with the very opposite connotations.)

256. The stage directions for Winchester are conjectural. The Q text does not indicate his entrance or exit in this scene. Perhaps Mortimer hands Winchester the *privy seal* (and then Winchester exits with the seal), or it may be that Mortimer dismisses Winchester (*Let me alone*) and then picks up the privy seal to indicate that he and Isabella have authority to act as they will. Mortimer may keep the privy seal in hand ready to authorize the letter that he instructs Matrevis to write at lines 47–50. The *privy seal* was the personal seal of the king (distinct from the Great Seal of the Realm).

257. "To frustrate the dull-brained Edmund's plot."

Matrevis. It shall be done, my lord.
    [Matrevis writes a letter.]
Mortimer.   Gurney.
Gurney.   My lord.
Mortimer. As thou intendest to rise by Mortimer,
    Who now makes Fortune's wheel turn as he please,[258]
    Seek all the means thou canst to make him° droop,   *(the king)*
    And neither give him kind word nor good look.
Gurney. I warrant you, my lord.
Mortimer. And this above the rest: because we hear
    That Edmund casts° to work his liberty,   *plots*
    Remove him still from place to place by night,
    Till at the last he come to Killingworth,   ·60
    And then from thence to Berkeley back again.
    And by the way° to make him fret the more,   *along the way*
    Speak curstly° to him, and in any case   *harshly*
    Let no man comfort him if he chance to weep,
    But amplify his grief with bitter words.
Matrevis. Fear not, my lord, we'll do as you command.
Mortimer. So now away; post thitherwards amain.°   *at once*
Queen. [Approaching]
    Whither goes this letter? To my lord the king?
    Commend me humbly to his majesty,
    And tell him that I labor all in vain   70
    To ease his grief and work his liberty;
    And bear him this as witness of my love.
    [She gives Matrevis a jewel.]
Matrevis. I will, madam.

      Exeunt Matrevis and Gurney. Isabella and Mortimer
      remain. Enter the young Prince and the Earl of Kent
      talking with him.

Mortimer. [Speaking privately to the Queen]
    Finely dissembled![259] Do so still, sweet queen.
    Here comes the young prince with the Earl of Kent.
Queen. Something he whispers in his childish ears.

---

258. These lines mark Mortimer as a disciple of Machiavelli. Traditionally, as in Boethius's *Consolation of Philosophy*, Lady Fortune was seen as subject to the will of Providence. Machiavelli, however, claims that an effective ruler can master Lady Fortune and make her submit to his will (see *The Prince*, ch. 25).

259. Mortimer compliments Isabella for her pretended concern for King Edward.

Mortimer. If he have such access unto the prince,
　　Our plots and stratagems will soon be dashed.
Queen. Use Edmund friendly, as if all were well.
Mortimer. [To Kent] How fares my honorable lord of Kent?　　　　80
Kent. In health, sweet Mortimer. *[To Qu.]* How fares your grace?
Queen. Well, if my lord your brother were enlarged.[260]
Kent. I hear of late he hath deposed himself.
Queen. The more my grief.
Mortimer. And mine.
Kent. [Aside] Ah, they do dissemble!
Queen. Sweet son, come hither; I must talk with thee.
　　[She takes Prince Edward aside.]
Mortimer. [To Kent] Thou, being his uncle and the next of blood,
　　Do look to be Protector over the prince.
Kent. Not I, my lord. Who should protect the son　　　　　　90
　　But she that gave him life—I mean the queen?
Prince Edward. Mother, persuade me not to wear the crown.
　　Let him be king.[261] I am too young to reign.
Queen. But be content, seeing 'tis his highness' pleasure.[262]
Prince Edward. Let me but see him first, and then I will.
Kent. Ay, do, sweet nephew.
Queen. Brother, you know it is impossible.
Prince Edward. Why, is he dead?
Queen. No, God forbid!
Kent. I would those words proceeded from your heart.　　　　100
Mortimer. Inconstant Edmund, dost thou favor him
　　That wast a cause of his imprisonment?[263]
Kent. The more cause have I now to make amends.
Mortimer. I tell thee 'tis not meet° that one so false　　　　*proper*
　　Should come about the person of a prince.
　　[To Prince Ed.] My lord, he hath betrayed the king his brother,
　　And therefore trust him not.
Prince Edward. But he repents and sorrows for it now.

260. *Enlarged* means "freed" (from prison), but the queen may pun on the secondary meaning of "freed from this life and sent into the next."

261. Prince Edward apparently refers to his absent father, but he could be referring to his uncle Kent on stage.

262. Isabella clearly misrepresents King Edward's willingness to abdicate.

263. Like Isabella, Mortimer misrepresents and exaggerates. Kent did indeed join the queen's rebellion, but Kent returned his loyalty to Edward before the king was captured and imprisoned (see 4.6.1–18).

Queen. Come son, and go with this gentle lord and me.
Prince Edward. With you I will, but not with Mortimer.   110
Mortimer. Why, youngling, 'sdain'st thou so of Mortimer?[264]
    Then I will carry thee by force away.
Prince Edward. Help, uncle Kent! Mortimer will wrong me.
    [Exit Mortimer with the Prince.]
Queen. Brother Edmund, strive not;° we are his friends.   *do not interfere*
    Isabel is nearer than the Earl of Kent.[265]
Kent. Sister, Edward is my charge; redeem him.°   *release him*
Queen. Edward is my son, and I will keep him.
    [Exit the Queen.]
Kent. Mortimer shall know that he hath wronged me.
    Hence will I haste to Killingworth Castle,
    And rescue agèd[266] Edward from his foes,   120
    To be revenged on Mortimer and thee.°   *(the queen)*
    [Exit Kent.]

ACT 5, SCENE 3

    Enter Matrevis and Gurney with the King
    [and Soldiers with torches].

Matrevis. My lord, be not pensive;° we are your friends.   *sad*
    Men are ordained to live in misery.
    Therefore come; dalliance dangereth° our lives.   *delay endangers*
Edward. Friends, whither must unhappy Edward go?
    Will hateful Mortimer appoint no rest?
    Must I be vexed° like the nightly bird°   *tormented / (the owl)*
    Whose sight is loathsome to all winged fowls?
    When will the fury of his mind assuage?°   *diminish*
    When will his heart be satisfied with blood?
    If mine will serve, unbowel° straight this breast,   *cut open*
    And give my heart to Isabel and him;   11
    It is the chiefest mark they level° at.   *aim*

---

264. "Why, youngster, do you so disdain Mortimer?"

265. "Isabel (as mother) is *nearer* in blood to the prince than Kent" (who is only his uncle).

266. *Agèd*, in this context, does not mean "elderly" but simply "older" (in comparison to the young prince). King Edward was 42 when he was deposed in 1327, and he died 8 months later at age 43.

Gurney. Not so, my liege. The queen hath given this charge°   command
    To keep your grace in safety.
    Your passions make your dolours° to increase.   sorrows
Edward. This usage makes my misery increase.
    But can my air° of life continue long   breath
    When all my senses are annoyed with stench?
    Within a dungeon England's king is kept,
    Where I am starved for want° of sustenance.   lack
    My daily diet is heartbreaking sobs,   21
    That almost rends the closet° of my heart.   tears the chamber
    Thus lives old Edward not relieved by any,
    And so must die, though pitièd by many.
    O water, gentle friends, to cool my thirst
    And clear my body from foul excrements.[267]
Matrevis. Here's channel water,° as our charge is given.   sewer water
    Sit down, for we'll be barbers to your grace.
Edward. Traitors, away! What, will you murder me,
    Or choke your sovereign with puddle water?   30
Gurney. No, but wash your face and shave away your beard,
    Lest you be known and so be rescuèd.
Matrevis. Why strive you thus? Your labor is in vain.
Edward. The wren may strive against the lion's strength,
    But all in vain; so vainly do I strive
    To seek for mercy at a tyrant's hand.

    They wash him with puddle water and
    shave his beard away.[268]

    Immortal powers, that knows the painful cares
    That waits upon my poor distressèd soul,
    O level all your looks upon these daring men,
    That wrongs their liege and sovereign, England's king!   40
    O Gaveston, it is for thee that I am wronged;

267. *Excrement* could refer to any discharge from the body, such as feces or human hair. Edward intends the first meaning (wanting to be cleansed of dirt and filth), but Matrevis assumes (with malevolent sarcasm) the second meaning and uses water from a sewage channel to shave the king's beard.

268. According to Stow's *Annals of England*, the tormenters of the king, in an effort to "disfigure him that he might not be known," shaved Edward with water from a "ditch" (see Related Texts). Marlowe makes the shaving of the king more degrading with the use of *puddle water* from a sewage channel. The scene may also suggest a perverse parody of baptism.

For me both thou and both the Spencers died,
And for your sakes a thousand wrongs I'll take.
The Spencers' ghosts, wherever they remain,°   *dwell*
Wish well to mine. Then tush, for them I'll die.
Matrevis. 'Twixt theirs and yours shall be no enmity.[269]
 Come, come, away. Now put the torches out.
 We'll enter in by darkness to Killingworth.
  [They extinguish their torches.]

 Enter Edmund [Earl of Kent].

Gurney. How now, who comes there?
Matrevis. Guard the king sure. It is the Earl of Kent.   50
Edward. O gentle brother, help to rescue me.
Matrevis. Keep them asunder! Thrust in the king.
  [Soldiers take the King aside.]
Kent. Soldiers, let me but talk to him one word.
Gurney. Lay hands upon the earl for this assault.
Kent. Lay down your weapons, traitors; yield the king.
Matrevis. Edmund, yield thou thyself, or thou shalt die.
  [Soldiers seize Kent.]
Kent. Base villains, wherefore do you grip me thus?
Gurney. Bind him, and so convey him to the court.
Kent. Where is the court but here?[270] Here is the king,
 And I will visit him. Why stay you me?   60
Matrevis. The court is where Lord Mortimer remains.
 Thither shall your honor go, and so, farewell.
  Exeunt Matrevis and Gurney with the King.
  Edmund [Earl of Kent] and the Soldiers remain.
Kent. O, miserable is that commonweal° where lords *state*
 Keep courts and kings are locked in prison!
Soldier. Wherefore stay we? On, sirs, to the court.
Kent. Ay, lead me whither you will, even to my death,
 Seeing that my brother cannot be released.
  Exeunt.

269. "Between their ghosts and yours there will be no tension" (because you will all be dead together).

270. Kent's claim that the dungeon is the *court* because the king is present is not entirely sophistic. In medieval and early modern England, the *court* was not a building or location but the assembly of the king and his advisers.

ACT 5, SCENE 4

Enter Mortimer alone [with a letter].

Mortimer. The king must die, or Mortimer goes down;
    The commons° now begin to pity him.   *common people*
    Yet he that is the cause of Edward's death
    Is sure to pay for it when his son is of age,
    And therefore will I do it cunningly.
    This letter, written by a friend of ours,[271]
    Contains his death, yet bids them save his life.
    [He reads] "*Edwardum occidere nolite timere bonum est.*"
    "Fear not to kill the king, 'tis good he die."
    But read it thus, and that's another sense: 10
    [He reads] "*Edwardum occidere nolite timere bonum est.*"
    "Kill not the king, 'tis good to fear the worst."
    Unpointed[272] as it is, thus shall it go,
    That, being dead,° if it chance to be found,   *after the king is dead*
    Matrevis and the rest may bear the blame,
    And we be quit° that caused it to be done.   *cleared of suspicion*
    Within this room is locked the messenger
    That shall convey it and perform the rest.
    And by a secret token that he bears,
    Shall he be murdered when the deed is done.   20
    Lightborn,[273] come forth!
        [Enter Lightborn.]
    Art thou as resolute as thou wast?
Lightborn. What else, my lord? And far more resolute.
Mortimer. And hast thou cast° how to accomplish it?   *planned*
Lightborn. Ay, ay, and none shall know which way he died.
Mortimer. But at his looks, Lightborn, thou wilt relent.

271. According to Holinshed, the letter was written by the bishop of Hereford, a friend and ally of Queen Isabella.

272. *Unpointed* means "without punctuation marks." Without comma marks, the Latin sentence can be interpreted in two opposite ways: advising the reader to kill the king, or not to kill the king.

273. *Lightborn* has no counterpart in Holinshed or any other historical source. The name appears in the Chester mystery plays (as one of the agents of Satan), but it is also possible the name circulated in popular oral culture, or Marlowe may have invented the name independently. In any case, "Lightborn" clearly evokes associations with "Lucifer" (both names mean "light-bearer").

Lightborn. Relent? Ha, ha! I use much to relent.[274]
Mortimer. Well, do it bravely,° and be secret.   *skillfully*
Lightborn. You shall not need to give instructions;
 'Tis not the first time I have killed a man.   30
 I learned in Naples how to poison flowers,
 To strangle with a lawn thrust through the throat,[275]
 To pierce the windpipe with a needle's point,
 Or, whilst one is asleep, to take a quill
 And blow a little powder in his ears,
 Or open his mouth and pour quicksilver° down.   *mercury*
 But yet I have a braver° way than these.   *more skillful*
Mortimer. What's that?
Lightborn. Nay, you shall pardon me; none shall know my tricks.
Mortimer. I care not how it is, so it be not spied.   40
 Deliver this to Gurney and Matrevis.
  [He hands Lightborn a letter.]
 At every ten miles' end thou hast a horse.[276]
  [He gives Lightborn a token.][277]
 Take this. Away, and never see me more.
Lightborn. No?
Mortimer. No,
 Unless thou bring me news of Edward's death.
Lightborn. That will I quickly do. Farewell, my lord.
  [Exit Lightborn.]
Mortimer. The prince I rule, the queen do I command,
 And with a lowly congè° to the ground   *bow*
 The proudest lords salute me as I pass.   50
 I seal,[278] I cancel, I do what I will.

274. "I often relent" (spoken ironically).

275. "To strangle (suffocate) with a linen cloth thrust down the throat." In the lines that follow, Lightborn boasts of several methods of committing murder, all of which would leave no evidence of how the deed was done. Naples and the other Italian city-states were notorious for such sinister methods. Marlowe's Barabas makes similar boasts about his exploits in Florence (see *Jew of Malta* 2.3.179–206).

276. To speed Lightborn's journey, Mortimer has arranged for a fresh horse every ten miles.

277. The *token*, as Mortimer indicated earlier in the scene, will seal Lightborn's fate (see lines 19-20).

278. Mortimer will use the king's privy seal or the Great Seal of the Realm to authorize official documents (see notes to 1.1.167 and 5.2.37).

Feared am I more than loved.[279] Let me be feared,
And when I frown, make all the court look pale.
I view the prince with Aristarchus' eyes,[280]
Whose looks were as a breeching° to a boy.   *whipping*
They thrust upon me the Protectorship
And sue to me for that that I desire.[281]
While at the council table, grave enough,
And not unlike a bashful Puritan,
First I complain of imbecility,°   *bodily weakness*
Saying it is *onus quam gravissimum*,   *a heavy burden (Latin)*
Till, being interrupted by my friends,   62
Suscepi that *provinciam*,° as they term it,   *I accept the office (Latin)*
And to conclude, I am Protector now.[282]
Now is all sure: the queen and Mortimer
Shall rule the realm, the king; and none rule us.
Mine enemies will I plague, my friends advance,
And what I list° command, who dare control?   *desire*
Maior sum quam cui possit fortuna nocere.[283]
And that this be the coronation day,   70
It pleaseth me and Isabel the queen.
        [Trumpets are sounded off stage.]
The trumpets sound; I must go take my place.

        *Enter the young King [Edward III], Bishop
        [of Canterbury], Champion, Nobles, Queen,
        [and Attendants].*[284]

279. Mortimer echoes Machiavelli's claim that the effective prince must be *feared* more than *loved* (see *The Prince*, ch. 17).

280. Aristarchus of Samothrace was a notoriously severe and strict schoolmaster in ancient Alexandria in the second century BC.

281. "And plead for me to do that which I desire to do anyway."

282. Mortimer claims that like a *bashful Puritan* he feigns modesty and virtue but secretly longs for wealth and power. Puritans were often satirized on the English stage as pious hypocrites—at least in part because Puritans often denounced stage plays as immoral. (The term *Puritan* is anachronistic since there were no Puritans until the Protestant Reformation in the sixteenth century.)

283. "I am too great for Fortune to harm" (Ovid, *Metamorphoses*, VI, 195). Mortimer's claim to invincibility seems highly ironic since the line he quotes from Ovid is spoken by the proud and boastful Niobe just before the gods punish her by killing all her children and turning her into stone.

284. A throne is probably brought on stage at this point for Edward III to ascend.

Canterbury. Long live King Edward, by the grace of god,
    King of England and Lord of Ireland!
Champion. If any Christian, Heathen, Turk, or Jew
    Dares but affirm that Edward's not true king,
    And will avouch his saying with the sword,
    I am the champion that will combat him.[285]
Mortimer. None comes. Sound, trumpets!
    [Trumpets sound.]
Edward III.   Champion, here's to thee.
    [Edward III raises a toast to the Champion.]
Queen. Lord Mortimer, now take him to your charge.[286]   80

    Enter Soldiers with the Earl of Kent, prisoner.

Mortimer. What traitor have we there with blades and bills?°   *swords and halberds*
Soldier. Edmund, the Earl of Kent.
Edward III.   What hath he done?
Soldier. He would have taken the king away perforce°   *by force*
    As we were bringing him to Killingworth.
Mortimer. Did you attempt his rescue, Edmund? Speak.
Kent. Mortimer, I did; he is our king,
    And thou compell'st this prince to wear the crown.
Mortimer. Strike off his head! He shall have martial law.[287]
Kent. Strike off my head? Base traitor, I defy thee!
Edward III. My lord, he is my uncle, and shall live.   90
Mortimer. My lord, he is your enemy, and shall die.
Kent. *[To Soldiers]* Stay, villains!
Edward III. Sweet mother, if I cannot pardon him,
    Entreat my Lord Protector for his life.
Queen. Son, be content. I dare not speak a word.
Edward III. Nor I, and yet methinks I should command;
    But seeing I cannot, I'll entreat for him.
    My lord, if you will let my uncle live,
    I will requite it when I come to age.

285. In feudal tradition, a *champion* would appear at the coronation ceremony and offer to defend in combat the legitimacy of the newly crowned king.

286. The line is ambiguous: either the queen tells Mortimer, as Lord Protector, to take charge of the young king, or she tells Mortimer to take charge of the champion (and reward him for his services).

287. Under *martial law*, the king could sentence a man to death without a court trial.

Mortimer. 'Tis for your highness' good, and for the realm's.   100
    [To Soldiers] How often shall I bid you bear him hence?
Kent. Art thou king? Must I die at thy command?
Mortimer. At our command.[288] Once more, away with him.
Kent. Let me but stay and speak; I will not go.
    Either my brother or his son is king,
    And none of both them° thirst for Edmund's blood.   *neither of them*
    And therefore, soldiers, whither will you hale me?

    *They hale Edmund [Earl of Kent] away, and
    carry him to be beheaded.*[289]

Edward III. [To Queen] What safety may I look for at his hands,
    If that my uncle shall be murdered thus?
Queen. Fear not, sweet boy; I'll guard thee from thy foes.   110
    Had Edmund lived, he would have sought thy death.
    Come, son, we'll ride a-hunting in the park.
Edward III. And shall my uncle Edmund ride with us?
Queen. He is a traitor; think not on him. Come.
    Exeunt.

ACT 5, SCENE 5

Enter Matrevis and Gurney [with torches].

Matrevis. Gurney, I wonder the king dies not,
    Being in a vault° up to the knees in water,   *dungeon*
    To which the channels° of the castle run,   *sewers*
    From whence a damp continually ariseth
    That were enough to poison any man,
    Much more a king brought up so tenderly.[290]

288. Mortimer's use of the plural—*At our command*—refers to himself and Isabella, but the phrase also suggests the royal plural and thus implies his overweening ambition for kingly power.

289. The historical Kent was not executed until 1330, three years after the coronation of King Edward III in 1327. Though three years had passed, Kent was charged with treason for attempting to restore Edward II to the throne.

290. In Holinshed, the king is imprisoned in a "chamber over a foul filthy dungeon, full of dead carrion" in which he suffers an "abominable stench" (see Related Texts). Marlowe increases the degradation of the king by placing him not above but in a filthy dungeon up to his knees in sewer water.

Gurney. And so do I, Matrevis. Yesternight
    I opened but the door to throw him meat,°   *food*
    And I was almost stifled with the savour.°   *smell*
Matrevis. He hath a body able to endure   10
    More than we can inflict, and therefore now
    Let us assail his mind another while.
Gurney. Send for him out thence, and I will anger him.

     Enter Lightborn.

Matrevis. But stay, who's this?
Lightborn.   My Lord Protector greets you.

    [Lightborn presents a letter.]

Gurney. What's here? I know not how to conster° it.   *interpret*
Matrevis. Gurney, it was left unpointed for the nonce.° *unpunctuated for this purpose*
    [He reads] "Edwardum occidere nolite timere"—
    That's his meaning.
Lightborn. [Showing the token]
    Know you this token? I must have the king.
Matrevis. Ay, stay a while; thou shalt have answer straight.   20
     [Matrevis and Gurney speak privately.]
    This villain's sent to make away° the king.   *kill*
Gurney. I thought as much.
Matrevis.   And when the murder's done,
    See how he must be handled for his labor.
    Pereat iste![291] Let him have the king.
    [To Lightborn] What else? Here is the keys; this is the lake.[292]
    Do as you are commanded by my lord.
Lightborn. I know what I must do. Get you away.
    Yet be not far off; I shall need your help.
    See that in the next room I have a fire,
    And get me a spit, and let it be red hot.   30
Matrevis. Very well.
Gurney. Need you anything besides?

291. Matrevis reads the Latin phrase, *Pereat iste* (let him perish), in the letter from
Mortimer—which instructs them to kill Lightborn after the murder of the king
is done. (Mortimer apparently wrote the instructions in Latin so that Lightborn
would not comprehend that the letter calls for his own death.)

292. *Lake* (from the Latin *lacus*) could refer to a "pit or cave" or a "body of water."
Matrevis seems to intend the first meaning—the pit or dungeon in which Edward
is imprisoned.

Lightborn. What else? A table and a featherbed.

Gurney. That's all?

Lightborn. Ay, ay; so when I call you, bring it in.

Matrevis. Fear not you that.

Gurney. Here's a light to go into the dungeon.[293]

    [He hands a torch to Lightborn.]

Lightborn. So.

    [Exeunt Gurney and Matrevis.]

    Now must I about this gear.° Ne'er was there any   *business*

    So finely handled as this king shall be.   40

    [He opens the door to the dungeon.]

    Foh! Here's a place indeed, with all my heart.

    [Enter Edward.][294]

Edward. Who's there? What light is that? Wherefore comes thou?

Lightborn. To comfort you and bring you joyful news.

Edward. Small comfort finds poor Edward in thy looks.

    Villain, I know thou com'st to murder me.

Lightborn. To murder you, my most gracious lord?

    Far is it from my heart to do you harm.

    The queen sent me to see how you were used,°   *treated*

    For she relents at this your misery.

    And what eyes can refrain from shedding tears   50

    To see a king in this most piteous state?

Edward. Weep'st thou already? List° a while to me,   *listen*

    And then thy heart, were it as Gurney's is,

    Or as Matrevis', hewn from the Caucasus,[295]

    Yet will it melt ere I have done my tale.

    This dungeon where they keep me is the sink

    Wherein the filth of all the castle falls.

Lightborn. O villains!

---

293. The *light* (torch) that Gurney hands to Lightborn would serve the practical purpose of indicating the darkness of the dungeon (which the audience needs to imagine on the daylit stage). But the *light* may also suggest a visual irony: the name Lightborn (like Lucifer) means "light-bearer."

294. It is possible that Edward emerges from under the stage (conventionally the location of hell) by way of the trap door, or Edward may enter from a curtained alcove or door at the back of the stage. The Q text includes no stage instructions for this entrance of the king.

295. *Caucasus:* mountain range east of the Black Sea renowned for its rocky terrain and cold climate.

Edward. And there in mire and puddle have I stood
  This ten days' space, and lest that I should sleep,   60
  One plays continually upon a drum.
  They give me bread and water, being a king,
  So that for want° of sleep and sustenance   *lack*
  My mind's distempered° and my body's numbed, *disturbed*
  And whether I have limbs or no, I know not.
  O, would my blood dropped out from every vein,
  As doth this water from my tattered robes.
  Tell Isabel the queen I looked not thus
  When for her sake I ran at tilt in France
  And there unhorsed the Duke of Cleremont.²⁹⁶   70
Lightborn. O speak no more, my lord; this breaks my heart.
  Lie on this bed and rest yourself a while.
Edward. These looks of thine can harbor nought but death;
  I see my tragedy written in thy brows.
  Yet stay a while; forbear thy bloody hand,
  And let me see the stroke before it comes,
  That even then when I shall lose my life,
  My mind may be more steadfast on my God.
Lightborn. What means your highness to mistrust me thus?
Edward. What means thou to dissemble with me thus?   80
Lightborn. These hands were never stained with innocent blood,
  Nor shall they now be tainted with a king's.²⁹⁷
Edward. Forgive my thought for having such a thought.
  One jewel have I left; receive thou this.²⁹⁸
   [He gives Lightborn a jewel.]
  Still fear I, and I know not what's the cause,
  But every joint shakes as I give it thee.
  O, if thou harbor'st murder in thy heart,
  Let this gift change thy mind and save thy soul.
  Know that I am a king. O, at that name
  I feel a hell of grief. Where is my crown?   90
  Gone, gone, and do I remain alive?

---

296. There is no mention of this jousting contest in Holinshed or the other historical sources.

297. Lightborn's reference to "hands . . . not stained with innocent blood" alludes to Pilate in his words to Christ: "When Pilate saw that he availed nothing, but that more tumult was made, he took water and washed his hands before the multitude, saying, 'I am innocent of the blood of this just man'" (Matt. 27:24, Geneva Bible).

298. This *jewel* may be the one sent by Isabella to Edward in 5.2.72.

Lightborn. You're overwatched,° my lord. Lie down and rest.   *overtired*
    [Edward lies on the bed.]
Edward. But that grief keeps me waking, I should sleep,
    For not these ten days[299] have these eyelids closed.
    Now as I speak they fall, and yet with fear
    Open again.
        [Lightborn sits on the bed.]
              O wherefore sits thou here?
Lightborn. If you mistrust me, I'll be gone, my lord.
Edward. No, no, for if thou mean'st to murder me,
    Thou wilt return again, and therefore stay.
    [Edward falls asleep.]
Lightborn. He sleeps.   100
Edward. [Waking] O let me not die! Yet stay, O stay a while!
Lightborn. How now, my lord?
Edward. Something still buzzeth in mine ears
    And tells me if I sleep I never wake.[300]
    This fear is that which makes me tremble thus;
    And therefore tell me, wherefore art thou come?
Lightborn. To rid thee of thy life. Matrevis, come!

    [Enter Matrevis with a spit, followed by Gurney.]

Edward. I am too weak and feeble to resist.
    Assist me, sweet God, and receive my soul![301]
Lightborn. Run for the table.   110
    [Matrevis and Gurney exit and return with a table.]
Edward. O spare me, or dispatch me in a trice!
Lightborn. So, lay the table down and stamp on it,
    But not too hard, lest that you bruise his body.

299. Twice Edward refers to his imprisonment for *ten days* (here and at line 60 above)—possibly an allusion to the book of Revelation: "behold, it shall come to pass, that the devil shall cast some of you into prison, that ye may be tried, and ye shall have tribulation ten days; be thou faithful unto the death, and I will give thee the crown of life" (Rev. 2:10).

300. It is not clear what *buzzeth* (whispers) in Edward's ear, but the audience might assume that a good angel is warning Edward of ominous dangers from the bad angel (Lightborn)—as happens repeatedly in Marlowe's *Doctor Faustus*.

301. Edward echoes the final words of Christ on the cross: "And Jesus cried with a loud voice, and said, 'Father, into thine hands I commend my spirit.' And when he thus had said, he gave up the ghost" (Luke 23:46).

[They set the table over Edward, and stamp on it,
while Lightborn penetrates Edward with the spit.
Edward screams and dies.][302]

Matrevis. I fear me that this cry will raise the town,
    And therefore let us take horse and away.
Lightborn. Tell me, sirs, was it not bravely° done?   *skillfully*
Gurney. Excellent well. Take this for thy reward.

    Then Gurney stabs Lightborn.

Come, let us cast the body in the moat,
And bear the king's to Mortimer, our lord.
Away!   120
    Exeunt [carrying the bodies].

ACT 5, SCENE 6

Enter Mortimer and Matrevis [from different sides].

Mortimer. Is't done, Matrevis, and the murderer dead?
Matrevis. Ay, my good lord; I would it were undone.
Mortimer. Matrevis, if thou now growest penitent,
    I'll be thy ghostly father.[303] Therefore choose
    Whether thou wilt be secret in this,
    Or else die by the hand of Mortimer.
Matrevis. Gurney, my lord, is fled, and will, I fear,
    Betray us both; therefore let me fly.
Mortimer. Fly to the savages!
Matrevis. I humbly thank your honor.   10
    [Exit Matrevis.]

302. The Q text includes no stage directions for the murder of Edward, though the method of execution is explicit in Holinshed (see Introduction and Related Texts). The "featherbed" mentioned by Lightborn (at line 33) poses a minor staging problem in the scene: it might be the "bed" (mentioned at line 72) on which Edward lies and on which he is murdered, or perhaps Gurney and Matrevis enter (at line 110) with both a table and a featherbed, and place the featherbed over the king and then place the table over the bed—so as not to bruise the body of the king.

303. *I'll be thy ghostly father*: a proverbial expression meaning "I will kill you" (based on the practice of priests hearing the last confessions and offering communion to men about to die).

Mortimer. As for myself, I stand as Jove's huge tree,
  And others are but shrubs compared to me.[304]
  All tremble at my name, and I fear none.
  Let's see who dare impeach° me for his death.   *accuse*

     Enter the Queen.

Queen. Ah, Mortimer, the king my son hath news
  His father's dead, and we have murdered him.
Mortimer. What if we have? The king is yet a child.
Queen. Ay, ay, but he tears his hair, and wrings his hands,
  And vows to be revenged upon us both.
  Into the council chamber he is gone   20
  To crave the aid and succour of his peers.   *support*
  Ay me, see where he comes, and they with him.
  Now, Mortimer, begins our tragedy.

     *Enter the King [Edward III], with the Lords
     [and Attendants].*

1 Lord. Fear not, my lord. Know that you are a king.
Edward III. *[To Mortimer]* Villain!
Mortimer. How now my lord?
Edward III. Think not that I am frighted with thy words.
  My father's murdered through thy treachery,
  And thou shalt die, and on his mournful hearse
  Thy hateful and accursèd head shall lie,   30
  To witness to the world that by thy means
  His kingly body was too soon interred.
Queen. Weep not, sweet son.
Edward III. Forbid not me to weep. He was my father,
  And had you loved him half so well as I,
  You could not bear his death thus patiently.
  But you, I fear, conspired with Mortimer.
1 Lord. *[To Mort.]* Why speak you not unto my lord the king?
Mortimer. Because I think it scorn to be accused.
  Who is the man dares say I murdered him?   40
Edward III. Traitor, in me my loving father speaks
  And plainly saith, 'twas thou that murd'redst him.
Mortimer. But hath your grace no other proof than this?

---

304. Once again Mortimer reveals his overweening ambition: comparing himself
to *Jove's huge tree* (the oak, the topmost tree in the hierarchy of the forest), he is
implicitly claiming the status of royalty.

Edward III. Yes, if this be the hand of Mortimer.
    [He presents the letter.]
Mortimer. [Aside to Qu.] False Gurney hath betrayed me and himself.
Queen. [Aside to Mort.] I feared as much. Murder cannot be hid.
Mortimer. 'Tis my hand.[305] What gather you by this?
Edward III. That thither thou didst send a murderer.
Mortimer. What murderer? Bring forth the man I sent.
Edward III. Ah, Mortimer, thou knowest that he is slain,   50
    And so shalt thou be too. *[To Lords]* Why stays he here?
    Bring him unto a hurdle, drag him forth;
    Hang him, I say, and set his quarters up.[306]
    But bring his head back presently to me.
Queen. For my sake, sweet son, pity Mortimer.
Mortimer. Madam, entreat not. I will rather die
    Than sue° for life unto a paltry° boy.   *plead / worthless*
Edward III. Hence with the traitor, with the murderer!
Mortimer. Base Fortune, now I see that in thy wheel
    There is a point to which when men aspire,   60
    They tumble headlong down. That point I touched,
    And seeing there was no place to mount up higher,
    Why should I grieve at my declining fall?
    Farewell, fair queen. Weep not for Mortimer,
    That scorns the world, and as a traveler
    Goes to discover countries yet unknown.
Edward III. What, suffer you the traitor to delay?
    *[Exit Mortimer, guarded by the First Lord
    and Attendants.]*

---

305. Mortimer's response that the letter was written in his own hand contradicts his earlier claim that it was "written by a friend" (see 5.4.6). Perhaps the audience is to believe that the unnamed "friend" wrote the unpunctuated Latin instructions to kill the king, but Mortimer with his own hand added more to the letter, in particular the Latin phrase, *Pereat iste* (let him perish), instructing Matrevis and Gurney to kill Lightborn.

306. The king orders that Mortimer be strapped to a *hurdle* (a wooden frame), dragged through the streets, hanged on the gallows, and then cut into *quarters* so his body parts can be put on public display as a warning to all—the standard punishment for high treason in medieval and early modern England. According to Holinshed, the historical Mortimer was hanged but not quartered or beheaded: "His body remained two days and two nights on the gallows, and after taken down was delivered to the friars minors, who buried him in their church the morrow after he was delivered to them, with great pomp and funeral exequies" (see Related Texts).

Queen. As thou received'st thy life from me,
  Spill not the blood of gentle Mortimer.
Edward III. This argues that you spilt my father's blood,   70
  Else would you not entreat for Mortimer.
Queen. I spill his blood? No!
Edward III. Ay, madam, you, for so the rumor runs.
Queen. That rumor is untrue; for loving thee
  Is this report raised on poor Isabel.
Edward III. *[To the Lords]* I do not think her so unnatural.
2 Lord. My lord, I fear me it will prove too true.
Edward III. Mother, you are suspected for his death,
  And therefore we commit you to the Tower
  Till further trial° may be made thereof.   *investigation*
  If you be guilty, though I be your son,   81
  Think not to find me slack or pitiful.
Queen. Nay, to my death, for too long have I lived
  Whenas my son thinks to abridge my days.
Edward III. Away with her! Her words enforce these tears,
  And I shall pity her if she speak again.
Queen. Shall I not mourn for my belovèd lord,[307]
  And with the rest accompany him to his grave?
2 Lord. Thus, madam: 'tis the king's will you shall hence.
Queen. He hath forgotten me. Stay, I am his mother.   90
2 Lord. That boots° not; therefore, gentle madam, go.   *matters*
Queen. Then come, sweet death, and rid me of this grief.[308]
  [Exit Queen with Second Lord and Attendants.]

  [Enter the First Lord with the head of Mortimer.]

1 Lord. My lord, here is the head of Mortimer.
Edward III. Go fetch my father's hearse, where it shall lie,[309]
  And bring my funeral robes. *[Exit Attendants.]*

---

307. Isabella claims she wants to mourn her *beloved lord*, apparently the dead king. But the phrase could also refer, with unconscious irony, to Mortimer (who has just been sent to his death).

308. Though the queen anticipates that she will die shortly, the historical Isabella lived a long life after the events depicted in the play. She was put under house arrest at Windsor Castle for two years, then allowed to retire to Norfolk where she lived in comfort and luxury until her death from natural causes in 1358.

309. "Go get my father's hearse, where it (Mortimer's head) shall lie." As young Edward had earlier warned Mortimer, "thou shalt die, and on his mournful hearse / Thy hateful and accursèd head shall lie" (5.6.29–30).

                                    Accursèd head!
Could I have ruled thee then, as I do now,
Thou hadst not hatched this monstrous treachery.

> *[Enter Attendants carrying the hearse of Edward II
> and funeral robes.]*

Here comes the hearse. Help me to mourn, my lords.
Sweet father, here unto thy murdered ghost
I offer up this wicked traitor's head,   100
And let these tears, distilling° from mine eyes,   *flowing*
Be witness of my grief and innocency.

> *[Exeunt, with a funeral march.]*

RELATED TEXTS

HISTORICAL SOURCES

Raphael Holinshed, *The Third Volume of Chronicles* (1587)[1]

The primary source for Marlowe's play is Holinshed's historical account of the reign of King Edward II and the early phase of the reign of Edward III. Holinshed's Chronicles *(also the main source for Shakespeare's history plays) was first published in 1577. After Holinshed's death in 1580, a second edition, with added materials from other authors, was printed in 1587. The differences between the two editions are minor, and there is no conclusive evidence indicating which edition Marlowe used—though the spelling of "Killingworth" in Marlowe's play matches the spelling in the 1587 edition (while the earlier edition used the spelling "Kenilworth"). Like Shakespeare, Marlowe drew heavily from Holinshed, but he freely selected, rearranged, and compressed Holinshed's sprawling narrative (covering more than twenty years of English history) into a cohesive and unified stage play.*

[Edward and Gaveston]

Edward, the second of that name, the son of Edward the First, born at Caernarfon in Wales, began his reign over England the seventh day of July, in the year of our Lord 1307, of the world 5273. . . . His father's corpse was conveyed from Burgh upon Sands unto the abbey of Waltham, there to remain till things were ready for the burial, which was appointed at Westminster.

Within three days after, when the Lord Treasurer Walter de Langton, Bishop of Coventry and Lichfield (through whose complaint Piers de Gaveston had been banished the land) was going towards Westminster to make preparation for the same burial, he was upon commandment from the new king arrested, committed to prison, and after delivered to the hands of the said Piers, being then returned again into the realm, who sent him from castle to castle as a prisoner. His lands and tenements were seized to the king's use, but his moveables were given to the foresaid Piers. . . .

---

1. Selections are from Raphael Holinshed, *The Third Volume of Chronicles* (London, 1587). Spelling and punctuation have been modernized.

But now concerning the demeanor of this new king, whose disordered manners brought himself and many others unto destruction: we find that in the beginning of his government, though he was of nature given to lightness, yet being restrained with the prudent advertisements of certain of his counselors, to the end he might show some likelihood of good proof, he counterfeited a kind of gravity, virtue, and modesty; but yet he could not thoroughly be so bridled, but that forthwith he began to play divers wanton and light parts, at the first indeed not outrageously, but by little and little, and that covertly. For having revoked again into England his old mate the said Piers de Gaveston, he received him into most high favor, creating him Earl of Cornwall, and Lord of Man, his principal secretary, and Lord Chamberlain of the realm, through whose company and society he was suddenly so corrupted that he burst out into most heinous vices. For then using the said Piers as a procurer of his disordered doings, he began to have his nobles in no regard, to set nothing by their instructions, and to take small heed unto the good government of the commonwealth, so that within a while he gave himself to wantonness, passing his time in voluptuous pleasure and riotous excess. And to help them forward in that kind of life, the foresaid Piers, who (as it may be thought, he had sworn to make the king to forget himself and the state to the which he was called) furnished his court with companies of jesters, ruffians, flattering parasites, musicians, and other vile and naughty ribalds, that the king might spend both days and nights in jesting, playing, banqueting, and in such other filthy and dishonorable exercises. And moreover, desirous to advance those that were like to himself, he procured for them honorable offices, all which notable preferments and dignities, sith[2] they were ill bestowed, were rather to be accounted dishonorable than otherwise, both to the giver and the receiver. . . .

[In 1307, Gaveston is married to the daughter of the Earl of Gloucester, and in the following year King Edward is married to Isabella, daughter of the French king. Later in 1308, "the Knights Templars in England were apprehended all in one day by the king's commandment, upon suspicion of heinous crimes and great enormities by them practiced, contrary to the articles of the Christian faith."]

[Banishment of Gaveston]

The malice which the lords had conceived against the Earl of Cornwall still increased, the more indeed through the high bearing of him, being now advanced to honor. For being a goodly gentleman and a stout, as

2. *sith*: since.

would not once yield an inch to any of them, which worthily procured him great envy amongst the chiefest peers of all the realm . . . which upon such wrath and displeasure as they had conceived against him, thought it not convenient to suffer the same any longer, in hope that the king's mind might happily be altered into a better purpose, being not altogether converted into a venomous disposition, but so that it might be cured, if the corrupter thereof were once banished from him.

Hereupon they assembled together in the parliament time [in 1308], at the New Temple, on Saturday next before the feast of St. Dunstan, and there ordained that the said Piers should abjure the realm, and depart the same on the morrow after the Nativity of St. John Baptist at the furthest, and not to return into the same again at any time then after to come. To this ordinance the king (although against his will), because he saw himself and the realm in danger, gave his consent, and made his letters patents to the said earls and lords, to witness the same. . . .

The Archbishop of Canterbury . . . did pronounce the said Piers accursed if he tarried within the realm longer than the appointed time, and likewise all those that should aid, help, or maintain him, as also if he should at any time hereafter return again into the land. To conclude, this matter was so followed that at length he was constrained to withdraw himself to Bristol, and so by sea as a banished man to sail into Ireland.

The king being sore offended herewith, as he that favored the earl more than that he could be without his company, threatened the lords to be revenged for this displeasure, and ceased not to send into Ireland unto Piers, comforting him both with friendly messages and rich presents, and as it were to show that he meant to retain him still in his favor, he made him ruler of Ireland as his deputy there. A wonderful matter that the king should be so enchanted with the said earl, and so addict himself, or rather fix his heart upon a man of such a corrupt humor, against whom the heads of the noblest houses in the land were bent to devise his overthrow. . . .

The lords, perceiving the king's affection, and that the treasure was spent as lavishly as before, thought with themselves that it might be that the king would both amend his past trade of life, and that Piers being restored home, [the king] would rather advise him thereto, than follow his old manners. . . . Hereupon, to retain amity, as was thought on both sides, Piers by consent of the lords was restored home again [in 1309], the king meeting him at Chester, to his great comfort and rejoicing for the time, although the malice of the lords was such that such joy lasted not long. . . .

[Return of Gaveston]

The king indeed was lewdly led, for after that the Earl of Cornwall was returned into England, he showed himself no changeling (as writers do affirm), but through support of the king's favor bare himself so high in his doings, which were without all good order, that he seemed to disdain all the peers and barons of the realm. And after the old sort he provoked the king to all naughty rule and riotous demeanor, and having the custody of the king's jewels and treasure, he took out of the king's jewelhouse a table and a pair of trestles of gold, which he delivered unto a merchant ... commanding him to convey them over the sea into Gascony. This table was judged of the common people to belong sometime unto King Arthur, and therefore men grudged the more that the same should thus be sent out of the realm.

[Edward raises an army to seek his adversary, Robert Bruce, in Scotland, but the mission does not succeed. Holinshed then mentions that King Edward I had commanded the earls to prevent Gaveston from ever returning to England: "Some write that King Edward the First upon his death-bed charged the earls of Lincoln, Warwick, and Pembroke to foresee that the foresaid Piers returned not again into England, lest by his evil example he might induce his son the prince to lewdness as before he had already done."]

The lords, perceiving the mischief that daily followed and increased by that naughty man (as they took it) the Earl of Cornwall, assembled at Lincoln, and there took counsel together, and concluded eftsoons[3] to banish him out of the realm, and so thereupon shortly after ... he [Gaveston] was exiled into Flanders, sore against the king's will and pleasure, who made such account of him that (as appeared) he could not be quiet in mind without his company, and therefore about Candlemas[4] he eftsoons revoked him home.

But he being nothing at all amended of those his evil manners, rather demeaned himself worse than before he had done, namely towards the lords, against whom using reproachful speech, he called the Earl of Gloucester, "bastard," the Earl of Lincoln lately deceased, "bursten belly," the Earl of Warwick, "the black hound of Arden," and the Earl of Lancaster, "churl." Such lords and other more that were thus abused at this Earl of Cornwall's hands determined to be revenged upon him, and to dispatch the realm of such a wicked person; and thereupon assembling their powers together, came towards Newcastle, whither the king from York was

3. *eftsoons*: soon afterward.
4. *Candlemas*: February 2.

removed, and now hearing of their approach, he [Edward] got him to Tynemouth, where the queen lay, and understanding there that Newcastle was taken by the lords, he leaving the queen behind him, took shipping and sailed from thence with his dearly beloved familiar, the Earl of Cornwall, unto Scarborough, where he left him in the castle, and rode himself towards Warwick. The lords, hearing where the Earl of Cornwall was, made thither with all speed, and besieging the castle, at length constrained their enemy to yield himself into their hands, requiring no other condition but that he might come to the king's presence to talk with him.

[Capture and death of Gaveston]

The king, hearing that his best beloved familiar was thus apprehended, sent to the lords, requiring them to spare his life, and that he [Gaveston] might be brought to his presence, promising withal that he would see them fully satisfied in all their requests against him. Whereupon, the Earl of Pembroke persuaded with the barons to grant to the king's desire, undertaking upon forfeiture of all that he had to bring him to the king and back again to them in such state and condition as he received him. When the barons had consented to his motion, he took the Earl of Cornwall with him to bring him where the king lay, and coming to Deddingon, left him there in safe keeping with his servants, whilst he for one night went to visit his wife, lying not far from thence.

The same night it chanced that Guy, Earl of Warwick, came to the very place where the Earl of Cornwall was left, and taking him from his keepers, brought him unto Warwick, where incontinently[5] it was thought best to put him to death, but that some, doubting[6] the king's displeasure, advised the residue to stay,[7] and so they did, till at length an ancient grave man amongst them exhorted them to use the occasion now offered, and not to let slip the mean to deliver the realm of such a dangerous person, that had wrought so much mischief, and might turn them all to such peril, as afterwards they should not be able to avoid, nor find shift how to remedy it. And thus persuaded by his words, they caused him straightways to be brought forth to a place called Blacklow, otherwise named by most writers Gaversley Heath, where he had his head smitten from his shoulders, the twentieth day of June [1312], being Tuesday. A just reward for so scornful and contemptuous a merchant,[8] [who] as in respect of himself (because

5. *incontinently*: immediately.

6. *doubting*: fearing.

7. *advised the residue to stay*: advised them to delay.

8. *merchant*: commoner.

he was in the prince's favor) esteemed the nobles of the land as men of such inferiority, as that in comparison of him they deserved no little jot or mite of honor. But to the vice of ambition, accompanied with a rabble of other outrages, even a reproachful end with an everlasting mark of infamy, which he pulled by violent means on himself with the cords of his own lewdness, and could not escape this fatal fall. . . .

When the king had knowledge hereof, he was wonderfully displeased with those lords that had thus put the said earl unto death, making his vow that he would see his death revenged, so that the rancor which before was kindled betwixt the king and those lords began now to blaze abroad, and spread so far, that the king ever sought occasion how to work them displeasure. This year, the thirteenth of November, the king's eldest son named Edward (which succeeded his father in the kingdom by the name of Edward the Third) was born at Windsor. King Edward now after that the foresaid Piers Gaveston, the Earl of Cornwall, was dead, nothing reformed his manners, but as one that detested the counsel and admonition of his nobles, chose such to be about him and to be of his privy council, which were known to be men of corrupt and most wicked living (as the writers of that age report). Amongst these were two of the Spensers, Hugh the father and Hugh the son, which were notable instruments to bring him unto the liking of all kind of naughty and evil rule.

By the counsel therefore of these Spensers, he was wholly led and governed, wherewith many were much offended, but namely Robert, the Archbishop of Canterbury, who foresaw what mischief was like to ensue; and therefore to provide some remedy in time, he procured that a parliament was called at London, in the which many good ordinances and statutes were devised and established, to oppress the riots, misgovernance, and other mischiefs which as then were used; and to keep those ordinances, the king first, and after his lords, received a solemn oath, that in no wise neither he nor they should break them. By this means was the state of the realm newly restored and new counselors placed about the king. But he, neither regarding what he had sworn, neither weighing the force of an oath, observed afterwards none of those things, which by his oath he had bound himself to observe. And no marvel, for surely (as it should seem by report of Thomas de la More), the lords wrested[9] him too much, and beyond the bounds of reason, causing him to receive to be about him whom it pleased them to appoint. For the younger Spenser, who in place of the Earl of Cornwall was ordained to be his chamberlain, it was known to them well enough that the king bare no good will at all to him at the

---

9. *wrested*: pressured or forced.

first, though afterwards through the prudent policy and diligent industry of the man, he quickly crept into his favor. . . .

[Edward's defeat at Bannockburn]

[In 1314, Robert Bruce recovers castles in Scotland that had been controlled by the English.]

King Edward, to be revenged hereof, with a mighty army bravely furnished and gorgeously appareled, more seemly for a triumph than meet to encounter with the cruel enemy in the field, entered Scotland, in purpose specially to rescue the castle of Stirling, as then besieged by the Scottish men. But at his approaching near to the same, Robert Bruce was ready with his power to give him battle. In the which King Edward, nothing doubtful of loss,[10] had so unwisely ordered his people and confounded their ranks, that even at the first joining, they were not only beaten down and overthrown by those that coped with them at hand, but also were wounded with shot afar off by those their enemies which stood behind to succor their fellows when need required, so that in the end the Englishmen fled to save their lives, and were chased and slain by the Scots in great number.

The king escaped with a few about him, in great danger to have been either taken or slain. Many were drowned in a little river called Bannockburn, near to the which the battle was foughten. . . . There were slain of all sorts upon the English part that day about ten thousand men, over and beside the prisoners that were taken. . . .

[The Scots continue to launch raids into England, and they also invade Ireland. For the first time in the narrative, Holinshed mentions Mortimer. In a battle against the Scots in Ireland in 1315, "the lord Roger Mortimer was discomfited by the foresaid Edward Bruce,[11] and many of the said Sir Roger's men were slain and taken." Meanwhile, England suffers from excess rain, crop failure, famine, and disease. The poor of England "were constrained through famine to eat the flesh of horses, dogs, and other vile beasts." In 1318 a man named John Poidras, son of a tanner, claimed to be the son and rightful heir of King Edward I. He alleged that "by means of a false nurse he was stolen out of his cradle, and this Edward the Second, being a carter's son, was brought in and laid in his place." The pretender to the throne was condemned to death by hanging, but only after he confessed that "in his house he had a spirit in likeness of a cat which amongst other things assured him that he should be King of England."]

---

10. *nothing doubtful of loss*: not fearing defeat.

11. *Edward Bruce*: younger brother of Robert Bruce, king of Scotland (r. 1306–29).

[Rise of the Spensers]

Thus all the king's exploits by one means or other quailed and came but to evil success, so that the English nation began to grow in contempt by the unfortunate government of the prince ... which thing so grieved the noblemen of the realm, that they studied day and night by what means they might procure him to look better to his office and duty, which they judged might well be brought to pass, his nature being not altogether evil, if they might find shift to remove from him the two Spensers, Hugh the father and Hugh the son, who were gotten into such favor with him, that they only did all things, and without them nothing was done, so that they were now had in as great hatred and indignation ... both of the lords and commons, as ever in times past was Piers de Gaveston. . . . Hugh the son was made High Chamberlain of England, contrary to the mind of all the noblemen, by reason whereof he bare himself so haughty and proud, that no lord within the land might gainsay that which in his conceit seemed good. . . .

About this season [in 1321], the lord William de Bruce, that in the marches of Wales enjoyed divers fair possessions to him descended from his ancestors, but through want of good government was run behindhand, offered to sell a certain portion of his lands called Gower's land, lying in the marches there, unto divers noblemen that had their lands adjoining to the same, as to the Earl of Hereford and to the two lords Mortimers. . . . But at length (as unhap would) Hugh Spenser the younger, Lord Chamberlain, coveting that land because it lay near on each side to other lands that he had in those parts, found such means through the king's furtherance and help, that he went away with the purchase, to the great displeasure of the other lords that had been in hand to buy it.

[The barons attack castles and manors held by the king's allies, including the Spensers. Eventually, the king agrees to banish the Spensers from the realm, but before long the Spensers return to England and are protected by the king. Edward continues to fight the barons, and he sends a letter to the Earl of Lancaster, reprimanding him for pride and disloyalty. Holinshed then comments: "Yet for that he [the king] tolerated such insolence of behavior, as was unseemly to be showed against the person of his prince, the king's clemency and patience is highly therein to be commended, though his forbearing and seeking means of quietness did never a whit amend the malignant mind of the earl, whose heart was so enchanted with ambition and super-eminent honor." Meanwhile, the castles of the Mortimers in Wales are taken by a Welsh army. The Mortimers then submit to the king, and they are sent as prisoners to the Tower of London.]

[Edward's victory at Boroughbridge]

[Edward and his loyal barons, including Kent, Pembroke, and Arundel, raise an army to fight the remaining rebel barons. In 1322, at the battle of Boroughbridge, Edward wins a great victory. The Earl of Lancaster is taken prisoner, arraigned for high treason, and sentenced to be "drawn, hanged, and headed." As the queen's uncle, he was spared hanging, but he was beheaded.]

Thus the king seemed to be revenged of the displeasure done to him by the Earl of Lancaster for the beheading of Piers de Gaveston, Earl of Cornwall, whom he so dearly loved, and because the Earl of Lancaster was the chief occasioner of his [Gaveston's] death, the king never loved him entirely after. So that here is verified the censure of the Scripture expressed by the wisdom of Solomon, that the anger and displeasure of the king is as the roaring of a lion, and his revenge inevitable [see Prov. 20:2]. Wherefore it is an high point of discretion in such as are mighty to take heed how they give edge unto the wrath of their sovereign, which if it be not by submission made blunt, the burden of the smart ensuing will lie heavy upon the offender, even to his utter undoing and loss (perhaps) of life. In this sort came the mighty earl of Lancaster to his end, being the greatest peer in the realm, and one of the mightiest earls in Christendom; for when he began to levy war against the king, he was possessed of five earldoms—Lancaster, Lincoln, Salisbury, Leicester, and Derby—beside other signatories, lands, and possessions, great to his advancement in honor and puissance.[12] But all this was limited within prescription of time, which being expired, both honor and puissance were cut off with dishonor and death....

[Holinshed includes a list of the lords and knights executed by order of King Edward.[13]]

But now touching the foresaid Earl of Lancaster, great strife rose afterwards amongst the people whether he ought to be reputed for a saint or no. Some held that he ought to be no less esteemed for that he did many almsdeeds in his lifetime, honored men of religion, and maintained a true quarrel till his life's end. Also, his enemies continued not long after but came to evil end. Others conceived an other opinion of him, alleging that he favored not his wife but lived in spouse-breach, defiling a great number of damsels and gentlewomen. If any offended him, he slew him shortly after in his wrathful mood.... yet by reason of certain miracles which were said to be done near the place both where he suffered and where he was buried, caused many to think he was a saint....

---

12. *puissance*: power.

13. See stage direction and note at 4.3.11.

[Edward restores the Spensers to their lands and offices, and he grants the title of Earl of Winchester to the Spenser Senior.]

At this time also, master Robert Baldock, a man evil beloved in the realm, was made Lord Chancellor of England. This Robert Baldock, and one Simon Reading, were great favorers of the Spensers, and so likewise was the Earl of Arundel, whereby it may be thought that the Spensers did help to advance them into the king's favor, so that they bare no small rule in the realm . . . and the queen for that she gave good and faithful counsel, was nothing regarded, but by the Spensers' means clearly worn out of the king's favor. . . .

[The Earl of Pembroke is arrested and accused of being a "secrete favorer of the barons' cause against the Spensers in the time of late troubles." But after paying a fine and taking an oath of fidelity to the king, Pembroke is set at liberty.]

Here is to be noted, that during the time whilst the civil war was in hand betwixt King Edward and his barons, the Scots and Frenchmen were not idle, for the Scots wasted and destroyed the country of the bishopric of Durham (as before ye have partly heard), and the Frenchmen made roads and incursions into the borders of Guienne, alleging that they did it upon good and sufficient occasion, for that King Edward had not done his homage unto the King of France, as he ought to have done, for the duchy of Aquitaine and the county of Ponthieu. . . .

[The Earl of Carlisle is accused of treason and executed, and Holinshed takes the occasion to comment on the divine right of kings: "for God, who hath placed princes in thrones of royalty to this end, hath vouchsafed them a superlative degree of dignity, that they might be obeyed; neither will his justice permit impunity to the disloyal enterprises and complots of malefactors, common peace-disturbers . . . or any lewd malcontent."]

About the same time, the lord Roger Mortimer of Wigmore, giving his keepers a drink that brought them into a sound and heavy sleep, escaped out of the Tower of London where he was prisoner. This escape of the lord Mortimer greatly troubled the king, so that immediately upon the first news, he wrote to all the sheriffs of the realm that if he chanced to come within their rooms,[14] they should cause hue and cry to be raised, so as he might be stayed and arrested. But he [Mortimer] made such shift, that he got over into France, where he was received by a lord of Picardy. . . .

14. *rooms*: lands.

[Queen Isabella in France]

[Concerned with the crisis in England, Edward refuses to travel to France to pay homage in person to King Charles IV. In response, the French seize English territories in Guienne. Kent goes to France to defend the English towns, but the French prevail. Queen Isabella is then sent to France to attempt a resolution. The French agree to give Prince Edward control over the disputed territories of Aquitaine and Ponthieu. Prince Edward then travels to France to join his mother and to pay homage to the French king.]

In the beginning of the next spring, King Edward sent into France unto his wife and son, commanding them, now that they had made an end of their business, to return home with all convenient speed. The queen, receiving the message from her husband, whether it was so that she was stayed by her brother, unto whom belike she had complained after what manner she was used at her husband's hands, being had in no regard with him, or for that she had no mind to return home because she was loth to see all things ordered out of frame by the counsel of the Spensers, whereof to hear she was weary, or whether (as the manner of women is) she was long about to prepare herself forward, she slacked all the summer, and sent letters ever to excuse her tarriance.[15] But yet because she would not run in any suspicion with her husband, she sent divers of her folks before her into England by soft[16] journeys. A lamentable case, that such division should be between a king and his queen, being lawfully married, and having issue of their bodies, which ought to have made that their copulation more comfortable, but (alas) what will not a woman be drawn and allured unto, if by evil counsel she be once assaulted? And what will she leave undone, though never so inconvenient to those that should be most dear unto her, so her own fancy and will be satisfied? And how hardly is she revoked from proceeding in an evil action if she have once taken a taste of the same? . . .

But to the purpose. King Edward, not a little offended with King Charles, by whose means he knew that the woman thus lingered abroad, he procured Pope John to write his letters unto the French king, admonishing him to send home his sister and her son unto her husband. But when this nothing availed, a proclamation was made in the month of December [1325], the nineteenth year of this king's reign, that if the queen and her son entered not the land by the octave of the Epiphany next ensuing in peaceable wise, they should be taken for enemies to the realm and crown of England. Here authors vary, for some write that upon knowledge had of

15. *tarriance*: delay.
16. *soft*: slow, leisurely.

this proclamation, the queen determined to return into England forthwith, that she might be reconciled to her husband.

Others write, and that more truly, how she being highly displeased, both with the Spensers and the king her husband, that suffered himself to be misled by their counsels, did appoint indeed to return into England, not to be reconciled, but to stir the people to some rebellion, whereby she might revenge her manifold injuries, which (as the proof of the thing showed) seemeth to be most true, for she being a wise woman, and considering that . . . she might well think that there was small hope to be had in her husband, who heard no man but the said Spensers, which she knew hated her deadly. Whereupon, after that the term prefixed in the proclamation was expired, the king caused to be seized into his hands all such lands as belonged either to his son or to his wife. . . .

King Edward, understanding all the queen's drift, at length sought the French king's favor, and did so much by letters and promise of bribes with him and his council, that Queen Isabel was destitute in manner of all help there, so that she was glad to withdraw into Hainault by the comfort of John, the lord Beaumont. . . .

[Queen Isabella's invasion of England]

But Queen Isabel and her son, with such others as were with her in Hainault, stayed not their journey for doubt of all their adversaries' provision, but immediately after that they had once made their purveyances, and were ready to depart, they took the sea, namely the queen, her son, Edmund of Woodstock, Earl of Kent,[17] Sir John de Hainault aforesaid, and the lord Roger Mortimer of Wigmore, a man of good experience in the wars, and divers others, having with them a small company of Englishmen, with a crew of Hainaulters and Almains,[18] to the number of 2,757 armed men, the which sailing forth towards England, landed at length in Suffolk . . . the twenty fifth day of September [1326]. Immediately after that the queen and her son were come to land, it was wonder to see how fast the people resorted unto them. . . .

[King Edward flees to Wales to raise an army. He issues a proclamation commanding all citizens to fight against the invading army, and he offers a thousand marks for the "head or dead corpse of the lord Mortimer." Queen Isabella issues a proclamation offering two thousand pounds for the "head of Spenser the younger."]

---

17. Holinshed provides no explanation about why Kent joined the queen's rebellion.

18. *Almains*: Germans.

Then, shortly after, the queen with her son making towards London wrote a letter to the mayor and the citizens, requiring to have assistance for the putting down of the Spensers, not only known enemies of theirs, but also common enemies to all the realm of England. To this letter no answer at the first was made, wherefore another was sent . . . containing, in effect, that the cause of their landing and entering into the realm at that time was only for the honor of the king and wealth of the realm, meaning hurt to no manner of person, but to the Spensers. . . .

[In London, an unruly mob forces the mayor to take an oath support-ing the cause of Queen Isabella. The mob executes the bishop of Exeter and sets free all prisoners and outlaws. The queen's army reaches Bristol, where the elder Spenser is captured and hanged. King Edward, Spenser Junior, Baldock, and Arundel attempt to sail to the Isle of Lundy or Ireland, but contrary winds force their return to Wales, where they take refuge in the abbey of Neath. Meanwhile, Prince Edward is made Lord Warden of the realm, and all men "made fealty in receiving an oath of allegiance to be faithful and loyal to him."]

[Capture and imprisonment of King Edward]

The queen remained about a month's space at Hereford, and in the mean-while sent the lord Henry, Earl of Leicester, and the lord William la Zouch, and one Rice ap Howell, that was lately delivered out of the Tower where he was prisoner, into Wales to see if they might find means to apprehend the king by help of their acquaintance in those parts, all three of them having lands thereabouts, where it was known the king for the more part kept. They used such diligence in that charge that finally with large gifts bestowed on the Welshmen, they came to understand where the king was, and so on the day of St. Edmund the Archbishop, being the sixteenth of November [1326], they took him in the monastery of Neath . . . together with Hugh Spenser the son, called Earl of Gloucester, the Lord Chancellor Robert de Baldock, and Simon de Reading, the king's marshal, not caring for other the king's servants, whom they suffered to escape.

The king was delivered to the Earl of Leicester, who conveyed him by Monmouth and Ledbury to Killingworth castle, where he remained the whole winter. The Earl of Gloucester, the Lord Chancellor, and Simon de Reading were brought to Hereford, and there presented to the queen, where on the four and twentieth of November, the said earl [Spenser Junior] was drawn and hanged on a pair of gallows of fifty foot in height. Then was his head striken off, his bowels taken out of his body and burnt, and his body divided in quarters. His head was sent to London, and set upon the bridge with other, and his quarters were sent to four several parts of the realm, and there pight[19] upon poles, to be seen of the people. . . .

[Arundel is put to death by the command of Lord Mortimer, and Baldock is sent to Newgate prison, where he dies from "inward sorrow and extreme grief of mind."]

[Deposition of King Edward]

[At a meeting of Parliament in 1327] it was concluded and fully agreed by all the states (for none durst speak to the contrary) that for divers articles which were put up against the king, he was not worthy longer to reign, and therefore should be deposed, and withal they willed to have his son Edward, Duke of Aquitaine, to reign in his place. This ordinance was openly pronounced in the great hall at Westminster by one of the lords . . . to the which all the people consented. The Archbishop of Canterbury, taking his theme *Vox populi, vox Dei* [the voice of the people is the voice of God], made a sermon exhorting the people to pray to God to bestow of His grace upon the new king. . . . [Prince Edward] protested that he would never take it [the crown] on him without his father's consent, and so thereupon it was concluded that certain solemn messengers should go to Killingworth to move the king to make resignation of his crown and title of the kingdom unto his son. . . .

The bishops of Winchester and Lincoln went before, and coming to Killingworth, associated with them the Earl of Leicester . . . that had the king in keeping. And having secret conference with the king, they sought to frame his mind, so as he might be contented to resign the crown to his son, bearing him in hand[20] that, if he refused so to do, the people in respect of the evil will which they had conceived against him would not fail but proceed to the election of some other that should happily not touch him in lineage. And sith[21] this was the only mean to bring the land in quiet, they willed him to consider how much he was bound in conscience to take that way that should be so beneficial to the whole realm.

The king, being sore troubled to hear such displeasant news, was brought into a marvelous agony, but in the end, for the quiet of the realm and doubt[22] of further danger to himself, he determined to follow their advice, and so when the other commissioners were come, and that the Bishop of Hereford had declared the cause wherefore they were sent, the

19. *pight*: placed or set upright.

20. *bearing him in hand*: manipulating him into believing.

21. *sith*: since.

22. *doubt*: fear.

king in presence of them all . . . [showed] how much it inwardly grieved him, yet after he was come to himself, he answered that he knew that he was fallen into this misery through his own offenses, and therefore he was contented patiently to suffer it, but yet it could not, he said, but grieve him that he had in such wise run into the hatred of all his people. Notwithstanding, he gave the lords most hearty thanks that they had so forgotten their received injuries and ceased not to bear so much good will towards his son Edward as to wish that he might reign over them. Therefore to satisfy them, sith otherwise it might not be, he utterly renounced his right to the kingdom and to the whole administration thereof. And lastly he besought the lords now in his misery to forgive him such offenses as he had committed against them. . . .

On the same day, Sir William Trussell, procurator for the whole parliament, did renounce the old king in name of the whole parliament, with all homages and fealties due to him. . . .

[The murder of Edward]

But now to make an end of the life, as well as of the reign of King Edward the Second, I find that after he was deposed of his kingly honor and title, he remained for a time at Killingworth in custody of the Earl of Leicester. But within a while the queen was informed by the Bishop of Hereford (whose hatred towards him had no end) that the Earl of Leicester favored her husband too much, and more than stood with the surety[23] of her son's state, whereupon he [Edward] was appointed to the keeping of two other lords, Thomas Berkeley and John Maltravers. . . .

But forsomuch as the lord Berkeley used him more courteously than his adversaries wished him to do, he was discharged of that office, and Sir Thomas Gurney appointed in his stead, who together with the lord Maltravers conveyed him secretly (for fear lest he should be taken from them by force) from one strong place to another, as to the castle of Corfe, and such like, still removing with him in the night season, till at length they thought it should not be known whither they had conveyed him. And so at length they brought him back again in secret manner unto the castle of Berkeley, where whilst he remained (as some write) the queen would send unto him courteous and loving letters with apparel and other such things, but she would not once come near to visit him, bearing him in hand that she durst not for fear of the people's displeasure, who hated him so extremely. Howbeit, she with the rest of her confederates had no doubt laid the plot of their device for his dispatch, though by painted words she

23. *surety*: safety.

pretended a kind of remorse to him in this his distress, and would seem to be faultless in the sight of the world. . . .

But as he thus continued in prison, closely kept, so that none of his friends might have access unto him, as in such cases it often happeneth when men be in misery some will ever pity their state, there were divers of the nobility (of whom the Earl of Kent was chief) began to devise means by secret conference had together how they might restore him to liberty, discommending greatly both Queen Isabel and such other as were appointed governors to the young king, for his father's strict imprisonment. The queen and other the governors understanding this conspiracy of the Earl of Kent, and of his brother, durst not yet in that new and green world go about to punish it, but rather thought good to take away from them the occasion of accomplishing their purpose. And hereupon the queen and the Bishop of Hereford wrote sharp letters unto his keepers, blaming them greatly, for that they dealt so gently with him, and kept him no strictlier,[24] but suffered him to have such liberty, that he advertised some of his friends abroad how and in what manner he was used, and withal the Bishop of Hereford under a sophistical form of words signified to them by his letters that they should dispatch him out of the way, the tenor whereof wrapped in obscurity ran thus:

> *Edwardum occidere nolite timere bonum est:*
> To kill Edward will not to fear it is good.

Which riddle or doubtful kind of speech, as it might be taken in two contrary senses, only by placing the point in orthography called comma, they construed in the worse sense, putting the comma after *timere*, and so presuming of this commandment as they took it from the bishop, they lodged the miserable prisoner in a chamber over a foul filthy dungeon, full of dead carrion, trusting so to make an end of him, with the abominable stench thereof. But he bearing it out strongly, as a man of a tough nature, continued still in life, so as it seemed he was very like to escape that danger, as he had by purging either up or down[25] avoided the force of such poison as had been ministered to him sundry times before of purpose so to rid him.

Whereupon when they saw that such practices would not serve their turn, they came suddenly one night into the chamber where he lay in bed fast asleep, and with heavy featherbeds or a table (as some write) being cast

---

24. *no strictlier:* not strict or harsh enough.

25. *by purging either up or down:* by vomiting or excreting.

upon him, they kept him down and withal put into his fundament an horn, and through the same they thrust up into his body an hot spit, or (as other have) through the pipe of a trumpet, a plumber's instrument of iron made very hot, the which passing up into his entrails, and being rolled to and fro, burnt the same, but so as no appearance of any wound or hurt outwardly might be once perceived. His cry did move many within the castle and town of Berkeley to compassion, plainly hearing him utter a wailful noise, as the tormentors were about to murder him, so that divers being awakened therewith (as they themselves confessed) prayed heartily to God to receive his soul, when they understood by his cry what the matter meant.

The queen, the bishop, and others, that their tyranny might be hid, outlawed and banished the lord Maltravers and Thomas Gurney, who fleeing unto Marseilles, three years after being known, taken and brought toward England, was beheaded on the sea, lest he should accuse the chief doers, as the bishop and other. John Maltravers, repenting himself, lay long hidden in Germany, and in the end died penitently. Thus was King Edward murdered in the year 1327 on the 22 of September. The fame went that by this Edward the Second, after his death, many miracles were wrought. So that the like opinion of him was conceived as before had been of earl Thomas of Lancaster, namely amongst the common people.[26] He was known to be of a good and courteous nature, though not of most pregnant wit.

And albeit in his youth he fell into certain light crimes, and after by the company and counsel of evil men was induced unto more heinous vices, yet was it thought that he purged the same by repentance, and patiently suffered many reproofs and finally death itself (as before ye have heard) after a most cruel manner. . . .

All these mischiefs and many more happened not only to him, but also to the whole state of the realm, in that he wanted judgment and prudent discretion to make choice of sage and discreet counselors . . . insomuch that by their covetous rapine, spoil, and immoderate ambition, the hearts of the common people and nobility were quite estranged from the dutiful love and obedience which they ought to have showed to their sovereign, going about by force to wrest him to follow their wills, and to seek the destruction of them whom he commonly favored, wherein surely they were worthy of blame, and to taste (as many of them did) the deserved punishment for their disobedient and disloyal demeanors.

26. The marginal gloss adds: "The fond opinion of the ignorant people."

[King Edward III and the fate of Kent, Mortimer, and Isabel]

[The following selections are from Holinshed's account of the reign of Edward III. In 1327 King Edward III is crowned at age fourteen. A council of twelve lords, including Kent, is selected to rule the realm until Edward comes of age. In 1328 Mortimer is created Earl of March.]

. . . the Earl of March took the most part of the rule of all things pertaining either to the king or realm into his own hands, so that the whole government rested in a manner betwixt the queen mother and him. The other of the council that were first appointed were in manner displaced, for they bare no rule to speak of at all, which caused no small grudge to arise against the queen and the said Earl of March, who maintained such ports[27] and kept among them such retinue of servants, that their provision was wonderful.

[In 1330 Kent is arrested] . . . and being arraigned upon certain confessions and letters found about him, he was found guilty of treason. . . . [Kent] upon his open confession before sundry lords of the realm, declared that not only by commandment from the Pope, but also by the setting on of divers nobles of this land (whom he named), he was persuaded to endeavor himself by all ways and means possible how to deliver his brother King Edward the Second out of prison, and to restore him to the crown. . . .

The earl [Kent] himself was had out of the castle gate at Winchester, and there lost his head the nineteenth day of March, chiefly (as was thought) through the malice of the queen mother and of the Earl of March, whose pride and high presumption the said Earl of Kent might not well abide. His death was the less lamented because of the presumptuous government of his servants and retinue which he kept about him, for that they riding abroad would take up things at their pleasure, not paying nor agreeing with the party to whom such things belonged. . . .

Also in a parliament holden at Nottingham about St. Luke's tide, Sir Roger Mortimer, the Earl of March, was apprehended the seventeenth day of October [1330] within the castle of Nottingham, where the king with the two queens, his mother and his wife, and divers other were as then lodged. . . . From Nottingham he was sent up to London . . . [and] committed to prison in the Tower. Shortly after was a parliament called at Westminster, chiefly (as was thought) for reformation of things disordered through the misgovernance of the Earl of March. But whosoever was glad or sorry for the trouble of the said earl, surely the queen mother took it most heavily above all other, as she that loved him more (as the fame

27. *ports*: extravagant luxuries.

went) than stood well with her honor: For, as some write, she was found to be with child by him. They kept as it were house together, for the earl to have his provision the better cheap laid his penny with hers, so that her takers served him as well as they did her, both of victuals and carriages. Of which misusage (all regard to honor and estimation neglected) every subject spake shame. For their manner of dealing, tending to such evil purposes as they continually thought upon, could not be secret from the eyes of the people. . . .

[In 1330 Mortimer is charged with high treason and other crimes.]

These articles with other being proved against him, he was adjudged by authority of the parliament to suffer death, and according thereunto, upon St. Andrew's Even next ensuing, he was at London drawn and hanged at the common place of execution, called in those days the Elms, and now Tyburn, as in some books we find. His body remained two days and two nights on the gallows, and after taken down was delivered to the friars minors, who buried him in their church the morrow after he was delivered to them, with great pomp and funeral exequies, although afterwards he was taken up and carried unto Wigmore, whereof he was lord. . . .

In this parliament holden at Westminster, the king took into his hand, by advice of the states there assembled, all the possessions, lands, and revenues that belonged to the queen his mother, she having assigned to her a thousand pounds by year for the maintenance of her estate, being appointed to remain in a certain place and not to go elsewhere abroad, yet the king to comfort her would lightly[28] every year once come to visit her.

John Stow, *The Annals of England* (1592)[29]

Holinshed provided almost all the material Marlowe needed for the play, though it is evident that Marlowe read other chronicles as well. The Scottish jig that Lancaster recites in 2.2.189–94 is taken almost verbatim from Robert Fabyan's Chronicle *(1559). And the fate of Mortimer at the end of the play may have been influenced by Richard Grafton's* Chronicle *(1569), which claims Mortimer was beheaded (as in the play) rather than hanged (as in Holinshed and the other chronicles).[30]*

---

28. *lightly*: customarily.

29. Selections are from John Stow, *Annals of England* (London, 1592). Spelling and punctuation have been modernized.

30. See Robert Fabyan, *The Chronicle of Fabyan* (London, 1559), Vol. 2, p. 169; and Richard Grafton, *The Chronicle and History of the Affairs of England* (London, 1569), Vol. 2, p. 223.

Aside from Holinshed, Marlowe's most substantial borrowing was from John Stow's Chronicles of England, *printed in 1580, with an expanded edition and a new title,* Annals of England, *appearing in 1592. Marlowe may have used either edition (the differences concerning the reign of Edward II are slight). Stow includes several details that seem to have influenced, at least indirectly, Marlowe's characterization of Gaveston. In Stow the nobles claim that Gaveston's father was executed as a "traitor to the king of France," his mother was "burned for a witch," and Gaveston had "bewitched the king himself" (Stow 321). Marlowe's play tells us nothing of Gaveston's parents, but the nobles do complain that the king is "bewitched" (1.2.55). Stow also mentions that the king called Gaveston "brother" and promised that Gaveston "should succeed him in the kingdom" (Stow 321). King Edward in the play never offers to make Gaveston his successor, but he does offer to "share the kingdom" with his "dearest friend" (1.1.2), and he indeed calls Gaveston "brother" (2.2.35). Stow also describes the followers of Gaveston as "outlandish men" (Stow 324), a phrase that seems to surface in the play when Mortimer refers to Gaveston's train of overdressed foreigners as "base outlandish cullions" (1.4.409).*

Marlowe's most significant borrowing from Stow, however, is from Stow's account of the humiliations inflicted on Edward after he is deposed. In the following excerpt, the king's jailors torment him with hunger and sleeplessness, and they forcibly cut off his hair and shave his beard with water from a ditch (an event that appears nowhere in the other chronicles).

[The tormenting and shaving of King Edward]

These tormentors of Edward [Gurney and Maltravers] exercised towards him many cruelties, unto whom it was not permitted to ride, unless it were by night, neither to see any man, or to be seen of any. When he rode, they forced him to be bareheaded; when he would sleep, they would not suffer him; neither when he was hungry would they give him such meats as he desired, but such as he loathed; every word that he spake was contraried by them, who gave it out most slanderously that he was mad. And, shortly to speak, in all matters they were quite contrary to his will, that either by cold, watching,[31] or unwholesome meats, for melancholy [or] by some infirmity he might languish and die. But this man being by nature strong to suffer pains, and patient through God's grace to abide all griefs, he endured all the devices of his enemies; for as touching poisons, which they gave him often to drink, by the benefit of nature he dispatched away.

---

31. *watching*: sleeplessness.

These champions bring Edward towards Berkeley, being guarded with a rabble of hell-hounds, along by the grange[32] belonging to the castle of Bristol, where that wicked man Gurney, making a crown of hay, put it on his [Edward's] head, and the soldiers that were present scoffed and mocked him beyond all measure, saying "Tprut, avaunt[33] Sir King," making a kind of noise with their mouths as though they had farted. They feared to be met of any that should know Edward; they bent their journey therefore towards the left hand, riding along over the marish[34] grounds lying by the river of Severn. Moreover, devising to disfigure him that[35] he might not be known, they determined for to shave as well the hair of his head as also of his beard; wherefore, as in their journey they travelled by a little water which ran in a ditch, they commanded him to light from his horse to be shaven, to whom, being set on a mole-hill, a barber came unto him with a basin of cold water taken out of the ditch to shave him withal, saying unto the king, that that water should serve for that time. To whom Edward answered, that . . . he would have warm water for his beard, and, to the end that he might keep his promise, he began to weep, and to shed tears plentifully. At length they came to Berkeley castle, where Edward was shut up close like an anchor.[36]

POWER AND POLITICS

St. Paul, Epistle to the Romans (c. 56)[37]

In Protestant England, there was no higher textual authority than the Bible, and biblical passages were often cited in defense of political positions. While the Gospels recorded the famous command of Jesus to "Give therefore to Caesar the things which are Caesar's, and give unto God those things which are God's" (Matt. 22:21), the letters of St. Paul included more explicit comments on how Christians should respond to political authorities. In the

32. grange: farm.

33. *Tprut, avaunt:* Go, move along.

34. *marish:* wet or marshy.

35. *that:* so that.

36. *anchor:* hermit or monk.

37. Selections are from the *Geneva Bible* (London, 1587). Spelling and punctuation have been modernized.

*Epistle to the Romans, St. Paul urges the Christian community to obey all
civil magistrates (in part because Paul did not want the Roman state to see
Christians as a pernicious threat to political and civic stability).[38]*

*In medieval and early modern Europe, St. Paul was often cited in sup-
port of the doctrine of the divine right of kings—the claim (affirmed by the
supporters of King Edward in the play) that the power of the king descends
from God above, and thus a king should never be judged or opposed by any
human authority. Of course the opponents of divine right could cite other
passages from St. Paul, in particular his ironic inversion of worldly power
and Christian humility in his First Epistle to the Corinthians: "But God
hath chosen the foolish things of the world to confound the wise, and God
hath chosen the weak things of the world to confound the mighty things"
(1 Cor. 1:27).*

*The text below is from the Geneva Bible (the English translation most
widely available in sixteenth-century England), with selected marginal glosses
from the 1587 edition. As the glosses indicate, Paul's letter can be read not
only as a demand for obedience to civil authorities, but also as an affirmation
of the higher authority of God and the reciprocal responsibilities between the
ruler and the ruled.*

Chapter 13:1–8

1. Let every soul be subject unto the higher powers, for there is no power
but of God, and the powers that be are ordained of God. [Marginal gloss:
Therefore the tyranny of the Pope over all kingdoms must down to the
ground.]

2. Whosoever therefore resisteth the power, resisteth the ordinance of God;
and they that resist shall receive to themselves condemnation.

3. For Magistrates are not to be feared for good works, but for evil. Wilt
thou then be without fear of the power? Do well, so shalt thou have praise
of the same. [Marginal gloss: By which words the Magistrates themselves
are put in mind of that duty which they owe to their subjects.]

4. For he is the minister of God for thy wealth. But if thou do evil, fear;
for he beareth not the sword for nought; for he is the minister of God to
take vengeance on him that doeth evil.

5. Wherefore ye must be subject, not because of wrath only, but also for
conscience sake. [Marginal gloss: So far as lawfully we may, for if unlawful
things be commanded us, we must answer as Peter teacheth us: It is better
to obey God than men.]

---

38. See Johnson, *History of Christianity*, 170.

6. For this cause ye pay also tribute, for they are God's ministers, applying themselves for the same thing.

7. Give to all men therefore their duty: tribute to whom ye owe tribute; custom to whom custom; fear to whom fear; honor to whom ye owe honor.

8. Owe nothing to any man, but to love one another; for he that loveth another hath fulfilled the Law. [Marginal gloss: He commendeth charity as an abridgement of the whole law.]

An Homily against Disobedience and Willful Rebellion (1570)[39]

In response to the attempted rebellion of the northern earls in 1569, the Elizabethan government issued the Homily against Disobedience *in the following year (the primary author was apparently Bishop John Jewel). The homily was later reprinted in* Certain Sermons or Homilies Appointed to Be Read in Churches *(1571). As the title indicates, the Tudor homilies were intended to be read from the pulpit (or used as guidelines for sermons) in all the churches in England on a regular basis. The* Homily against Disobedience *served as a powerful and insistent affirmation of the divine right of kings—a doctrine that is echoed repeatedly in Marlowe's play by King Edward and his supporters in their struggles against the rebellious barons.*

As God the Creator and Lord of all things appointed his angels and heavenly creatures in all obedience to serve and to honor his Majesty, so was it his will that man, his chief creature upon the earth, should live under the obedience of him his Creator and Lord; and for that cause God, as soon as he had created man, gave unto him a certain precept and law, which he, being yet in the state of innocency and remaining in Paradise, should observe as a pledge and token of his due and bounden obedience, with denunciation of death if he did transgress and break the said law and commandment. . . . Whereby it is evident that obedience is the principal virtue of all virtues, and indeed the very root of all virtues, and the cause of all felicity.

But as all felicity and blessedness should have continued with the continuance of obedience, so with the breach of obedience and breaking in of rebellion, all vices and miseries did withal break in and overwhelm the world. The first author of which rebellion, the root of all vices and mother

---

39. Selections are from *An Homily against Disobedience and Willful Rebellion* (London, 1570). Spelling and punctuation have been modernized.

of all mischiefs, was Lucifer, first God's most excellent creature and most bounden subject, who, by rebelling against the Majesty of God, of the brightest and most glorious angel is become the blackest and most foulest fiend and devil, and from the height of heaven is fallen into the pit and bottom of hell. Here you may see the first author and founder of rebellion, and the reward thereof. Here you may see the grand captain and father of all rebels, who, persuading the following of his rebellion against God their creator and lord, unto our first parents, Adam and Eve, brought them in high displeasure with God, wrought their exile and banishment out of Paradise, a place of all pleasure and goodness, into this wretched earth and vale of all misery. . . . Thus became rebellion, as you see, both the first and greatest, and the very root of all other sins, and the first and principal cause both of all worldly and bodily miseries, sorrows, diseases, sicknesses, and deaths, and, which is infinitely worse than all these, as is said, the very cause of death and damnation eternal also.

After this breach of obedience to God and rebellion against his Majesty, all mischiefs and miseries breaking in therewith and overflowing the world, lest all things should come unto confusion and utter ruin, God forthwith, by laws given unto mankind, repaired again the rule and order of obedience thus by rebellion overthrown; and, besides the obedience due unto his Majesty, he not only ordained that in families and households the wife should be obedient unto her husband, the children unto their parents, the servants unto their masters, but also, when mankind increased and spread itself more largely over the world, he by his Holy Word did constitute and ordain in cities and countries several and special governors and rulers, unto whom the residue[40] of his people should be obedient.

As in reading of the Holy Scriptures we shall find in very many and almost infinite places, as well of the Old Testament as of the New, that kings and princes, as well the evil as the good, do reign by God's ordinance, and that subjects are bound to obey them; that God doth give princes wisdom, great power, and authority; that God defendeth them against their enemies, and destroyeth their enemies horribly; that the anger and displeasure of the prince is as the roaring of a lion, and the very messenger of death; and that the subject that provoketh him to displeasure sinneth against his own soul; with many other things concerning both the authority of princes and the duty of subjects.

But here let us rehearse two special places out of the New Testament, which may stand in stead of all other. The first out of St. Paul's Epistle to the Romans, and the thirteenth chapter, where he writeth thus unto all

---

40. *residue*: remainder.

subjects: "Let every soul be subject unto the higher powers, for there is no power but of God, and the powers that be are ordained of God. Whosoever therefore resisteth the power, resisteth the ordinance of God; and they that resist shall receive to themselves damnation. For princes are not to be feared for good works, but for evil. Wilt thou then be without fear of the power? Do well, so shalt thou have praise of the same. For he is the minister of God for thy wealth. But if thou do evil, fear; for he beareth not the sword for naught; for he is the minister of God to take vengeance upon him that doth evil. Wherefore you must be subject, not because of wrath only, but also for conscience sake. For this cause you pay also tribute, for they are God's ministers, serving for the same purpose. Give to every man therefore his duty: tribute to whom tribute belongeth; custom to whom custom is due; fear to whom fear belongeth; honor to whom you owe honor" [Rom. 13:1–7]. Thus far are St. Paul's words. The second place is in St. Peter's first Epistle, and the second chapter, whose words are these: "Submit yourselves unto all manner [of] ordinance of man for the Lord's sake, whether it be unto the king, as unto the chief head, either unto rulers, as unto them that are sent of him for the punishment of evildoers. . . . Honor all men, love brotherly fellowship, fear God, honor the king. Servants, obey your masters with fear, not only if they be good and courteous, but also though they be froward"[41] [1 Pet. 2:13–18]. Thus far out of St. Peter. . . .

And as God himself, being of an infinite majesty, power, and wisdom, ruleth and governeth all things in heaven and in earth, as the universal Monarch and only King and Emperor over all . . . so hath he constituted, ordained, and set earthly princes over particular kingdoms and dominions in earth, both for the avoiding of all confusion, which else would be in the world if it should be without such governors, and for the great quiet and benefit of earthly men their subjects, and also that the princes themselves in authority, power, wisdom, providence, and righteousness in government of people and countries committed to their charge, should resemble his heavenly governance, as the majesty of heavenly things may by the baseness of earthly things be shadowed and resembled. . . .

What shall subjects do then? Shall they obey valiant, stout, wise, and good princes, and condemn, disobey, and rebel . . . against undiscreet and evil governors? God forbid. For first, what a perilous thing were it to commit unto the subjects the judgment [of] which prince is wise and godly, and his government good, and which is otherwise. As though the foot must judge of the head, an enterprise very heinous, and must needs breed rebellion. For who else be they that are most inclined to rebellion,

---

41. *froward*: harsh and demanding.

but such haughty spirits? . . . What an unworthy matter were it then to make the naughtiest subjects, and most inclined to rebellion and all evil, judges over their princes, over their government, and over their councilors, to determine which of them be good or tolerable, and which be evil and so intolerable that they must needs be removed by rebels, being ever ready as the naughtiest subjects soonest to rebel against the best princes, specially if they be young in age, women in sex, or gentle and courteous in government. . . . But whereas indeed a rebel is worse than the worst prince, and rebellion worse than the worst government of the worst prince that hitherto hath been, both are rebels . . . and rebellion an unfit and unwholesome medicine to reform any small lacks in a prince, or to cure any little griefs in government, such lewd remedies being far worse than any other maladies and disorders that can be in the body of a commonwealth. . . .

Nay let us either deserve to have a good prince, or let us patiently suffer and obey such as we deserve. And whether the prince be good or evil, let us according to the counsel of the Holy Scriptures pray for the prince, for his continuance and increase in goodness if he be good, and for his amendment if he be evil.

John Ponet, *A Short Treatise of Politic Power* (1556)[42]

In medieval and early modern Europe, the doctrine of divine right was never uniformly accepted in theory or in practice. In the thirteenth century, St. Thomas Aquinas argued that it is not sinful for subjects to depose a tyrant king in the interest of the common good (see Summa Theologiae *II.2.42). Resistance to divine right, however, grew in intensity during the Reformation, especially among Protestants living under Catholic monarchs.*

John Ponet (c. 1514–1556) was the bishop of Winchester and an ardent Protestant reformer. When the Catholic Queen Mary ascended to the throne in 1553, Ponet was deprived of his office. He went into exile on the continent, and he eventually settled in Strasburg, where he wrote A Short Treatise of Politic Power *(published anonymously in the year of his death). Basing his arguments on biblical and historical precedents, as well as Greek and Roman concepts of natural law, Ponet argues against the doctrine of divine right and in favor of a nonsacred and nonsacramental view of royal authority. Ponet never justifies popular insurrection, but he claims that the nobles and church authorities have the right to depose or kill a tyrant king—and he cites King Edward II as an example: "they deprived King Edward the Second, because without law he killed his subjects, spoiled them of their goods, and*

42. Selections are from John Ponet, *A Short Treatise of Politic Power* (Strasburg, 1556). Spelling and punctuation have been modernized.

wasted the treasure of the realm." The treatise would have been welcomed by many Protestants during the reign of the Catholic Mary, but Ponet's arguments against divine right fell out of favor during the reign of Elizabeth (a Protestant monarch who supported divine right).

In Marlowe's play the issue of tyranny extends beyond the king and thus becomes murky and problematic. King Edward is twice called a "tyrant" by the nobles (1.2.3, 3.4.21), but the nobleman Mortimer is also called a "tyrant" (4.7.91, 5.3.36), and indeed Mortimer proves more ruthless than the king he deposes.

Chapter VI: Whether It Be Lawful to Depose an Evil Governor, and Kill a Tyrant

As there is no better nor happier commonwealth, nor no greater blessing of God, than where one ruleth if he be a good, just, and godly man; so is there no worse nor none more miserable, nor greater plague of God, than where one ruleth that is evil, unjust, and ungodly. . . . And as a good physician earnestly seeketh the health of his patient and a shipmaster the wealth and safeguard of those he hath in his ship, so doth a good governor seek the wealth of those he ruleth. And therefore the people, feeling the benefit coming by good governors, used in time past to call such good governors, fathers; and gave them no less honor than children owe to their parents. An evil person coming to the government of any state, either by usurpation or by election or by succession, utterly neglecting the cause why kings, princes, and other governors in commonwealths be made (that is, the wealth of the people) seeketh only or chiefly his own profit and pleasure. And as a sow coming into a fair garden rooteth up all the fair and sweet flowers and wholesome simples, leaving nothing behind, but her own filthy dirt; so doth an evil governor subvert the laws and orders, or maketh them to be wrenched or racked to serve his affections, that they can no longer do their office. He spoileth the people of their goods, either by open violence, making his ministers to take it from them without payment therefore, or promising and never paying, or craftily under the name of loans, benevolences, contributions, and such like gay painted words. . . . And when he hath it, consumeth it, not to the benefit and profit of the commonwealth, but on whores, whoremongers, dicing, carding, banqueting, unjust wars, and such like evils and mischiefs, wherein he delighteth. . . .

Now for as much as there is no express positive law for punishment of a tyrant among Christian men, the question is, whether it be lawful to kill such a monster and cruel beast covered with the shape of a man. And first for the better and more plain proof of this matter, the manifold and continual examples that have been from time to time of the deposing of kings and killing of tyrants do most certainly confirm it to be most true, just, and consonant to God's judgment. The history of kings in the Old Testament is full of it. And as Cardinal Pole[43] truly citeth, England lacketh not the practice and experience of the same. For they deprived King Edward the Second, because without law he killed his subjects, spoiled them of their goods, and wasted the treasure of the realm. And upon what just causes Richard the Second was thrust out, and Henry the Fourth put in his place, I refer it to their own judgment. Denmark also now in our days did nobly the like act, when they deprived Christian the Tyrant,[44] and committed him to perpetual prison.

. . . And this law of nature to depose and punish wicked governors hath not been only received and exercised in politic matters, but also in the church. For the canonists (the pope's own champions), grounding themselves upon this law of nature, say that popes who may be in deed (by their saying) the lieutenants of the devil, albeit they call themselves the vicars of God, may be deprived by the body of the church. And so at one clap, in the council held in Constance in Germany in the year of our Lord 1415, were three popes popped out of their places—Gregory, John, and Benedict—and the fourth (called Martin the fifth) chosen. . . .

Now if it be lawful for the body of the Church to depose and punish a pope, being the chief priest, anointed not on the arm or shoulder, as kings be, but on the head and hands, to declare a higher authority than kings have; nor crowned with a simple crown, as emperors and kings be, but with a triple crown, to show his regality and power above all others; how much more by the like arguments, reasons, and authority may emperors, kings, princes and other governors abusing their office be deposed and removed out of their places and offices by the body or state of the realm or commonwealth? . . .

Kings, princes, and governors have their authority of the people, as all laws, usages, and policies do declare and testify. For in some places and countries they have more and greater authority, in some places less. And in some the people have not given this authority to any other, but retain and exercise it themselves. And is any man so unreasonable to deny that the whole may do as much as they have permitted one member to do? Or those that have appointed an office upon trust, have not authority upon just occasion (as the abuse of it) to take away that they gave? All laws do agree

43. Cardinal Reginald Pole was the Catholic archbishop of Canterbury from 1556 to 1558, during the reign of Queen Mary I.

44. Christian the Tyrant became the king of Denmark and Norway in 1513 but was deposed by the nobility in 1523.

that men may revoke their proxies and letters of attorney when it pleaseth them, much more when they see their proctors and attorneys abuse it.

But now to prove the later part of this question affirmatively, that it is lawful to kill a tyrant, there is no man can deny, but that the Ethnics[45] (albeit they had not the right and perfect true knowledge of God) were endued with the knowledge of the law of nature. For it is no private law to a few or certain people, but common to all; not written in books, but grafted in the hearts of men; not made by man, but ordained of God; which we have not learned, received or read, but have taken, sucked, and drawn it out of nature; where unto we are not taught, but made; not instructed, but seasoned; and (as St. Paul sayeth) man's conscience bearing witness of it.[46]

This law testifieth to every man's conscience, that it is natural to cut away an incurable member, which (being suffered) would destroy the whole body. Kings, princes, and other governors, albeit they are the heads of a politic body, yet they are not the whole body. And though they be the chief members, yet they are but members; neither are the people ordained for them, but they are ordained for the people. . . .

Vindiciae contra Tyrannos: A Defense of Liberty against Tyrants (1579)[47]

On the evening before St. Bartholomew's Day in 1572, hundreds of Protestants were massacred by Catholics on the streets of Paris, and in the weeks that followed thousands of Protestants were killed throughout France. The horrific events inspired a series of treatises against the Catholic King Charles IX of France (and his mother Catherine de Medici). The most influential and widely read of these treatises was the Defense of Liberty against Tyrants, *published in Latin in 1579, followed by a French edition in 1581. Like John Ponet's* Short Treatise, *the* Defense of Liberty *rejects the sacred and sacramental concept of royal authority, arguing (at greater length and with a higher level of political subtlety) in favor of popular sovereignty, limited royal power, and the right of the people (by way of Parliament) to depose a tyrannical and immoral king.*

The title page lists the author as "Junius Brutus," a politically charged pseudonym, and a double reference to two famous Romans who fought against tyranny: Lucius Junius Brutus (who deposed the last king of Rome,

---

45. Ethnics: pagans (ancient Greeks and Romans).

46. See 2 Corinthians 3:2–3.

47. Selections are from the first English translation: *Vindiciae contra Tyrannos: A Defense of Liberty against Tyrants* (1579; translated into English, London, 1648). Spelling and punctuation have been modernized.

Tarquin the Proud, and established the Roman Republic in 509 BC) and Marcus Junius Brutus (who participated in the assassination of Julius Caesar in 44 BC). The Defense of Liberty *was probably written by Hubert Languet or his friend Phillippe de Mornay—both were Huguenots (French Protestants) who wanted to limit the power of the Catholic king. Though the treatise anticipates some of the arguments in the social contract theories of Hobbes and Locke, the foundational arguments in the* Defense of Liberty *are primarily biblical and theological (and thus more akin to the contrary arguments in the Elizabethan* Homily against Disobedience*). Moreover, the arguments are not entirely new. The* Defense of Liberty *reaffirms and extends the traditional rights of the nobility and Parliament—rights that naturally tended to conflict with the powers of the king.*

Marlowe's play straddles the political fault line between the powers of the king and the rights of the nobility (an ongoing tension that was never resolved in medieval and early modern Europe). The rebellious barons in the play do not articulate a political theory, but their threats against King Edward often cohere with the arguments found in the Defense of Liberty. *Elizabethans would likely have responded to the treatise with conflicted reactions: Many would have felt sympathy for the Protestant cause in France, but many (not all) would have been wary of the radical arguments against the doctrine of divine right.*

Whether subjects are bound and ought to obey princes, if they command that which is against the law of God

This question happily may seem at the first view to be altogether superfluous and unprofitable, for that it seems to make a doubt of an axiom always held infallible amongst Christians, confirmed by many testimonies in Holy Scripture, divers examples of the histories of all ages, and by the death of all the holy martyrs. For it may be well demanded wherefore Christians have endured so many afflictions, but that they were always persuaded that God must be obeyed simply and absolutely, and kings with this exception, that they command not that which is repugnant to the law of God. Otherways wherefore should the apostles have answered that God must rather be obeyed than men?[48] And also seeing that only the will of God is always just, and that of men may be, and is, oftentimes unjust, who can doubt but that we must always obey God's commandments without any exception, and men's ever with limitation? But for so much as there are many princes in these days, calling themselves Christians, which arrogantly assume an unlimited power, over which God himself hath no command,

---

48. The marginal gloss refers to Acts 4:19.

and that they have no want of flatterers which adore them as gods upon earth, many others also, which for fear, or by constraint, either seem, or else do believe, that princes ought to be obeyed in all things, and by all men. . . .

Now is there any man that sees not this: if a man disobey a prince commanding that which is wicked and unlawful, he shall presently be esteemed a rebel, a traitor, and guilty of high treason? Our Savior Christ, the apostles, and all the Christians of the primitive church were charged with these calumnies.[49] If any, after the example of Ezra and Nehemiah, dispose himself to the building of the temple of the Lord, it will be said he aspires to the crown, hatches innovations, and seeks the ruin of the state. Then you shall presently see a million of these minions and flatterers of princes tickling their ears with an opinion, that if they once suffer this temple to be rebuilded, they may bid their kingdom farewell, and never look to raise impost[50] or taxes on these men. But what a madness is this! There are no estates which ought to be esteemed firm and stable but those in whom the temple of God is built, and which are indeed the temple itself, and these we may truly call kings which reign with God, seeing that it is by him only that kings reign.

On the contrary, what beastly foolishness it is to think that the state and kingdom cannot subsist if God Almighty be not excluded, and his temple demolished. From hence proceeds so many tyrannous enterprises, unhappy and tragic deaths of kings, and ruins of people. If these sycophants knew what difference there is between God and Caesar, between the King of Kings, and a simple king, between the lord and the vassal, and what tributes this lord requires of his subjects, and what authority he gives to kings over those his subjects, certainly so many princes would not strive to trouble the kingdom of God, and we should not see some of them precipitated from their thrones by the just instigation of the Almighty, revenging himself on them, in the midst of their greatest strength, and the people should not be sacked and pillaged and trodden down.

It then belongs to princes to know how far they may extend their authority, and to subjects in what they may obey them, lest the one encroaching on that jurisdiction, which no way belongs to them, and the others obeying him which commandeth further than he ought, they be both chastised when they shall give an account thereof before another judge. Now the end and scope of the question propounded, whereof the Holy Scripture shall principally give the resolution, is that which followeth. The question is, if subjects be bound to obey kings in case they command

---

49. *calumnies*: slanderous misrepresentations.

50. *impost*: a type of tax.

that which is against the law of God . . . to which of the two (God or king) must we rather obey? . . .

It may be that the flatterers of the court will reply that God has resigned his power unto kings, reserving heaven for himself, and allowing the earth to them to reign, and govern there according to their own fancies. . . . This discourse, I say, is worthy of that execrable Domitian who (as Suetonius recites)[51] would be called God and Lord, but altogether unworthy of the ears of a Christian prince, and of the mouths of good subjects. That sentence of God Almighty must always remain irrevocably true—"I will not give My glory to any other" [Isaiah 42:8]— that is, no man shall have such absolute authority, but I will always remain Sovereign. . . .

Now if we consider what is the duty of vassals, we shall find that what may be said of them agrees properly to kings. The vassal receives his fee[52] of his lord with right of justice, and charge to serve him in his wars. The king is established by the Lord God, the King of Kings, to the end [that] he should administer justice to his people and defend them against all their enemies. The vassal receives laws and conditions from his sovereign. God commands the king to observe his laws and to have them always before his eyes, promising that he and his successors shall possess long the kingdom if they be obedient, and, on the contrary, that their reign shall be of small continuance if they prove rebellious to their sovereign king. The vassal obligeth himself by oath unto his lord, and swears that he will be faithful and obedient. In like manner, the king promises solemnly to command according to the express law of God. Briefly, the vassal loses his fee if he commit felony, and by law forfeiteth all his privileges. In the like case the king loses his right, and many times his realm also, if he despise God, if he complot with his enemies, and if he commit felony against that Royal Majesty. . . .

Kings are made by the people

We have showed before that it is God that doth appoint kings, which chooseth them, which gives the kingdom to them. Now we say that the people establish kings, putteth the scepter into their hands, and with their suffrages approveth the election. God would have it done in this manner to the end that the kings should acknowledge that after God they held their power and sovereignty from the people, and that it might the rather

51. *Domitian* was a Roman emperor (81–96 AD), and *Suetonius* a Roman historian (c. 69–122 AD).

52. *fee*: a fief, usually in the land, that a lord grants his vassal in return for military services.

induce them to apply and address the utmost of their care and thoughts for the profit of the people, without being puffed with any vain imagination that they were formed of any matter more excellent than other men. . . . But let them remember and know that they are of the same mold and condition as others, raised from the earth by the voice and acclamations now as it were upon the shoulders of the people unto their thrones, that they might afterwards bear on their own shoulders the greatest burdens of the commonwealth. . . .

The whole body of the people is above the king

Now, seeing that the people choose and establish their kings, it follows that the whole body of the people is above the king. For it is a thing most evident, that he which is established by another is accounted under him that has established him, and he which receives his authority from another is less than he from whom he derives his power. . . . In a commonwealth, commonly compared to a ship, the king holds the place of pilot, the people in general are owners of the vessel, obeying the pilot, whilst he is careful of the public good; although this pilot neither is nor ought to be esteemed other than servant to the public; as a judge or general in war differs little from other officers, but that he is bound to bear greater burdens, and expose himself to more dangers. . . .

Besides, the kingdom of France has the peers (so called either for that they are the king's companions or because they are the fathers of the commonwealth) taking their denominations from the several provinces of the kingdom, in whose hands the king at his inauguration takes his oath as if all the people of the kingdom were in them present, which shows that these twelve peers are above the king. They on the other side swear that they will preserve not the king but the crown, that they will assist the commonwealth with their counsel, and therefore will be present with their best abilities to counsel the prince both in peace and war, as appears plainly in the patentee of their peership. . . .

The assembly of the three estates

Besides all this, anciently[53] every year, and since less often, to wit when some urgent necessity required it, the general or three estates were assembled, where all the provinces and towns of any worth, to wit, the burgesses, nobles, and ecclesiastical persons, did all of them send their deputies, and there they did publicly deliberate and conclude of that which concerned

53. *anciently*: traditionally.

the public state. Always the authority of this assembly was such that what was there determined, whether it were to treat peace, or make war, or create a regent in the kingdom, or impose some new tribute, it was ever held firm and inviolable; nay, which is more by the authority of this assembly, the kings convinced of loose intemperance, or of insufficiency, or so great a charge, or tyranny, were disthronized;[54] yea, their whole races were forever excluded from their succession to the kingdom, no more nor less, as their progenitors were by the same authority formerly called to that administration of the same kingdom. Those whom the consent and approbation of the estates had formerly raised were by the dissent and disallowing of the same afterwards cast down. Those which tracing in the virtuous steps of their ancestors were called to that dignity, as if it had been their inheritance, were driven out and disinherited for their degenerate ingratitude, and for that being tainted with insupportable vices, they made themselves incapable and unworthy of such honor.

LOVE, FRIENDSHIP, AND HOMOEROTICISM

Plato, *The Symposium* (c. 380 BC)[55]

Most of the works of Plato were unknown to Western Europe until the fifteenth century, when Byzantine scholars, fleeing the Turkish conquest of Constantinople in 1453, immigrated to Italian city-states and brought with them the texts of Plato, as well as expertise in ancient Greek. By the sixteenth century, newly printed editions of the works of Plato were widely available in the West. At the University of Cambridge, Marlowe would have had ready access to Henri Estienne's 1578 edition of the dialogues of Plato in Greek, as well as Marsilio Ficino's 1484 edition of the works of Plato translated into Latin.

Plato's views on homoerotic desire seem inconsistent and continue to provoke scholarly debate. In The Republic *he forbids sexual relations among the guardians (see III.403a–c), and in* The Laws *he refers to same-sex relations as an offense against nature that must be forbidden by law (see I.636a–e and VIII.838e–839d). Plato's most detailed account of the subject,*

54. *disthronized*: deposed.

55. Selections are from Plato, *Symposium*, trans. Alexander Nehamas and Paul Woodruff (Indianapolis: Hackett Publishing, 1989), 27–29, 57–60. By permission of the publisher.

however, is in The Symposium—*a text that stands apart as the most positive and philosophically developed treatment of homoerotic love in the ancient world. Early modern writers, such as Montaigne, tended to see Plato's* Symposium *as a definitive description of Greek attitudes and practices.[56] Montaigne's assumptions are based on scant evidence and are certainly too reductive to account for the variety of attitudes and practices in ancient Greece. Nevertheless, Plato's* Symposium *(when read in isolation) seems to represent homoerotic desire as entirely normative and natural—and indeed superior to heterosexual desire. In the dialogue, the speakers take a variety of positions, but all speak of homoerotic desire with frank and unabashed acceptance. Even Socrates argues that the highest form of love—love of transcendent beauty and goodness—begins with homoerotic physical attraction.*

In The Symposium *(the title means "drinking party"), Plato describes a social gathering of Socrates and his friends in which each man gives a speech in praise of love. Phaedrus, the first to speak, claims that Eros, the god of love, is one of the most ancient gods (after Chaos and Earth), and he claims that love is the most powerful force in inspiring human beings to attain virtue. In the next speech, Pausanias responds by claiming that there are two types of love, expressed in the two goddesses named Aphrodite. Common Aphrodite is the goddess of carnal love, and she inspires those who seek physical satisfaction with women or young boys. Heavenly Aphrodite inspires those who seek a higher, intellectual love: Such relationships involve a man and a more mature boy (who shows the traces of a beard), and the relationship is beneficial to both. The man enjoys the favors of the boy, and the boy is instructed by the man in virtue and wisdom. Eryximachus, the physician, is the next to speak, and he describes love not only as a force in human nature but as a force that pervades the entire universe: animals, plants, the seasons, and even the movements of planets and stars.*

Aristophanes follows with a mythical explanation of love. He claims that originally all humans were double creatures—round in shape, with two faces, four arms, four legs, and two sets of sexual organs. According to Aristophanes, there were three types: double males, double females, and hybrid male-females. They were all fast and powerful (as they spun around in cartwheel motions), but at one point they tried to ascend to heaven to depose the gods. Fearing their power, Zeus used his thunderbolts to split them into halves. He then commanded Apollo to stitch together their wounds and turn their faces around in the direction of their stomachs. Zeus then took pity on them by moving their genitals to the front so they could copulate with each other and breed

---

56. See Montaigne's essay, *On Friendship*, in Related Texts.

inwardly. (Originally, the double creatures cast their seed on the ground, and their offspring were born out of the earth.)

After narrating the story, Aristophanes explains that love is the desire for one human being to reunite with his or her other half.

[The speech of Aristophanes]

Each of us, then, is a "matching half" of a human whole, because each was sliced like a flatfish, two out of one, and each of us is always seeking the half that matches him. That's why a man who is split from the double sort (which used to be called "androgynous") runs after women. Many lecherous men have come from this class, and so do the lecherous women who run after men. Women who are split from a woman, however, pay no attention at all to men; they are oriented more towards women, and lesbians come from this class. People who are split from a male are male-oriented. While they are boys, because they are chips off the male block, they love men and enjoy lying with men and being embraced by men; those are the best of boys and lads, because they are the most manly in their nature. Of course, some say such boys are shameless, but they're lying. It's not because they have no shame that such boys do this, you see, but because they are bold and brave and masculine, and they tend to cherish what is like themselves. Do you want me to prove it? Look, these are the only kind of boys who grow up to be politicians. When they're grown men, they are lovers of young men, and they naturally pay no attention to marriage or to making babies, except insofar as they are required by local custom. They, however, are quite satisfied to live their lives with one another unmarried. In every way, then, this sort of man grows up as a lover of young men and a lover of Love, always rejoicing in his own kind.

And so, when a person meets the half that is his very own, whatever his orientation, whether it's to young men or not, then something wonderful happens: the two are struck from their senses by love, by a sense of belonging to one another, and by desire, and they don't want to be separated from one another, not even for a moment.

These are the people who finish out their lives together and still cannot say what it is they want from one another. No one would think it is the intimacy of sex—that mere sex is the reason each lover takes so great and deep a joy in being with the other. It's obvious that the soul of every lover longs for something else; his soul cannot say what it is, but like an oracle it has a sense of what it wants, and like an oracle it hides behind a riddle. Suppose two lovers are lying together and Hephaestus[57] stands over them

---

57. *Hephaestus*: the craftsman god.

with his mending tools, asking, "What is it you human beings really want from each other?" And suppose they're perplexed, and he asks them again: "Is this your heart's desire, then—for the two of you to become parts of the same whole, as near as can be, and never to separate, day or night? Because if that's your desire, I'd like to weld you together and join you into something that is naturally whole, so that the two of you are made into one. Then the two of you would share one life, as long as you lived, because you would be one being, and by the same token, when you died, you would be one and not two in Hades, having died a single death. Look at your love, and see if this is what you desire: wouldn't this be all the good fortune you could want?"

Surely you can see that no one who received such an offer would turn it down; no one would find anything else that he wanted. Instead, everyone would think he'd found out at last what he had always wanted: to come together and melt together with the one he loves, so that one person emerged from two. Why should this be so? It's because, as I said, we used to be complete wholes in our original nature, and now "Love" is the name for our pursuit of wholeness, for our desire to be complete.

[*After Aristophanes, Agathon claims that Eros is not the oldest but instead the youngest of the gods, and he claims that love desires only the company of the young and the beautiful. Socrates praises the eloquence of Agathon's speech, but he argues that love is not a god at all. Socrates claims that a woman named Diotima taught him all that he knows about love. According to Diotima, love is the offspring of Poverty and Resourcefulness. Love is a spirit (above humans but below the gods) that does not possess beauty but desires beauty, and is resourceful in trying to attain beauty. Love does not seek its other half (as in the myth of Aristophanes) but instead seeks a higher ideal of beauty. Diotima claims that all lovers are "pregnant" and desire to give birth to that which is beautiful. Ordinary male lovers turn to women and give birth to children, but the lovers of ideal beauty become pregnant in their souls and give birth to forms of beauty that are indeed immortal, such as the poetry of Homer and the law code of Solon. Socrates then explains the highest mysteries of love, as revealed to him by Diotima.*]

[The speech by Socrates]

[Quoting Diotima:] "Even you, Socrates, could probably come to be initiated into these rites of love. But as for the purpose of these rites when they are done correctly—that is the final and highest mystery, and I don't know if you are capable of it. I myself will tell you," she said, "and I won't stint any effort. And you must try to follow if you can.

"A lover who goes about this matter correctly must begin in his youth to devote himself to beautiful bodies. First, if the leader[58] leads aright, he should love one body and beget beautiful ideas there; then he should realize that the beauty of any one body is brother to the beauty of any other and that if he is to pursue beauty of form he'd be very foolish not to think that the beauty of all bodies is one and the same. When he grasps this, he must become a lover of all beautiful bodies, and he must think that this wild gaping after just one body is a small thing and despise it.

"After this he must think that the beauty of people's souls is more valuable than the beauty of their bodies, so that if someone is decent in his soul, even though he is scarcely blooming in his body, our lover must be content to love and care for him and to seek to give birth to such ideas as will make young men better. The result is that our lover will be forced to gaze at the beauty of activities and laws and to see that all this is akin to itself, with the result that he will think that the beauty of bodies is a thing of no importance. After customs he must move on to various kinds of knowledge. The result is that he will see the beauty of knowledge and be looking mainly not at beauty in a single example—as a servant would who favored the beauty of a little boy or a man or a single custom (being a slave, of course, he's low and small-minded)—but the lover is turned to the great sea of beauty, and, gazing upon this, he gives birth to many gloriously beautiful ideas and theories, in unstinting love of wisdom, until, having grown and been strengthened there, he catches sight of such knowledge, and it is the knowledge of such beauty. . . .

"Try to pay attention to me," she said, "as best you can. You see, the man who has been thus far guided in matters of Love, who has beheld beautiful things in the right order and correctly, is coming now to the goal of Loving: all of a sudden he will catch sight of something wonderfully beautiful in its nature; that, Socrates, is the reason for all his earlier labors:

"First, it always is and neither comes to be nor passes away, neither waxes nor wanes. Second, it is not beautiful this way and ugly that way, nor beautiful at one time and ugly at another, nor beautiful in relation to one thing and ugly in relation to another; nor is it beautiful here but

---

58. *The leader.* Love.

ugly there, as it would be if it were beautiful for some people and ugly for others. Nor will the beautiful appear to him in the guise of a face or hands or anything else that belongs to the body. It will not appear to him as one idea or one kind of knowledge. It is not anywhere in another thing, as in an animal, or in earth, or in heaven, or in anything else, but itself by itself with itself, it is always one in form; and all the other beautiful things share in that, in such a way that when those others come to be or pass away, this does not become the least bit smaller or greater nor suffer any change. So when someone rises by these stages, through loving boys correctly, and begins to see this beauty, he has almost grasped his goal. This is what it is to go aright, or be led by another, into the mystery of Love: one goes always upwards for the sake of this Beauty, starting out from beautiful things and using them like rising stairs: from one body to two and from two to all beautiful bodies, then from beautiful bodies to beautiful customs, and from customs to learning beautiful things, and from these lessons he arrives in the end at this lesson, which is learning of this very Beauty, so that in the end he comes to know just what it is to be beautiful.

"And there in life, Socrates, my friend," said the woman from Mantinea, "there if anywhere should a person live his life, beholding that Beauty. If you once see that, it won't occur to you to measure beauty by gold or clothing or beautiful boys and youths—who, if you see them now, strike you out of your senses, and make you, you and many others, eager to be with the boys you love and look at them forever, if there were any way to do that, forgetting food and drink, everything but looking at them and being with them. But how would it be, in our view," she said, "if someone got to see the Beautiful itself, absolute, pure, unmixed, not polluted by human flesh or colors or any other great nonsense of mortality, but if he could see the divine Beauty itself in its one form? Do you think it would be a poor life for a human being to look there and to behold it by that which he ought,[59] and to be with it? Or haven't you remembered," she said, "that in that life alone, when he looks at Beauty in the only way that Beauty can be seen—only then will it become possible for him to give birth not to images of virtue (because he's in touch with no images), but to true virtue (because he is in touch with the true Beauty). The love of the gods belongs to anyone who has given birth to true virtue and nourished it, and if any human being could become immortal, it would be he."

This, Phaedrus and the rest of you, was what Diotima told me. I was persuaded. And once persuaded, I try to persuade others too that human nature can find no better workmate for acquiring this than Love. That's

---

59. *by that which he ought*: by the higher faculties of the mind.

why I say that every man must honor Love, why I honor the rites of Love myself and practice them with special diligence, and why I commend them to others. . . .

[At the end of Socrates's speech, the drunken Alcibiades arrives and begins to tease Socrates for sitting next to the young and handsome Agathon. In response, Socrates complains of the tempestuous and jealous nature of Alcibiades. After drinking more wine, Alcibiades agrees to give a speech in praise of Socrates. In a playfully mocking tone, he claims that Socrates has tormented him with philosophical speeches. Socrates has told him that his political career has been misspent and his life is not worth living. Alcibiades finds Socrates's speeches impossible to resist, but he admits that when he departs from Socrates he quickly reverts to his old ways of trying to curry favor with the Athenian crowd. Alcibiades also complains that Socrates is immune to his youthful charms and good looks, and to his dismay Socrates did not once make a sexual advance at him. Toward the end of his speech, Alcibiades's playful mockery turns to genuine praise as he describes Socrates's indifference to the needs of the flesh. In their military campaigns together, Socrates was never bothered by hunger, and in the coldest weather he wore only a light cloak and walked about in bare feet over icy ground. Socrates was also exceedingly courageous in battle and even saved the life of Alcibiades.

Marlowe's play refers to the intimate friendship between "Grave Socrates" and "wild Alcibiades" (1.4.397), characterizations derived primarily from Alcibiades's speech at the end of the Symposium, in which Socrates is indeed "Grave" in his self-control and dedication to the highest forms of human love, while Alcibiades is "wild" in his drunken recklessness and inability to appreciate true beauty and goodness.[60]]

---

60. Plato depicts the wild behavior of Alcibiades in the *Symposium* as a preview of things to come. The time frame of the dialogue is 417 BC. In the following year, Alcibiades convinced the Athenian assembly to send a military expedition to Sicily. Before the fleet departed, however, statues of the gods were vandalized in Athens, and Alcibiades and his followers were suspected of the impious desecrations. Alcibiades departed for Sicily but was soon called back to face charges. Instead of returning, Alcibiades fled to Sparta and served as a military adviser in Sparta's defeat of Athens.

Marcus Tullius Cicero, *Of Friendship* (44 BC)[61]

Marcus Tullius Cicero (106–43 BC) was one of the most widely read and admired ancient writers in early modern Europe. Not only was Cicero praised as a paragon of literary style and eloquence, but he was seen by Renaissance humanists as an ideal embodiment of the philosophical life combined with civic duty and active engagement in the world. In England his works were studied in grammar schools and were included in the curriculum at the universities of Cambridge and Oxford. His philosophical dialogue, Of Friendship, *was especially popular—printed in the English translation of John Tiptoft in 1481, followed by the translation of John Harrington in 1550. Marlowe, as a university student at Cambridge, certainly would have known the original Latin.*

Like Plato's Symposium, *Cicero's work is in dialogue form (though all the selections below are taken from the main speaker, Laelius, who describes his intimate friendship with the recently deceased Scipio Africanus the Younger). Cicero's philosophy of friendship is influenced not only by Plato (especially the* Lysis) *but also by Cicero's wide reading in the philosophy of Aristotle, the Stoics, and the Epicureans. The friendship that Cicero describes is never erotic or sexual but nevertheless involves the complete devotion of one man to another.*

Cicero's description of ideal friendship seems implicitly evoked throughout Edward II. *The terms "friend" and "friendship" appear fifty-eight times in the play. Moreover, Edward twice refers to Gaveston as his other "self" (see 1.1.142 and 1.4.118), a concept clearly developed in Cicero (and in Plato). The friendship of Edward and Gaveston can certainly be faulted—indeed, they are not especially virtuous men, as Cicero would require. And yet Edward and Gaveston may come closer to the ideals of Cicero than any other characters in the play.*

. . . Still, such is my enjoyment in the recollection of our friendship that I feel as if my life has been happy because it was spent with Scipio, with whom I shared my public and private cares; lived under the same roof at home; served in the same campaigns abroad, and enjoyed that wherein lies the whole essence of friendship—the most complete agreement in policy, in pursuits, and in opinions. Hence, I am not so much delighted by my

61. Selections are from Cicero's "Of Friendship," reprinted by permission of the publishers and the Trustees of the Loeb Classical Library, from *Cicero: Volume XX, De Senectute, De Amicitia, De Divination,* Loeb Classical Library, Vol. 154, translated by William Armistead Falconer (Cambridge, MA: Harvard University Press, 1923), pp. 125–35, 155–59, 179–89.

reputation for wisdom . . . as I am by the hope that the memory of our friendship will always endure; and this thought is the more pleasing to me because in the whole range of history only three or four pairs of friends are mentioned; and I venture to hope that among such instances the friendship of Scipio and Laelius will be known to posterity. . . .

This, however, I do feel first of all—that friendship cannot exist except among good men; nor do I go into that too deeply, as is done by those who . . . say that no one is good unless he is wise.[62] We may grant that; but they understand wisdom to be a thing such as no mortal man has yet attained. I, however, am bound to look at things as they are in the experience of everyday life and not as they are in fancy or in hope. Never could I say that Gaius Fabricius, Manius Curius, and Tiberius Coruncanius, whom our ancestors adjudged to be wise, were wise by such a standard as that. Therefore, let the Sophists keep their unpopular and unintelligible word to themselves, granting only that the men just named were good men. . . . Let us then proceed "with our own dull wits," as the saying is. Those who so act and so live as to give proof of loyalty and uprightness, of fairness and generosity; who are free from all passion, caprice, and insolence, and have great strength of character—men like those just mentioned—such men let us consider good, as they were accounted good in life, and also entitled to be called by that term because, in as far as that is possible for man, they follow Nature, who is the best guide to good living. . . .

For friendship is nothing else than an accord in all things, human and divine, conjoined with mutual goodwill and affection, and I am inclined to think that, with the exception of wisdom, no better thing has been given to man by the immortal gods. Some prefer riches, some good health, some power, some public honors, and many even prefer sensual pleasures. This last is the highest aim of brutes; the others are fleeting and unstable things and dependent less upon human foresight than upon the fickleness of fortune. Again, there are those who place the "chief good" in virtue and that is really a noble view; but this very virtue is the parent and preserver of friendship and without virtue friendship cannot exist at all. To proceed then, let us interpret the word "virtue" by the familiar usage of our everyday life and speech, and not in pompous phrase apply to it the precise standards which certain philosophers use; and let us include in the number of good men those who are so considered—men like Paulus, Cato, Gallus, Scipio, and Philus—who satisfy the ordinary standard of life; but let us pass by such men as are nowhere to be found at all.

62. Cicero is referring to philosophers such as Plato who attempted to define ideal and perfect virtues.

Therefore, among men like those just mentioned, friendship offers advantages almost beyond any power to describe. In the first place, how can life be what Ennius calls "the life worth living," if it does not repose on the mutual goodwill of a friend? What is sweeter than to have someone with whom you may dare discuss anything as if you were communing with yourself? How could your enjoyment in times of prosperity be so great if you did not have someone whose joy in them would be equal to your own? Adversity would indeed be hard to bear, without him to whom the burden would be heavier even than to yourself. In short, all other objects of desire are each, for the most part, adapted to a single end—riches, for spending; influence, for honor; public office, for reputation; pleasures, for sensual enjoyment; and health, for freedom from pain and full use of the bodily functions; but friendship embraces innumerable ends; turn where you will it is ever at your side; no barrier shuts it out; it is never untimely and never in the way. . . . I am not now speaking of the ordinary and commonplace friendship—delightful and profitable as it is—but of that pure and faultless kind, such as was that of the few whose friendships are known to fame. For friendship adds a brighter radiance to prosperity and lessens the burden of adversity by dividing and sharing it.

Seeing that friendship includes very many and very great advantages, it undoubtedly excels all other things in this respect, that it projects the bright ray of hope into the future, and does not suffer the spirit to grow faint or to fall. Again, he who looks upon a true friend, looks, as it were, upon a sort of image of himself. Wherefore friends, though absent, are at hand; though in need, yet abound; though weak, are strong; and—harder saying still—though dead, are yet alive; so great is the esteem on the part of their friends, the tender recollection and the deep longing that still attends them. These things make the death of the departed seem fortunate and the life of the survivors worthy of praise. But if you should take the bond of goodwill out of the universe no house or city could stand, nor would even the tillage of the fields abide. If that statement is not clear, then you may understand how great is the power of friendship and of concord from a consideration of the results of enmity and disagreement. For what house is so strong, or what state so enduring that it cannot be utterly overthrown by animosities and division? . . .

Therefore let this be ordained as the first law of friendship: Ask of friends only what is honorable; do for friends only what is honorable and without even waiting to be asked; let zeal be ever present, but hesitation absent; dare to give true advice with all frankness; in friendship let the influence of friends who are wise counsellors be paramount, and let that influence be employed in advising, not only with frankness, but, if the occasion demands, even with sternness, and let the advice be followed when given. I say this because certain men who, I am informed, are considered sages in Greece, have approved certain views, which, in my opinion, are astonishing (but there is nothing that those men will not pursue with their subtleties).[63] Some of these men teach that too much intimacy in friendships should be avoided, lest it be necessary for one man to be full of anxiety for many; that each one of us has business of his own, enough and to spare; that it is annoying to be too much involved in the affairs of other people; that it is best to hold the reins of friendship as loosely as possible, so that we may either draw them up or slacken them at will; for, they say, an essential of a happy life is freedom from care, and this the soul cannot enjoy if one man is, as it were, in travail for many.

Again, there are others, I am told, who, with even less of human feeling, maintain (and I briefly touched on this point just now) that friendships must be sought for the sake of the defense and aid they give and not out of goodwill and affection; therefore, that those least endowed with firmness of character and strength of body have the greatest longing for friendship; and consequently, that helpless women, more than men, seek its shelter, the poor more than the rich, and the unfortunate more than those who are accounted fortunate. O noble philosophy! Why, they seem to take the sun out of the universe when they deprive life of friendship, than which we have from the immortal gods no better, no more delightful boon. . . .

Wherefore, if distress of mind befalls a wise man (as it certainly does unless we assume that human sympathy has been rooted out of his heart), why should we remove friendship entirely from our lives in order that we may suffer no worries on its account? For when the soul is deprived of emotion, what difference is there—I do not say between man and the beasts of the field, but between man and a stock or a stone, or any such thing? . . .

But it is of the utmost importance in friendship that superior and inferior should stand on an equality. For oftentimes a certain pre-eminence does exist, as was that of Scipio in what I may call "our set." But he never affected any superiority over Philus, or Rupilius, or Mummius, or over his other friends of a lower rank. For example, his brother Quintus Maximus, a distinguished man, no doubt, though by no means his equal, was treated by him as a superior, because he was older than himself. Indeed Scipio desired that he might be the cause of enhancing the dignity of all his friends. And this course every man should adopt and imitate, so that if he is endowed with any superiority in virtue, intellect, or fortune he may impart it to his

63. Cicero has in mind Epicurean philosophers who advocated the avoidance of all sources of worry and anxiety in order to maximize contentment and pleasure.

relatives and share it with his next of kin; or if, for example, his parents are of a lowly station and his relatives are less favored in mind or estate than himself, he may increase the means of the one and be the source of honor and influence to the other. . . .

As, therefore, in the intimacy existing between friends and relatives the superior should put himself on a level with his inferior, so the latter ought not to grieve that he is surpassed by the former in intellect, fortune, or position. . . . Now, in the first place, you must render to each friend as much aid as you can, and, in the second place, as much as he whom you love and assist has the capacity to bear. For however eminent you may be, you cannot lead all your friends through the various grades to the highest official rank, as Scipio was able to do when he made Publius Rupilius consul, though he could not accomplish this result in the case of his brother, Lucius Rupilius. But even if you could bestow upon another any honor you chose, yet you must consider what he is able to bear.

. . . Now they are worthy of friendship who have within their own souls the reason for their being loved. A rare class indeed! And really everything splendid is rare, and nothing is harder to find than something which in all respects is a perfect specimen of its kind. But the majority of men recognize nothing whatever in human experience as good unless it brings some profit and they regard their friends as they do their cattle, valuing most highly those which give hope of the largest gain. Thus do they fail to attain that loveliest, most spontaneous friendship, which is desirable in and for itself; and they do not learn from their own experience what the power of such friendship is and are ignorant of its nature and extent. For everyone loves himself, not with a view of acquiring some profit for himself from his self-love, but because he is dear to himself on his own account; and unless this same feeling were transferred to friendship, the real friend would never be found; for he is, as it were, another self.

Now if it is evident in animals, whether of the air, the water, or the land, and whether tame or wild, first, that they love themselves—for this feeling is born alike in every living creature—and, secondly, that they require and eagerly search for other animals of their own kind to which they may attach themselves—and this they do with a longing in some degree resembling human love—then how much more, by the law of his nature, is this the case with man who both loves himself and uses his reason to seek out another whose soul he may so mingle with his own as almost to make one [soul] out of two! . . .

Michel de Montaigne, *Of Friendship* (1580)[64]

Of Friendship *appeared in Montaigne's first edition of his* Essays *in 1580 (and was expanded in the editions of 1588 and 1595). The essay focuses on the intimate friendship between Montaigne and Etienne de La Boétie, a judge, poet, translator, and political philosopher. The two men enjoyed a brief but intense friendship, cut short when La Boétie died at age thirty-three. Expanding on Cicero's ideal of friendship between adult males, Montaigne argues for the supreme value of friendship over all forms of family and marital relations.*

In Marlowe's play, Edward's exclusive devotion to Gaveston—to the neglect of his wife, his brother, and the barons of England—may be politically reckless and irresponsible but nevertheless resonates with the ideals of friendship that Montaigne explores in his essay.

To compare the affection toward women unto it [male friendship] . . . a man cannot, nor may it be placed in this rank. Her fire [of passions], I confess it . . . to be more active, more fervent, and more sharp. But it is a rash and wavering fire, waving and diverse, the fire of an ague[65] subject to fits and stints, and that hath but slender holdfast of us. . . . On the other side, friendship [between men] is enjoyed according as it is desired, it is neither bred nor nourished, nor increaseth but in jouissance,[66] as being spiritual, and the mind being refined by use and custom. . . . So are these two passions entered into me in knowledge one of another, but in comparison never: the first [male friendship] flying a high and keeping a proud pitch, disdainfully beholding the other to pass her points far under it.

Concerning marriage, besides that it is a covenant which hath nothing free but the entrance, the continuance being forced and constrained, depending elsewhere than from our will, and a match ordinarily concluded to other ends, a thousand strange knots are therein commonly to be unknit, able to break the web, and trouble the whole course of a lively affection. Whereas in friendship there is no commerce or business depending on the same, but itself. Seeing (to speak truly) that the ordinary sufficiency of women cannot answer this conference and communication, the nurse of this sacred bond; nor seem their minds strong enough to endure the

---

64. Selections are from the first English translation: *The Essays of Montaigne,* trans. John Florio (London, 1603). Spelling and punctuation have been modernized. Marlowe would have had access only to the 1580 and 1588 editions of Montaigne's *Essays.* Florio's translation is based on the slightly expanded 1595 edition.

65. *ague:* fever or sickness.

66. *jouissance:* joy, delight.

pulling of a knot so hard, so fast, and durable. And truly, if without that, such a genuine and voluntary acquaintance might be contracted where not only minds had this entire jouissance, but also bodies a share of the alliance, and where [a] man might wholly be engaged, it is certain that friendship would thereby be more complete and full. But this sex could never yet by any example attain unto it, and is by ancient schools rejected thence.

And this other Greek license[67] is justly abhorred by our customs, which notwithstanding—because according to use it had so necessary a disparity of ages and difference of offices between lovers—did no more sufficiently answer the perfect union and agreement which here we require. . . . For even the picture the Academy[68] makes of it will not (as I suppose) disavow me to say thus in her behalf: that this first fury, inspired by the son of Venus in the lover's heart upon the object of tender youth's flower . . . was simply grounded upon an external beauty, a false image of corporal imagination. For in the spirit it had no power, the sight whereof was yet concealed, which was but in his infancy and before the age of budding. For if this fury did seize upon a base-minded courage, the means of its pursuit were riches, gifts, favor to the advancement of dignities, and suchlike vile merchandise, which they reprove. If it fell into a more generous mind, the interpositions were likewise generous: philosophical instructions, documents to reverence religion, to obey the laws, to die for the good of his country, examples of valor, wisdom, and justice. The lover endeavoring and studying to make himself acceptable by the good grace and beauty of his mind (that of his body being long since decayed[69]), hoping by this mental society to establish a more firm and permanent bargain. When this pursuit attained the effect in his due season . . . then by the interposition of a spiritual beauty was the desire of a spiritual conception engendered in the beloved. . . . To conclude, all that can be alleged in favor of the Academy is to say that it was a love ending in friendship, a thing which hath no bad reference unto the Stoical definition of love: "That love is an endeavor of making friendship by the show of beauty" [Cicero, *Tusculan Disputations*].

I return to my description [of friendship] in a more equitable and equal manner: "Clearly friendships are to be judged by wits and ages already strengthened and confirmed" [Cicero, *Of Friendship*].[70] As for the rest, those

67. *Greek license*: pederastic love between men and boys.

68. The *Academy* was the school started by Plato. The lines that follow describe aspects of love as depicted in Plato's *Symposium*.

69. *Decayed* in this context means "aged" (not dead or decomposed).

70. Agreeing with Cicero, Montaigne argues for friendship that is *more equitable and equal*—between two mature men (not, as in Plato, between a mature man and a younger man).

we ordinarily call friends and amities are but acquaintances and familiarities tied together by some occasion or commodities by means whereof our minds are entertained. In the amity I speak of, they intermix and confound themselves one in the other with so universal a commixture that they wear out, and can no more find the seam that hath conjoined them together. If a man urge me to tell wherefore I loved him, I feel it cannot be expressed but by answering, "Because it was he, because it was myself." . . . We sought one another before ever we had seen one another, and by the reports we heard one of another . . . I think by some secret ordinance of the heavens we embraced one another by our names. And at our first meeting, which was by chance at a great feast and solemn meeting of a whole township, we found ourselves so surprised, so known, so acquainted, and so combinedly bound together, that from thenceforward nothing was so near unto us as one unto another. . . . Since it must continue so short a time, and begun so late (for we were both grown men, and he some years older than myself), there was no time to be lost.[71] And it was not to be modeled or directed by the pattern of regular and remiss friendship wherein so many precautions of a long and preallable[72] conversation are required.

. . . For this perfect amity I speak of is indivisible. Each man doth so wholly give himself unto his friend that he hath nothing left him to divide elsewhere. Moreover, he is grieved that he is [not] double, triple, or quadruple, and hath not many souls, or sundry wills, that he might confer them all upon this subject. Common friendships may be divided; a man may love beauty in one, facility of customs in another, liberality in one, and wisdom in another, paternity in this, fraternity in that man, and so forth. But this amity which possesseth the soul and sways it in all sovereignty, it is impossible it should be double. If two at one instant should require help, to which would you run? Should they crave contrary offices of you, what order would you follow? Should one commit a matter to your silence, which if the other knew would greatly profit him, what course would you take? Or how would you discharge yourself? A singular and principal friendship dissolveth all other duties and freeth all other obligations.

. . . But knowing how far such an amity is from the common use, and how seldom seen and rarely found, I look not to find a competent judge. For even the discourses which stern antiquity hath left us concerning this subject seem to me but faint and forceless in respect of the feeling I have of it. And in that point the effects exceed the very precepts of philosophy. . . .

---

71. Etienne de La Boétie (1530–1563) was three years older than Montaigne (1533–1592).

72. *preallable*: preliminary.

Ancient Menander accompted[73] him happy that had but met the shadow of a true friend. Verily he had reason to say so, especially if he had tasted of any. For truly, if I compare all the rest of my forepassed life, which although I have by the mere mercy of God passed at rest and ease, and, except [for] the loss of so dear a friend, free from all grievous affliction . . . if, as I say, I compare it all unto the four years I so happily enjoyed the sweet company and dear, dear society of that worthy man, it is nought but a vapor, nought but a dark and irksome light. Since the time I lost him . . . I do but languish, I do but sorrow. And even those pleasures all things present me with, instead of yielding me comfort, do but redouble the grief of his loss. We were copartners in all things. All things were with us at half; methinks I have stolen his part from him. . . . I was so accustomed to be ever two and so inured to[74] be never single that methinks I am but half myself.

John Calvin, *Commentary upon the First Book of Moses Called Genesis* (1554)[75]

In 1534 the English Parliament passed an "Act for the Punishment of the Vice of Buggery," making sodomy a felony punishable by death and confiscation of property. The act brought the sin of sodomy, traditionally handled by ecclesiastical courts (as were most moral offenses), under the direct control of the Tudor state.

Christian theologians, such as St. Augustine and St. Thomas Aquinas, had long condemned any form of nonprocreative sexuality as an offense against God's created order (see Summa Theologiae *II.2.154, 11–12). Though the Bible has relatively little to say about homoerotic love, the biblical passages on the subject were well known and often cited (see Lev. 18:22 and 20:13, Rom. 1:24–32, and 1 Cor. 6:9–10). The most significant biblical text on the subject, however, was the story of Sodom and Gomorrah (Gen. 19), a dominant narrative that informed virtually all discussions of homoeroticism in early modern Europe—and certainly a narrative that would linger in the minds of audience members watching Marlowe's play in the sixteenth century.*

John Calvin's Commentary upon Genesis, *translated into English in 1578, was widely known and often consulted. Though a staunch reformer,*

73. *accompted*: considered.

74. *inured to*: used to.

75. Selections are from John Calvin, *Commentary upon the First Book of Moses Called Genesis*, trans. Thomas Tymme (1554; translated into English, London, 1578). Spelling and punctuation have been modernized.

Calvin perceives sodomy in traditional theological terms—not as the behavior or inclination of a particular group, but as a symptom of the depraved and fallen condition of all humanity. Calvin follows the logic of medieval theologians who considered sins as essentially contagious—one sin leads to the next, and then the next. The logic was compelling in its simplicity and circularity: Sodomites offend the natural order of God's creation and therefore are in league with the devil; those in league with the devil are likely to promote heresy and sedition; those who promote heresy and sedition are likely to commit sodomy, and so on.

According to Richard Baines, Marlowe expressed a variety of radical opinions, including a blasphemous defense of sodomy: "That St. John the Evangelist was bedfellow to Christ and leaned always in his bosom; that he used him as the sinners of Sodom. That all they that love not tobacco and boys were fools."[76] We cannot be sure of the veracity of Baines's report. The accusations may have been contrived or exaggerated—or Marlowe indeed may have been a bold and rebellious defender of sodomites. In any case, however, Marlowe certainly knew that most of his audience members held no such views, or at least understood that such views were heretical. Even the most illiterate theatergoers would have arrived at the playhouse knowing the biblical account of God's wrath on the cities of Sodom and Gomorrah. If Marlowe intended to generate sympathy for Edward and Gaveston, he must have known that sympathy would be hard won.

Chapter 19

[In Calvin's *Commentary*, each chapter begins with the relevant text from the book of Genesis, followed by Calvin's interpretation of key passages.]

1. And in the evening there came two angels to Sodom; and Lot sat at the gate of Sodom, and Lot saw them, and rose up to meet them, and he bowed himself with his face to the ground.

2. And he said, See my lords, I pray you turn in now into your servant's house, and tarry all night, and wash your feet, and ye shall rise up early and go your ways. Who [the angels] said, Nay, but we will abide in the street all night.

3. Then he pressed upon them earnestly, and they turned in to him, and came to his house, and he made them a feast, and did bake unleavened bread, and they did eat.

---

76. See the Baines Note and similar comments by Thomas Kyd in the introduction on the "Life of Marlowe."

4. But before they went to bed, the men of the city, even the men of Sodom compassed[77] the house round about, from the young even to the old, all the people from all quarters.

5. Who crying unto Lot said unto him, Where are the men which came to thee this night? Bring them out unto us, that we may know them.

6. Then Lot went out at the door unto them, and shut the door after him,

7. And said, I pray you, my brethren, do not so wickedly.

8. Behold now, I have two daughters, which have not known man; them will I bring out now unto you, and do to them as seemeth you good; only unto these men do nothing. . . .

9. Then they said, Away hence. And they said, He [Lot] is come alone as a stranger, and shall he judge and rule? We will now deal worse with thee than with them. So they pressed sore upon Lot himself, and came to break the door.

10. But the men [the angels] put forth their hands, and pulled Lot into the house to them, and shut to the door.

11. Then they smote the men that were at the door of the house with blindness, both small and great, so that they were weary in seeking the door.

12. Then the men [the angels] said unto Lot, Whom hast thou yet here? Either son in law, or thy sons, or thy daughters, or whatsoever thou hast in the city, bring it out of this place.

13. For we will destroy this place, because the cry of them is great before the Lord, and the Lord hath sent us to destroy it.

14. Then Lot went out and spake unto his sons in law, which married his daughters, and said, Arise, get you out of this place, for the Lord will destroy the city; but he seemed unto his sons in law as though he had mocked.

15. And when the morning arose, the angels hasted Lot, saying, Arise, take thy wife and thy two daughters which are here, lest thou be destroyed in the punishment of the city.

16. And as he prolonged the time, the men caught both him and his wife and his two daughters by the hands (the Lord being merciful unto him), and they brought him forth, and set him without[78] the city.

17. And when they had brought them out, the angel said, Escape for thy life; look not behind thee, neither tarry thou in all the plain; escape into the mountain, lest thou be destroyed. . . .

24. Then the Lord rained upon Sodom and upon Gomorrah, brimstone and fire from the Lord out of heaven,

---

77. *compassed*: surrounded.

78. *without*: outside.

25. And overthrew those cities, and all the plain, and all the inhabitants of the cities; and that which grew upon the earth.

26. Now his wife behind him looked back, and she became a pillar of salt.

27. And Abraham, rising up early in the morning, went to the place where he had stood before the Lord.

28. And looking toward Sodom and Gomorrah, and toward all the land of the plain, behold, he saw the smoke of the land mounting up as the smoke of a furnace.

4. *But before they went to bed*: Here in one wicked fact Moses setteth forth a lively image of Sodom. For hereby it doth evidently appear what a devilish consent was among them to all wickedness, in that they all conspired together to commit such horrible and detestable filthiness. How great their wickedness was, it doth hereby appear in that, as it were with an army, they beseige the house of Lot. How blind and beastly is their lust insomuch that like brute beasts, void of all shame, they run to and fro? How great is their fierceness and cruelty in threatening so shamefully the holy father, and in assaying all extremities. Hereby also we gather that they were not infected with one vice alone, but also that they were fallen to all boldness of sinning, insomuch that they were devoid of all shame. And Ezekiel . . . doth notably declare from what beginnings and entrances of evils they fell to extreme filthiness [see Ezek. 16:49–50]. Hereunto also pertaineth the saying of Paul, how that God punisheth the ungodliness of men when he giveth them over into so great blindness that they fall into divers lusts and defile their bodies [Rom. 1:24–28]. But whenas shame being set aside, the reins are loosed to lust, filthy and beastly barbarousness must needs by and by follow, and divers kinds of wickednesses must of necessity be therewithal mingled that there may be more than a deformed confusion. . . .

From the young to the old: Moses concealeth many things which the reader may call to mind of himself, as this, that he maketh no mention by whom the multitude was stirred up. For it is very likely that there were certain provokers, but notwithstanding, we hereby perceive how willing and ready they were to commit wickedness, who, as it were with a watchword, came by and by together. It also showeth that there was no manner of shame left in them, because neither gravity restrained the old men, nor that modesty the young men, which became that age. To be short, he meaneth that all care of honesty was abolished and that the order of nature was perverted, when he saith that from the young to the old they came together from the furthest parts of the city. . . .

12. *Whom hast thou yet here?* Now at the last the angels show wherefore they came, and what they intended to do. For so heinous was the last act,

that Lot should now persuade himself, that this people was to be suffered no longer.

And first they say, that they came to destroy the city because their cry was great. By which words they give to understand that God was not provoked with one wickedness alone, but after he spared them a long time, he now at the last being almost constrained, through the great heap of wickedness, cometh to take punishment. For we are thus to think, the more sins that men do heap together, the higher their wickedness doth arise, and the nearer it cometh unto God, to call for vengeance. Wherefore, as the angels hitherto testify, that God hath been long suffering; so again, they give to understand, what manner of end all they shall have, which daily heaping one wickedness upon another, do still with greater boldness more and more rebel against God. . . .

24. *Then the Lord rained upon Sodom*: Moses here very briefly toucheth the destruction of Sodom and of the other cities. The grievousness of the matter required a larger treatise, yea, a tragical discourse. But Moses simply, according to his manner, reciting the judgment of God, those things which he could not vehemently enough express with words, he leaveth to the consideration of the readers. Therefore it is our part to have a full consideration of that horrible vengeance, the which seeing it happened not without the wonderful shaking of heaven and earth, we ought to be afraid at the only naming of it, and therefore mention is so oftentimes made of the same in the Scriptures. And the Lord would not have those cities to be swallowed up with an earthquake only, but to the end he might make a more notable example of his judgment, he cast fire and brimstone from heaven. . . . The lord raineth then not after the usual order of nature, but, as it were, with an outstretched arm, he openly thundered contrary to his wonted manner, to the end it might plainly enough appear that the same rain of fire and brimstone came not of any natural causes. It is very true that the air is never troubled by chance, and God is to be acknowledged the author of every little rain. . . . And whereas it was always wont to be demanded out of this place, what the infants deserved, which were destroyed together with their parents, the answer is easy to be made: that mankind is in the hand of God, insomuch that he appointeth to destruction whom he will, and upon whom he will he showeth mercy. Also we ought to submit unto his secret judgment whatsoever we cannot comprehend within the compass of our understanding and reach. Last of all, all that seed was accursed and execrable, in so much that of right he spared not the least.

Henri Estienne, *A World of Wonders* (1566)[79]

Henri Estienne (1528–1598)—also known by the Latin form of his name, Henricus Stephanus—was a prolific French Protestant writer, editor, and printer. He was famous for his many editions of ancient Greek texts, including works by Aristotle, Herodotus, Sophocles, and Plato. In his popular A World of Wonders *(published in fourteen editions during the late sixteenth century), Estienne argues that the wonders reported by the ancient historian Herodotus are no more astonishing than the events of his own age. Estienne's claims are often ironic and satirical in that the wondrous events of his own time are depicted as far more degraded and sinful than anything in the ancient past.*

His chapter on sodomy presents the widespread Protestant view that the offense is most common among Italians and Roman Catholics. In 1551 the English bishop John Bale argued the point in somewhat contrived but amusing terms: "If ye spell 'Roma' backward, ye shall find it love in this prodigious kind, for it is preposterous 'amor,' a love out of order or a love against kind."[80] For Bale and Estienne and many Elizabethans, sodomy (like venereal disease) was conceived as a foreign contagion. Moreover, Estienne shares with John Calvin the conception of sodomy as a manifestation of the overall depravity of human nature (and thus, for Estienne, sodomy is associated with other disorders, such as bestiality and transvestism).

In Marlowe's play, Gaveston is not Italian, but he dresses in Italian style, with a "short Italian hooded cloak" and "Tuscan cap" (1.4.413–14), and he intends to seduce the king with "Italian masques" (1.1.54). From the perspective of the barons, Gaveston is a source of foreign contamination and degeneracy in the English court.

Chapter 13: Of Sodomy, and the sin against nature, committed at this day

Moreover, if there were nothing else but such swinish sodomy as is committed at this day, might we not justly term this age the paragon of abominable wickedness? The heathens (I confess) were much addicted to this vice, but can it be showed that it was ever accounted among Christians as

---

79. Selections are from Henri Estienne, *A World of Wonders, or An introduction to a treatise touching the conformity of ancient and modern wonders, or A preparative treatise to the Apology for Herodotus,* trans. R. C. [Richard Carew] (1566; translated into English, London, 1607). Spelling and punctuation have been modernized.

80. See John Bale, *First Two Parts of the Acts of English Votaries* (London, 1551), part 2, Preface. The book is a fierce attack on Catholic monasticism.

a virtue? Yet some in these days have not only accounted it a virtue but also written in commendation of it and published their writings in print to the view of the world. For we may not forget how that John de la Casa, a Florentine and Archbishop of Benevento, wrote a book[81] in Italian rhyme wherein he sings forth a thousand praises in commendation of this sin which good Christians cannot so much as think of without horror, calling it (among other epithets which he giveth it) *a heavenly work*. . . .

But to return to this so foul and infamous a sin. Is it not great pity that gentlemen, who before they travelled into Italy abhorred the very naming of it, should after they have continued there a time, delight themselves not only in talking and discoursing, but in practicing and professing it as a thing which they have learned in a happy time? As for those who through bad custom have only kept the Italian phrase there commonly spoken (though borrowed from such wicked villainy), they have (I grant) some colorable excuse. But what can the rest allege for themselves? Yet I dare not affirm that all who are tainted with this sin learned it in Italy or Turkey: for our M. Maillard was never there and yet he made profession of it. . . .

But I were much to blame if I should forget Peter Lewis . . . son to Pope Paul the third. This Prince of Sodom, Duke of Parma and Placentia, that he might not degenerate from the Popish progeny (whence he was descended) was so addicted to this horrible and hellish sin and so carried away with the burning thereof, that he did not only forget the judgments of God and the provident care he should have had of his good name (at least with such as make no conscience to give themselves to such villainy). Nay (which is more), he did not only forget that he was a man, but even the daily danger of death itself, whereof brute beasts do stand in fear. For not content to satiate his lawless lust with innumerable persons of all sorts, sexes, and degrees, he went a wooing at the last to a young man called Cosmus Cherius, then Bishop of Fano, and perceiving that he could not otherwise have his pleasure of him and work him to his will, he caused his men to hold him. Shortly after which fact, he received the reward due to such monsters. And as he had led a wicked and shameful life, so they made for him so infamous and villainous an epitaph that the reader had need of a pomander[82] in his pocket, or some preservative, lest his stomach should rise at the reading thereof.

Concerning bestiality, or the sin against nature (which was ever more common among shepherds than others) who so list to make inquiry into the examples of later times shall find as great store of them as of the rest.

---

81. The book is no longer extant.

82. *pomander*: ball of perfume (used to ward off the plague and other diseases).

But if any desire examples of fresher memory, let him go to the Italian soldiers of the camp that would have beleaguered Lyon during the civil wars, and ask them what they did with their goats. Notwithstanding an accident happened in our time far more strange than any that can be alleged in this kind, of a woman burned at Toulouse (about seven and twenty years ago) for prostituting herself to a dog, which was also burned with her for company, which I account a most strange fact considering her sex. Now this sin I call *the sin against nature*, having respect rather to the common use and phrase of speech than to the proper signification of the word, according to which sodomy is as well a sin against nature as bestiality. But not to enter into a warfare of words, let this suffice that brute beasts do condemn us herein.[83]

Now albeit the former example be very strange, yet we have here another far more strange (though not altogether so wicked) committed about thirty years ago by a maid born at Fountains (between Blois and Romorantin), who having disguised herself like a man served as an hostler at an inn in the suburbs of Foy for the space of seven years, and afterwards married a maid of the town, with whom she companied for the space of two years or thereabout, attempting much, but effecting nothing. After which time her cozenage[84] and knavery in counterfeiting the office of a husband being discovered, she was apprehended, and having confessed the fact, was burned. By which examples we see that our age may well boast that (notwithstanding the vices of former times) it hath some proper and peculiar to itself. For this fact of hers hath nothing common with that which was practiced by those famous strumpets who in old time were called tribades.[85]

---

83. Brute beasts (since they do not fornicate outside of their own species) are better than degraded humans.

84. *cozenage*: fraud or trickery.

85. *tribades*: a term for lesbians.